Double Agency

ASIAN AMERICA
A series edited by Gordon H. Chang

The increasing size and diversity of the Asian American population, its growing significance in American society and culture, and the expanded appreciation, both popular and scholarly, of the importance of Asian Americans in the country's present and past—all these developments have converged to stimulate wide interest in scholarly work on topics related to the Asian American experience. The general recognition of the pivotal role that race and ethnicity have played in American life, and in relations between the United States and other countries, has also fostered this heightened attention.

Although Asian Americans were a subject of serious inquiry in the late nineteenth and early twentieth centuries, they were subsequently ignored by the mainstream scholarly community for several decades. In recent years, however, this neglect has ended, with an increasing number of writers examining a good many aspects of Asian American life and culture. Moreover, many students of American society are recognizing that the study of issues related to Asian America speaks to, and may be essential for, many current discussions on the part of the informed public and various scholarly communities.

The Stanford series on Asian America seeks to address these interests. The series will include works from the humanities and social sciences, including history, anthropology, political science, American studies, law, literary criticism, sociology, and interdisciplinary and policy studies.

Double Agency

ACTS OF IMPERSONATION IN
ASIAN AMERICAN LITERATURE
AND CULTURE

Tina Chen

STANFORD UNIVERSITY PRESS
STANFORD, CALIFORNIA
2005

Stanford University Press
Stanford, California
© 2005 by the Board of Trustees of the
Leland Stanford Junior University

Library of Congress Cataloging-in-Publication Data

Chen, Tina (Tina Yih-Ting).
   Double agency : acts of impersonation in Asian American
literature and culture / Tina Chen.
       p. cm.
   Includes bibliographical references and index.
   ISBN 0-8047-5185-4 (alk. paper) —
   ISBN 0-8047-5186-2 (pbk. : alk. paper)
   1. American literature—Asian American authors—History
and criticism.   2. Impostors and imposture in literature.
3. Stereotype (Psychology) in literature.   4. Asian Americans—
Intellectual life.   5. Identity (Psychology) in literature.   6. Asian
Americans in literature.   7. Group identity in literature.
8. Impersonation in literature.   9. Race in literature.   I. Title.
PS153.A84C47   2005
810.9'353—dc22

                                                2005000563

Printed in the United States of America
Original Printing 2005
Last figure below indicates year of this printing:
14   13   12   11   10   09   08   07   06   05

Typeset at Stanford University Press in 11/14 Garamond

To my family, with love

Contents

Acknowledgments

During the many years I spent working on this project, I often fantasized about what it would feel like to be able to write the acknowledgments and know that, finally, I was nearing completion of the manuscript. Now that the time has actually arrived to write this document, I am overwhelmed and humbled by the many acts of support, inspiration, and mentorship that have made this study possible.

I was lucky enough to begin my doctoral work at UC Berkeley and even luckier to be a member of Samuel Otter's "methods" course. From the beginning, Sam has provided me with invaluable guidance and support and his many kindnesses have extended far beyond the classroom. I count myself fortunate to have him as a mentor and a friend, one whose professional advice I value tremendously. I am grateful, too, to Sau-ling C. Wong, whose example as a researcher and teacher is one that continues to impact me. In addition to Sam and Sau-ling, I am indebted to the members of my dissertation committee—Anne Anlin Cheng, Martin Jay, and Genaro Padilla—for their support of the project in its earliest stages and for their enthusiasm for my scholarship. Graduate school can be an exhausting experience and having the encouragement of scholars whose work I so admire has made a tremendous difference.

Although I begin by thanking Vereen Bell, my first chair, for bringing me to Vanderbilt University, the list of people there to whom I owe my thanks is extensive. For professional guidance and first-rate mentorship, I am grateful to Jay Clayton, Teresa Goddu and Virginia Scott. Each of these senior colleagues provided welcome professional advice at key moments in my career; additionally, all of them have extended their friendship to me and helped me through the challenges of being an assistant professor. It has been a privilege working in the English department and I am grateful for the various kinds of support offered by my colleagues, among them Thadious Davis, Sam Girgus, Michael Kreyling, Lorraine Lopez, Leah Marcus, Mark Schoenfield, and Sheila Smith McKoy. My heartfelt gratitude goes, too, to Janis May, who not only keeps the department running smoothly but has always looked out for me and given me guidance of the most welcome sort. My thanks and appreciation go to the 2002–2003 Robert Penn Warren Center for the Humanities fellows who provided stimulating intellectual conversation and positive feedback on my work on comfort women. Also, I owe a special word of thanks to my friend and colleague Charles Morris for our lunches and talks; they have made a great difference in my life.

Beyond Vanderbilt, I have been fortunate enough to encounter a number of generous souls who have given me great encouragement and support. Foremost among this group is Garrett Hongo who, in his (too brief!) time as visiting writer at Vanderbilt, offered me his backing, friendship, and mentorship in unstinting measure. He has extended his generosity to me in myriad ways and my work is better as a result of his interest and his enthusiasm. Thanks, too, to Leslie Bow for her astute criticisms of the manuscript; her careful suggestions about each chapter have helped me to re-think and improve my work and I am grateful for her intellectual rigor coupled with kindness. I would like to acknowledge Gay Gibson Cima for helping me get into this profession; she started out as my teacher and, to my great delight, ended up being my friend. I am grateful, as well, for the advice and solidarity offered by Viet Thanh Nguyen. My appreciation goes to my editors at Stanford University Press, Carmen Borbón-Wu and John Feneron, who shepherded the project through the publication process expertly.

Chapter 2 and chapter 6 were published previously in different forms. Chapter 2 appeared in *Re/Collecting Early Asian America: Essays in Cultural History,* edited by Josephine Lee, Imogene L. Lim and Yuko Matsukawa (Philadelphia: Temple University Press, 2002): 218–37. Chapter 6 was published in *MFS: Modern Fiction Studies* 48.3 (Fall 2002): 637–66. I thank

Temple University Press, The Johns Hopkins University Press, and *MFS* for allowing me to include this revised material in the study.

This book could not have been completed without the generous financial support I enjoyed at the University of California, Berkeley, where I received a Chancellor's Opportunity Predoctoral Fellowship and a Mellon Dissertation Year Fellowship. At Vanderbilt University, I am grateful for the support provided by a Robert Penn Warren Center for the Humanities fellowship and a University Research Scholar grant. I am deeply appreciative for the time to research and write that such generous funding made possible.

I cannot express adequately what I owe to my parents, Jason Chien-Hsu Chen and Sophie M. C. Chen, whose love and concern have made all things possible. Their wonderful example to me has provided the foundation for all of my accomplishments; their unwavering support (through this long, long process!) has been critical to not only the completion of this project but all aspects of my life. My appreciation goes, too, to John, Kim, and Kylie Chen for their love and support; both have meant a lot to me. I also extend grateful thanks to my many families—the Chens, the Chuangs, the Goudies, the Tropeanos and the Wus—for their interest in my work and their appreciation of my endeavors. Although a project like this is pretty foreign to most of them, they have not let that get in the way of caring about its successful fruition. As I was finishing this project, Nora Sabella Goudie came into my life and her presence has made the work, and my life, richer and more meaningful.

Above all, my love and appreciation go to Sean X. Goudie for his devotion, his intellectual energy, his faith and his love. He is the best life partner one could ask for and I cannot imagine my life without him.

Preface: On Impersonation and the Nature of the Not-so-secret Agent

What is called "intelligence" cannot be divined from spirits, nor from gods, nor by analogy with past events, nor from [the] hocus-pocus of calculations. Intelligence is obtained from men [sic] inside the enemy situation.

Now there are five sorts of secret agents: (1) native; (2) inside; (3) doubled; (4) expendable; (5) living. Use them all.

from *The Art of War*, Sun Tzu, as quoted by Frank Chin

Frank Chin opens *Bulletproof Buddhists* (1998), his collection of essays, with a piece about his experience of being detained in Cuba in 1960 as a suspected *Yanqui* spy. Using excerpts from Sun Tzu's famous treatise on *The Art of War* to punctuate his narrative, Chin weaves an improbable tale about his hemispheric adventure—one that takes him from Berkeley to Mexico, involves his arrest in Cuba and return to the United States via Miami, and finally concludes (as well as begins) with his being questioned by an MP interested in discerning his qualifications for service in the U.S. military. Chin's narrative, replete with his characteristic *braggadocio* stylizations and his wryly heroic portrayal of himself as "the Lone Chinaman" (a.k.a. "Mr. Supervisible!"), is one of great irony. After all, his "mistaken" identity in Cuba as a spy for the United States—one that depends upon Cuban suspicions that he could be an effective *Yanqui* spy by posing as a Chinese national whose Communist sympathies make other Cubans willing to embrace him in "international brotherhood"—simply mirrors the dilemma he poses to those he encounters in the United States, many of whom believe him to be a Native American since "the idea of a Chinaman six feet tall offends their religion, shakes their faith, and sorely dislocates the shoulders of their reality" (5).

The seeming absurdity of Chin's adventures in identity is neither laugh-able nor remarkable within the context of this project. As the subtitle of the book suggests, *Double Agency* is concerned with the acts of impersonation Asian Americans have enacted in order to perform into existence their iden-tities *as Asian Americans.* Understanding the constructed nature of Asian American identities makes the performative dimensions of such construc-tions necessary aspects of study; attending to the complex negotiations be-tween always already articulated roles and emerging paradigms of perfor-mance encourages a consideration of how such roles both limit and make possible the emergence of self-reflexive strategies of enactment. Both imper-atives are addressed by the process of impersonation, a critical trope, I be-lieve, in Asian American literary and cultural production. What exactly does it mean, though, to come to Asian Americanness through a politics of im-personation? What are the disciplinary stakes of understanding imperson-ation not just as a performative strategy adopted by Asian American subjects but also as a strategy of reading to be taken up by Asian Americanist critics? And finally, how does a politics of impersonation help us address the issues of agency and subjecthood that have been so critical in the field of Asian American studies but have increasingly come under attack in the wake of antihumanist and poststructuralist discourses? Such questions motivate this study and the reading practices it offers; such questions are particularly rel-evant at a moment when Asian American studies has begun rethinking some of its traditional assumptions and refiguring itself to address the complexi-ties and contradictions embodied by the field itself as well as the subjects and objects it examines.

As an academic discipline that prides itself on its intimate connections with the communities from which it emerged and that it continues to in-vestigate, Asian American studies must consider ever more carefully the re-lationship between the objects it reads and the interpretive practices it pro-motes. Although these two emphases of critical inquiry have always been related, their relationship and (dis)articulation have increasingly come under scrutiny. Recent arguments by Viet Thanh Nguyen and Kandice Chuh, for example, have suggested the importance of reconceptualizing the theoretical practices that have characterized the field. Such practices, which yoke the texts we study to a specific political agenda privileging resistance and an-tiracist work, must be considered anew not to jettison either the possibility of mounting resistance or engaging in antiracism but to account for the ways in which the field itself has compromised its ability to perform effectively such goals through its inattention to the multiple and competing discourses that make up its formation. In *Race and Resistance* (2002), Nguyen asserts that "in order for Asian American intellectual work to grow in vitality[,] not only must it continue the vital task of criticizing American society's methods of racial and class domination, but it must also engage in a self-critique that results in an understanding of Asian America's limits" (11). Such self-critique can only happen, Chuh asserts in *Imagine Otherwise* (2003), if we recognize the importance of conceiving Asian American studies as a "subjectless discourse," one that acknowledges and depends upon understanding "Asian American" as "a term *in difference from itself*—at once making a claim of achieved subjectivity and referring to the impossibility of that achievement—[one that] deconstructs itself, is itself deconstruction" (9, 8).

Considering these injunctions together, it seems clear that Asian American studies is at a crossroads and must envision ways of engineering its own rebirth or run the risk of reifying the very hermeneutic practices to which it has traditionally been opposed. *Double Agency* contributes to this endeavor by developing impersonation as both textual and metatextual tactic, a strategic performance calculated to foreground the limits of subjectivity even as it insists upon the undeniable importance of subjecthood. Holding in visible tension these two, paradoxical aims is precisely the possibility that impersonation—not imposture—offers us. Indeed, I assert that it is imperative that we de-couple imposture from impersonation and understand these two types of performances as very different in intent if not always in effect. Such decoupling exposes how Asian American performances have often been misinterpreted, read as acts of betrayal rather than those of multiple allegiance. The paradox that comprises one of the book's framing concepts—impersonation as a performance of divided allegiance that simultaneously pays homage to and challenges authenticity and authority—becomes a site for reconsidering the implications of Asian Americans as double agents. By thinking about impersonation and the options it offers for resisting the binary logics of loyalty/disloyalty, real/fake, and Asian/American, *Double Agency* attends to the possibilities of reading such acts as ones of *im-personation,* a performance by which Asian Americans are constituted and constitute themselves as speaking and acting subjects.

Obviously not all Asian Americans are spies or foreigners and most of them are certainly not double agents in the traditional sense of the term. While the book's title plays with the popular connotations of the term double agent, the project's concerns are as much about quotidian performances as they are about the spec(tac)ular nature of such cases. The book focuses on ways in which we might read double agency not as the mark of a spy's betrayal or compromised loyalty but as a sign of the multiple allegiances that Asian Americans have maintained in order to construct themselves as agents capable of self-articulation and -determination. Thus, *Double Agency* explores the usefulness of impersonation as a way of investigating the contexts to which Asian Americans have been subject and the strategies by which they embrace Asian Americanness as a viable category of identity. If we assume Asian American impersonation to be a specific act that involves the assumption of a public identity that does not necessarily belong to "someone else" but that has been assigned to and subsequently adopted by the performer in question in order to articulate an identity comprehensible to the public, the manifest possibilities of how impersonation and identity are not only related but in some sense mutually constitutive become key sites for thinking through the complicated process of performing into being Asian Americanness. By attending to the multiple histories of Asian America and considering the possibilities of performance inherent in the coalitional practices that comprise the field of Asian American studies, *Double Agency* identifies an Asian American politics of impersonation that derives from the impossible subject known as "Asian American."

Given the pervasive ideas of Asian Americans as somehow never being able to be "American" enough, the very nature of Asian American identity might be thought of as *one that requires one to impersonate fundamentally oneself.* These particular ideas of Asian Americans being alien to U.S. American identity—stemming, in part, from "the historical racialization of Asian-origin immigrants as nonwhite 'aliens ineligible to citizenship'" (Lowe 20)—are accompanied by related stereotypes of Asians as "sneaky," "secretive," and "inscrutable." Such characterizations coalesce into the figure of the Asian American as spy or alien, a figure whose foreign allegiances make it not only possible but probable that his/her claims to American-ness are suspect or, in other words, impostured.

Double Agency argues for differentiating impersonation from perfor-

mances of imposture and of passing in order to expose the rhetorical and
narrative blind spots that make such ontological definitions so problematic
for Asian Americans. In the process, the book undertakes a more systematic
interrogation of the ways in which the performance of Asian American identities both relates to and challenges the dynamics by which U.S. American
identities are constructed in the first place. Crucial to this endeavor is characterizing imposture as the seamless performance of an adopted public identity that is understood to belong to someone else and considering impersonation as an act that makes apparent, in particular contexts, its own
origins and confounds the issues of betrayal that are so seemingly clear in
calling out imposture. By differentiating imposture from impersonation,
this study attempts to delineate a praxis through which Asian American
identities can be performed into being and agency claimed.

Double Agency conceptualizes Asian Americans as "double agents" who
work both to establish their own claims to a U.S. American identity and to
critique the American institutions that have designated them as "aliens"
whose incorporation into the body politic is thus always already suspect.
While suggesting that Asian Americans are "double agents" might seem to
adopt, in naïve or problematic ways, the hegemonic logic of those who
imagine Asian secrecy and stealth as defining characteristics that make Asian
Americans seemingly fitting subjects of exclusionary policies, I would like to
risk this potential danger in order to propose another way of thinking about
the problems and possibilities of double agency.

By theorizing Asian American subjects as impersonators who manifest a
doubled agency, I intend to highlight several significant aspects of Asian
American identity formation. Double agency gestures to the multiple allegiances that impersonation makes evident; it exposes the fear of betrayal
that is at the heart of charges of imposture to which Asian Americans have
been subject. Additionally, the concept highlights the precarious but pivotal
position occupied by Asian Americans as a "swing minority group" in American racial politics and demands that we acknowledge for Asian Americans
the possibility of making choices and claiming agency despite the conditions
circumscribing the options available to them. I encourage us to consider the
double agent as impersonator as a trope for thinking through the complexi-
ties of Asian American identities that are constructed not solely in reaction
to the outside impositions of the U.S. imagination but emerge *in the process*

of performing themselves. In this way, I hope to theorize agency not as some inviolable and discrete force that exerts itself from either inside or outside the subject in question, but as a matrix of effect and effort that emerges in the act of *acting like* a person. Accordingly, impersonation usefully encompasses a range of performative possibilities and, in the final analysis, offers Asian Americans an option that has, at times, been denied them: the opportunity to im-personate themselves, to perform themselves into being as persons recognized by their communities and their country. Significantly, Asian Americans have im-personated themselves as subjects and agents, *not by imposturing whiteness, but by performing into existence their multiple allegiances and identities—often fractured, sometimes incoherent, but always necessary—as Asian Americans.*

Overview of Chapters

In order to make these claims about double agency and how a politics of impersonation operates in contemporary Asian American literature and culture, the book pursues a double focus. Stereotype—both its pleasures and its dangers—preoccupies the first half of *Double Agency.* Thus, section one, "Impersonation and Stereotype," develops impersonation as both a hermeneutic strategy as well as a strategy of performance deployed on the Asian American stage in the re-presentation of stereotype. Critical to the readings in this section is an elaboration of how Asian Americans have developed a politics of impersonation that emerges from the specific histories of Asian America and affects contemporary Asian American reading and artistic practices. The first chapter, "Impersonation and Double Agency: Theorizing the Practice, Practicing the Theory," delineates the historical and theoretical grounding of the book. In this chapter, I derive a politics of impersonation from specific Asian American historical practices before suggesting the ways in which impersonation provides a conceptual tool for addressing the problem Susan Koshy has identified as "the fiction of Asian American literature." In the process of making this argument, I show how the establishment of Chinese American paper families during the Exclusion era and the practice of arranged marriages using picture brides in a Japanese American context help lay the groundwork for the impersonative practices that help us re-figure contemporary Asian American literary and cultural production. The chapter concludes with an assessment of the "uncomfortable fit" between performer and role that impersonation addresses, a discomfort nowhere more apparent than in the performance of stereotype.

Chapter 2, "Dissecting the 'Devil Doctor': Stereotype and Sensationalism in Sax Rohmer's Fu Manchu," delves into the stereotype of Fu Manchu, deconstructing a performance calculated to expose as well as hide the "Asian" body. In this chapter, I argue that the seemingly simple surface of stereotype in Rohmer's texts masks a complex web of signification that makes his work undeniably important in understanding and negotiating Asian American representation. The anxiety that Fu Manchu creates for Asian Americans— an anxiety that Daniel Kim terms "the legacy of Fu"—finds its most vociferous voice in Frank Chin, whose mission to remasculinize Asian American men has led him to target specifically Fu Manchu as a "homosexual menace." I argue that only by really looking at Rohmer's Fu Manchu and the ways in which such a character impostures Chinese identity can we confront the anxiety that Chin articulates. Without careful examination, we are left, like Chin, to rant at an empty image that remains powerful despite our rage. As James Moy asserts, "[T]o ignore the stereotype is to leave the geography littered with awkward figurations of Asianness that recall a bitter past which continues to affect the present in subtle ways" (5). By deploying impersonation as a metacritical strategy for understanding Fu Manchu as stereotype, this chapter demonstrates that Rohmer's interest in visual culture—represented by music hall performance, ethnographic display, and museum culture—had a major impact on his conceptualization and delineation of Fu Manchu. The first part of the chapter outlines how Rohmer's exposure to and interest in visual display and performance dictate much of how he develops and presents his "Asian" characters, focusing specifically on how music hall staging and practice—a theatrical tradition dependent upon yellowface performance and the imposture of Asianness as a stylization of a hypervisible Asian body—translate into the structure of the early Fu Manchu novels. The second half of the chapter points out the ways in which Rohmer's texts cultivate a systematic visual misrecognition that is masked by the many acts of both textual and metatextual imposture strewn throughout the texts.

The next chapter of *Double Agency* investigates the difficult process of deconstructing stereotype theatrically by noting both the pleasures and problems inherent in such a project. In addition to the stereotype of Asian villainy as embodied in Fu Manchu, Rohmer's literary legacy also includes the figure of Fu's desirable, manipulative, and dangerously alluring daughter Fah Lo Suee, the prototypical Asian "Dragon Lady." In chapter 3, "De/Posing Stereotype on the Asian American Stage," I explore how contemporary Asian American dramatists have staged acts of impersonation in order to address the complicated relationship that exists between Asian American performance and the re-enactment of stereotypes like that of the dragon lady and the effeminized Asian American man. Arguing that stereotype and identity are in some respects mutually constitutive, I consider the importance of pursuing multiple strategies of impersonation in order to de/pose the poses of stereotype. This chapter discusses a set of dramatic texts—Elizabeth Wong's "China Doll" (1996), David Henry Hwang's *M. Butterfly* (1989), Philip Kan Gotanda's *Yankee Dawg You Die* (1991), and Diana Son's "R.A.W. ('Cause I'm a Woman)" (1996)—in order to demonstrate how contemporary Asian American theater works to expose the issues of mastery and desire at the heart of stereotype in order to deconstruct stereotype's mastery, if not its pervasiveness. Although these playwrights and performance artists achieve varied measures of success in deconstructing stereotype, this chapter considers how their concerted efforts to undermine stereotype on the level of the performative constitute an effective approach to interrogating the notions of pretense, authenticity, and desire that stereotype so powerfully embodies.

The second section of the book focuses on Asian American acts of impersonation that move beyond the reiteration of stereotype. Entitled "Double Agents, Double Agency," this section emphasizes how Asian American characters im-personate themselves into subjects who resist the ways in which their identities as Asian Americans are legally and socially over-determined. The focus of each chapter in this section is on tracking the process of how characters who have been marginalized—as illegal aliens, as crazy immigrants, as invisible members of U.S. American society—perform into being viable roles that grant them both space to maneuver and the ability to resist singular interpretation. In this way, the last half of the book concentrates on the double agency of characters who, through their acts of impersonation, focus our attention on the always already constructed identities that are thrust upon them as well as on the necessity of taking on those roles in order to subvert them from within the moment of performance.

Thus, the fourth chapter takes up the performative tensions that undergird what it means for a subject to enact citizenship and alienness. In Hualing Nieh's *Mulberry and Peach* (1988), the possibilities of impersonation as an act of doubled agency are embodied by double subjects: Mulberry/Peach, two women whose different identities are trapped within a single body, two women whose attempts to make themselves known as different individuals are always read as an act of imposture that must be discounted as either duplicity or madness. In this novel, identity is charted on two levels—the bodily, where identity is tied to the body and its visual registers, and then again on a performative level, where acts and their consequences make present Peach's invisible presence. It is the visibility afforded to the body, a visibility manifesting itself as Mulberry's identity, that withholds from Peach the possibility of acknowledgment and recognition. I contend that through Mulberry/Peach's confrontation and embrace of "madness," the fragmentation made apparent through constantly existing as a "being-in-difference" reveals itself as schizophrenia, being-in-relation to an/Other who is also oneself. The existence of both Mulberry and Peach in the same body raises questions of authenticity and identity, and the struggle of the two women for recognition, both from others as well as from each other, reflects identity itself as an act of impersonation.

Chapter 5 further explores the intersections between "madness" and female identity. The existence of "comfort women"—women who were coerced into sexual slavery by the Japanese military during World War II—has gained international attention in the last decade. Nora Okja Keller's 1997 novel *Comfort Woman* explores the legacy of trauma and suffering caused by this experience. *Comfort Woman* is the story of two women: Akiko, whose horrific experiences in the "recreation camps" of the Japanese army dislocate her from her home and her former identity as Soon Hyo, and her daughter Beccah, who fears her mother is crazy and who will not fully understand her painful relationship with Akiko until she learns of the ways in which the comfort woman experience has affected them both. This chapter focuses on the ways in which Keller draws on Korean shamanistic religious rituals as a way of responding to the injustices Akiko suffers. I argue that Keller uses shamanistic rituals and practices to refigure what Beccah (mis)understands as Akiko's "madness." Significantly, Akiko's openness to possession by the gods and spirits of Korean shamanism enables her to accomplish impersonation's most difficult feat: an im-personation that gives her back her sense of personhood. In this chapter, impersonation becomes an imaginative act that helps to redress the wrongs of history. To put oneself in the place of the silenced, even as one keeps in mind the impossibility of *becoming* that subject: that is the double allegiance of impersonation and the lived theory that it offers us.

The final chapter of the book, "Impersonation and Other Disappearing Acts: The Double(d) Agent of Chang-rae Lee's *Native Speaker*," explores the disjunctions and conjunctions between Asian American impersonation and the practice of espionage. In *Native Speaker* (1995), Henry Park's effectiveness as a spy stems from his racial and cultural heritage as a Korean American. Working for a firm that specializes in providing undercover ethnic operatives, Park's job capitalizes on the in/visibility that his race affords him in order to expose "whatever grit of an ethnicity" (130) he can. I argue that in recasting his spy, Lee must also rewrite the conventions of the spy story in order to expose the ways in which the masquerade necessitated by Park's job (as well as his failure to perform it as successfully as he might) is one that he lives as an effect of his race. By asserting that the "fantasy of invisibility" promising a spy power through voyeurism, self-concealment, and license is impossible for the Asian American spy, I contend that Henry's (pre)occupation with serial identity renders him no longer able to distinguish between "real" and "fake" performances—even when those performances are ones of his own staging. Without the ability to figure out the paradox that makes each act of impersonation a false act founded upon a "true ontological bearing," Henry feels cut off from the identities he would claim as his own.

The connections between in/visibility and Asian American bodies, a connection mediated through performance as both somatic and textual practice, are best understood by thinking of performance as a politics of impersonation. As Robyn Wiegman notes in *American Anatomies* (1995), her cultural critique of American studies, it is "unthinkable" to "imagine ourselves outside . . . regimes of corporeal visibility" (4). Although this is, on one level, a statement of the obvious, it is the obviousness it bespeaks that interests me. The power of naturalization finds its greatest expression in the body, which often becomes a site of essential rights and essential differences. The intimate connections between body and sight—the regime of corporeal visibility—demand extended scrutiny because such a juncture proves a most powerful location for what seems obvious and unquestionable.

Chin's meditation makes clear the ways in which, on fundamental levels, his identity as "Mr. Supervisible!" results in his being continually subject to the charges of imposture and betrayal. Equally significantly, Chin demonstrates how such charges are ones that are predicated upon the suspicion that Asian American loyalties are always somehow in question and Asian Americans are particularly prone to acts of betrayal. One of the great ironies of Chin's detention as a spy in Cuba (besides the fact that he isn't a spy) is that his "foreign" experience in Cuba meshes so perfectly with the suspicion and discomfort his identity causes others as he moves through different U.S. geographies. In high school when he takes the Minnesota Multi-Phasic Personality Inventory, he discovers that he has "no personality at all" and is in fact the possessor of what he terms a "stealth personality" (6). In New Orleans, he confounds the racial distinctions of the lunch counter and discovers that the only place where he can "eat like a king" and not throw both customers and waiters into confusion is at "gay joints" (15). In Iowa, he finds himself in a "state full of white women, all strangers to me who sit down next to me and ask me, 'What are you?' and refuse to believe me when I tell them I'm a Chinaman" (4).

The incredulity of the white women Chin encounters and the ways in which Chin both does and does not accommodate himself to the public performance of what it means to be a Chinaman encapsulate the nature of impersonation as an act that holds in visible tension the "real" and the "fake" in order to question the foundations of both identity and identification. Rather than acquiescing to the binary logic of imposture—a logic that suggests the duplicity and betrayal that are figured so prominently in the character of the Asian/American spy but that underlies a number of other stereotypes about Asian Americans—impersonation speaks to the ways in which the uneven histories, struggling subjects, and partial practices of Asian America work both to construct and deconstruct the category of identity itself. Indeed, impersonation's dependence upon the interrelationship between the real and the fake, and its recognition of how both are inextricably intertwined in the formation of Asian American identities, constitute the directive for the double agents examined in this study.

Traise Yamamoto reminds us that at the heart of the scholarly and theoretical forays we make are the very real subjects of Asian America. This reminder—so simple but so very important—is embodied in both the spectacular flamboyance of Chin's persona as well as in the unremarkable daily acts of the Asian American immigrants who first laid the foundations of the politics of impersonation that this book treats. The "stealth personality" that Chin eventually claims for himself is one that has long been ascribed to Asian Americans; it is also one, among many, that Asian American subjects have sought to remake to their own ends through the possibilities of impersonation. As the epigraph with which this preface begins suggests, there are many kinds of secrecy and many kinds of agents. As the writers studied in *Double Agency* demonstrate, the key to mobilizing effectively is to "*[u]se them all.*"

PART I

Impersonation and Stereotype

Impersonation and Double Agency: Theorizing the Practice, Practicing the Theory

VINCENT . . . You are walking along, minding your own business, your head filled with poems and paintings—when what do you see coming your way? Some ugly "rumor," dressed in your clothes, staggering down the street impersonating you. And it is *not* you but no one seems to care. They want this impersonator—who is drinking from a brown paper bag, whose pant zipper is down to here and flapping in the wind—to be you. Why? They like it. It gives them glee. They like the lie. And the more incensed you become, the more real it seems to grow. Like some monster in a nightmare. If you ignore it, you rob it of its strength. It will soon disappear. *(Beat)* You will live. We all go to bed thinking, "The pain is so great, I will not last through the night." *(Beat)* We wake up. Alive. *C'est dommage.*

Yankee Dawg You Die, Philip Kan Gotanda

II. (Noh mask of benign woman)
   Over my mask
   is your mask
   of me
   an Asian woman
   grateful
   gentle
   in the pupils of your eyes
   as I gesture with each
   new play of
   light
   and shadow
   this mask be
   comes you.
   "Masks of Woman," Mitsuye Yamada

As the epigraphs taken from works by poet Mitsuye Yamada and playwright Philip Kan Gotanda elucidate, a central aspect of the experience of Asian Americanness involves the doubly conscious awareness of playing parts that seem distasteful and unnatural, but are perceived by others to be somehow representative of one's identity. Vincent Chang of *Yankee Dawg You Die* (1991), an older actor who has made a name playing stereotypes, seems to suggest that the stereotypes and "rumors" that haunt him as a minority subject are impersonations in that they embody the ugly desires of those who insist on their right to know him by virtue of what they think he must be. In this case, impersonation is a simple act of disguise, a ruse that bears watching but is perhaps not worthy of significant critique. After all, despite the fact that "they"—members of the dominant social order—"like the lie" and that the impersonation manifests a realness and a strength that is undeniable, it *is* a lie, it can be denied entirely as a construction and, according to Vincent, you can ultimately make it disappear if only "you ignore it."

In "Masks of Woman" (1992), Yamada's speaker reveals the impersonation that she performs daily as an act that is more complicated than the one Vincent decries.[1] Indeed, in acknowledging that the mask of "an Asian woman" is one that doesn't necessarily fall away to reveal some inner, essential truth of personality, Yamada articulates impersonation as an act whose daily performance both obscures and acknowledges the multiple, complex affiliations and contradictions that underlie the rather "benign" mask of identity. By emphasizing the fact that "your mask" covers not some essentially "real" identity but *"my mask,"* the poem's speaker insists upon impersonation as a double construction of identity: a performance always involving the acting out of roles, the contestation of the performances that we both wish to participate in and would like to somehow disavow.[2] Embedded in this seemingly simple statement about the disciplinary power of the outside gaze and the nature of stereotype as a form of psychic projection is a radical interrogation of what it means to come to identity through a politics of impersonation and a suggestion that Asian Americans—those of us who wear masks that are not always, *but also sometimes,* of our own choosing—are, fundamentally, impersonators. Indeed, despite Vincent's relatively complacent response to Bradley, his younger actor friend, about the nature and function of impersonation, he eventually comes to realize that the acts of impersonation he has performed cannot always be easily disavowed, that he too occupies the vexed role of the impersonator whose impersonations both cover and help him to discover the complicated issues of desire, mastery, and resistance that Yamada gestures toward in her poem.

As *Double Agency* demonstrates, acts of impersonation have been critical to constructing and deconstructing what it means to be Asian American in the United States. Understanding the constructed nature of Asian American identities makes the performative dimensions of such constructions necessary aspects of study; attending to the complex negotiations between always already articulated roles and emerging paradigms of performance encourages a consideration of how such roles both limit and make possible the emergence of self-reflexive strategies of enactment. Both imperatives are addressed by the process of impersonation, a critical trope, I believe, in Asian American literary and cultural production. Martin Manalansan urges that we consider performance not only to be positioned in divergent ways in particular communities but also as an analytical concept that helps us move beyond the artifice of the "staged event" (158) to an understanding of the quotidian dramas that constitute the on-going survival of specific, oppressed populations.[3] I develop the concept of impersonation as one that stems— with uneven results and applications—from key historical encounters in the Asian American past and continues to engage the problems and possibilities of contemporary Asian America. In this way, impersonation becomes both a way of *reading into* some of the enforced performances—of self and of community—to which Asian Americans have been subjected and a way of *acting out* the imbricated relationships that determine how Asian Americanness is constituted via a dynamic exchange between competing definitions of itself.

As both discursive and kinesthetic strategy, performance proves an extremely effective analytical tool for illuminating the effects of the gaze as a determinant of Asian American bodily expression. After all, the omnipresence of the gaze implies constant witness, an audience always already waiting to "see the show." Significantly, performance (and a sister term, "performativity") have generated new and exciting interdisciplinary conversations. Theorists such as Judith Butler, Jane Gallop, Elin Diamond, Sue-Ellen Case, Joseph Roach, and Peggy Phelan have popularized performance as a mode of inquiry as well as an epistemology.[4] The proliferating discussion of what constitutes performance makes it necessary to limit the ways in which I mobilize performance as a frame for my own project. Rather than arguing for "real" performances—of bodies, identities, or subjectivities—in Asian American literature and culture, I hope to elucidate the performance of Asian American bodies as a *politics of impersonation*. Such a politics would not assume impersonation as a false act or that which is not "real" so much as insist on impersonation's "genuineness" through an attention to its blurring of the authentic and inauthentic. In other words, impersonation demands performance itself to be self-aware, to be made visible.

The discourses that continually produce and reproduce Asian American bodies as visual icons represent what Peggy Phelan has termed "the ideology of the visible." In her book *Unmarked: The Politics of Performance* (1993), Phelan attempts to "expose the ways in which the visible real is employed as a truth-effect for the establishment of . . . discursive and representational notions of the real" (3) by critiquing the traditional emphasis on visibility as a sign of empowerment. Rather than cultivating the notion of visibility as a mark of power, Phelan advocates the politics of being "unmarked, unspoken, unseen" (7). Although Phelan's injunction to "give up the mark" gestures to some tantalizing prospects for those who have hitherto been "unseen," such a practice is difficult, perhaps even impossible, for those whose bodies have been marked as *in/visible,* a condition wherein the hypervisibility of race is the precondition for the ways in which one is mis-seen or unseen.[5] *Double Agency* interrogates the notions of performance and bodily representation in twentieth-century literary and dramatic texts by highlighting the ways in which an Asian American politics of impersonation both derives from and revises the in/visibility of Asian American bodies in U.S. American culture.

Impostors or Impersonators?—Acting Asian American

Asian Americans have repeatedly been seen in American culture as impostors of a particular sort. Concomitantly, they have been subject to a series of impostures perpetrated against them. What exactly does it mean to be charged as an impostor? To be identified as an impostor is to be named a fake, to be called out as a pretender who doesn't belong to whatever group is evaluating the performance in question, to be somehow found *inauthentic.* This is a powerful charge and can take on divergent forms; significantly, it has been leveled at Asian Americans both by outsiders and by those within the group.[6] One of the main ideas I propose in this book is to suggest that while Asian Americans have indeed been pressured into acts of imposture, they have through their performances wrestled with the ideologies that subject them to the charge of imposture and have struggled to make imposture something other than a mark of foreignness, secrecy, and falsehood. They have identified impersonation as a performance that articulates the circumscribed conditions of its emergence as a way of challenging static notions of racial authenticity even as it legitimates the truth of Asian American identities that emerge within a context of enforced performances of a particular nature. They have, in other words, rejected the logic of imposture—a logic based on binary notions of "real" and "fake"—in favor of enacting a politics of impersonation. In this way, impersonation disrupts and disputes the impositions of social hegemony, in part by acknowledging the interrelationships that exist between truth and falsity, the truth of identities that are always partly fictions of our own devising. Impersonation's dependence upon the interrelationship between the real and the fake, and its recognition of how both are inextricably intertwined in the formation of Asian American identities, constitute the directive for the double agents examined in this study.

What distinctions can be made between impersonation and imposture derive from different attitudes toward authority and the relationship each type of performance bears to the very notion of "authenticity." As I've noted, imposture depends upon a particular belief in the power of the authentic. As such, deception of this kind requires a seamless performance; the object is to fool others, to "pull one over" by convincing your audience (and maybe even yourself) of the rightness of your performance. Impersonation, on the other hand, challenges the notion of the seamless performance; it is a paradoxical act whereby the notions of authenticity and originality are simultaneously paid homage to and challenged. Impersonation, by its very nature as an act of divided allegiance, lends itself to more resistant possibilities—one of the reasons Asian Americans have adopted and adapted it for their uses in contemporary literary and artistic production.[7]

Clearly, determining impersonation's usefulness as a paradigm depends upon denoting the similarities and differences between such enactments and the performance of imposture. According to Webster's New Universal

Unabridged Dictionary, imposture is defined as:

1. The action or practice of imposing fraudulently upon others
2. Deception using an assumed character, identity, or name, as by an impostor; and
3. An instance or piece of fraudulent imposition.

Inherent in each of these definitions is the notion of imposture as an act that is, at its heart, about mendacity and duplicity. More concretely, imposture always involves some kind of betrayal. Alternatively, the definitions offered regarding impersonation vary somewhat; to impersonate means

1. to assume the character or appearance of; pretend to be
2. to mimic the voice, mannerisms, etc. of a person in order to entertain
3. to act or play the part of; personate
4. to represent in personal or bodily form; personify
5. embodied in a person; invested with personality.

While several of these definitions suggest impersonation as an act wherein the role being performed is taken on in order to pretend to be something one is not, impersonation, unlike imposture, is not equivalent to deception and fraudulence. This distinction is critical and constitutes the grounds from which we can use impersonation to examine possibilities that imposture would otherwise occlude for the performance of self. More exciting than seeing impersonation as an act that promises a possibility beyond betrayal for its performers are the strategies it proffers for establishing both subjectivity and agency. The last two definitions offered also gesture to the possibility of conceptualizing impersonation as an act through which identity itself is grounded in the body, "personified," and given "personality." In attending to the possibilities articulated in the act of personification, I would argue that impersonation requires that we move beyond the binary distinctions structuring any performance of imposture to sketch out the multiple performances—sometimes conflicted, often contradictory, and almost always of varied allegiance—that are both necessary and possible in the enactment of self-constitution. In other words, impersonation offers us more than a way of thinking about the performance of identity as that which is either essentialized or constructed: it affords us a paradigm for considering the mutually constitutive dimensions of identity and performance—the im-personation that is not about performing someone's else's identity but about performing into being a sense of one's own personhood.

Before I elaborate further upon the distinctions between imposture and impersonation, it is critical to note that while the usefulness of elucidating such differences can result in a *qualitatively different hermeneutic practice* (something I go on to demonstrate in the next chapter), imposture and impersonation do not always result in qualitatively different kinds of acts. I suggest that this site of potential overlap is critical to keep in mind even as this project begins with the assertion that understanding how such performances are distinct is paramount. The paradox of these two contentions should reflect not theoretical confusion but a productive site whose ambivalences and accretions will yield a flexible framework for considering the multiple aspects of Asian American identities. By focusing on the divergences in both intent and effect of imposture and impersonation, as well as by recognizing the spectrum of performance and response the two kinds of enactments share, *Double Agency* articulates a theory of how to re-consider literary and cultural representation by attending to both the quotidian and exceptional dramas from which such representational strategies emerge in the first place.

For many, imposture and impersonation suggest similar if not the same practices. Thus, in order to elaborate upon the issues of betrayal, subjectivity, and doubled allegiance that distinguish impersonation from imposture, it will be efficacious to consider how other critics have conceptualized these two kinds of performances. David Crane, for instance, differentiates imposture from impersonation by focusing on the visibility of the act; "(true) imposture—unlike impersonation—can't be seen too easily" (ix–x). While Crane's emphasis on imposture's secret nature in contradistinction to impersonation's more public performance of deception is extremely useful in considering the qualitatively different functions and effects of such acts, what seem to be clearly identifiable criteria for distinguishing such divergent performances are transformed into a site of unresolved concern when considered within an Asian American context. U.S. anxieties about how Asian Americans can or cannot be "seen" have regularly manifested themselves in a cultural history of considering Asian Americans both "excessively visible" and "inscrutable."

One of the most infamous examples of this racial anxiety concerning Asian Americanness's (in)visible differences is the oft-cited article from the December 1941 issue of *Life* magazine. The article—"How to Tell Japs from the Chinese"—is notable for many reasons: a concern about the ways in which members of the U.S. populace have revealed a "distressing ignorance on the delicate questions of how to tell a Chinese from a Jap"; a caution about proposed action on the part of the Chinese consulates to "tag their nationals with identification buttons" in order to prevent the United States's "staunch all[ies]" from being victimized; and a lesson derived from "anthropomorphic conformations" that will enable *Life*'s readers to distinguish with relative "scientific" accuracy between "friendly Chinese" and "enemy alien Japs." Accompanying the brief article is a set of pictures that demarcates the physical features and characteristics by which "Japs" and Chinese are supposedly to be differentiated. Despite the assurances in the article that such information is provided by physical anthropologists who are "devoted debunkers of race myths," clearly the text and pictures operate to *expose* the race myths that are founded on the simultaneously "excessively visible" and "inscrutable" features that make Asian Americanness troubling to U.S. notions of nation. As the markings on the pictures reveal, the public's ability to differentiate between what can or can't be seen too easily—Crane's basis for defining impersonation and imposture as discrete types of performances— is effective not so much in making clear the facial distinctions that determine the "Chinese type" from the "Japanese type" but in clarifying the anxiety of making even more visible (or rather, more "legible") the visibly disruptive difference Asian Americanness poses to U.S. hegemony. Significantly, such anxiety foregrounds the reasons Asian Americans have been subject to being called (out as) impostors and provides us a context within which to consider the implications of impersonation as a trope in contemporary Asian American literary and cultural production.

At the heart of Asian American impersonation, I posit, is *the deliberate confounding of both visible difference and visible sameness.* Such a paradox grants Asian American acts of impersonation a double foundation and makes such acts particularly effective in both critiquing the impositions placed upon Asian American subjects via the roles in the U.S. imaginary that they have been historically asked to perform and foregrounding the ways in which these very roles might be utilized to disrupt the codes of conduct they ostensibly uphold or to seduce the performer into playing a so-cially sanctioned part. What the *Life* sketch attempts to foreground are the ways in which the visually disruptive difference of Asian (American) faces, a difference that emerges from the uncanny sameness such faces pose to the untrained non-Asian U.S. observer, might be rendered clearly discernable so as to maintain the myth of a uniform national identity. What the *Life* sketch actually exposes are the white origins of the myths themselves, an originary act of imposture that forms one of the frameworks within which Asian American acts of impersonation take place and which such acts challenge. The threats being addressed in the sketch thus have as much to do with how dominant society is hostage to its own acts of racial and cultural imposture as with how Asian/Americans have somehow impostured their way into po-sitions that can undermine the sanctity of the U.S. body politic. In such a way, one of this study's central concerns is to expose the ways in which Asian American acts of impersonation paradoxically vivify dominant American so-ciety's manifold acts of racial and cultural imposture.

Echoing Crane's idea of a *visible* difference between the two kinds of per-formances, Hillel Schwartz understands imposture as "the compulsive as-sumption of invented lives" whereas impersonation involves "the concerted assumption of another's public identity" (72). Here, visibility becomes trans-lated into a public/private issue in order to make apparent what is at stake in differentiating the two kinds of performances. Thus, Schwartz goes on to suggest that distinctions between impostors and impersonators, while man-ifold, are ultimately critical because of how their actions impact those with whom they interact: "Impersonation, not imposture, is at home with quiet deceit and may breed underground. Both may be impeccably costumed, yet in the final dressing down, impostors want attention and love, and we be-tray them; impersonators want our money, our secrets, our family line, and they betray us" (73). Although Schwartz's assertion that distinctions must be made between imposture and impersonation is of critical importance, I con-tend that his bases for making such moral evaluations about betrayal and de-sire are complicated and problematized by the context of how such differ-ences operate in Asian American experience and representation. In suggesting that by the theft of "another's public identity" the impersonator ultimately betrays *us,* the key identifications of who "we" and "they" are must, of necessity, be addressed. While an emphasis on *public identity* is crucial to understanding the nature, practice, and possibilities of Asian American impersonation, the issue of "betrayal" becomes much less clearly assignable when the public identity in question does not so much belong to someone else as it is *the one that has already been assigned to you by the public*. To that end, I would turn Schwartz's provocative starting point around. The disjunctive and dislocating effects of assuming a public identity compel Asian Americans to resist imposture's insistence that the seams between performance and identity can disappear and instead to consider impersonation's self-reflexive efforts to maintain a kind of double agency that all-too-often gets interpreted as the desire to betray.

Betrayal is a complicated charge, one that works not only to "regulate group belonging" but also to "constitute subversion of another kind, a subversion of repressive authority that depends on upholding strict borders between groups and individuals" (Bow 8, 3). Leslie Bow's suggestion that accusations of betrayal are intimately connected to the development and maintenance of group affiliations thus exposes the dangerous ground occupied by Asian American impersonators. Threatened by and threatening to more than a single group, such subjects always run the risk of violating multiple affiliations.[8] Since Asian American impersonation is fundamentally a performance that holds in visible tension multiple allegiances, impersonators must forgo the illusory pleasures of identity as a singular performance in favor of enacting the messiness of such multiplicity. Additionally, they must recognize that the consequences of such behavior will be both to pacify and disrupt the conventional codes of identity and belonging assigned them. Indeed, the paradox of betrayal—that boundaries can only be determined through their transgression, affiliations strengthened and maintained by virtue of their violation—structurally parallels the paradox of Asian American acts of impersonation: that only by contesting legal, social, and political institutions that have sought to determine Asians in the United States as aliens have Asian Americans been able to make the United States accountable for the rhetoric of welcome and democratic inclusion that it ostensibly claims for itself. So it is that Asian American acts of impersonation become not simply a locus for the interrogation of U.S. legal and political structures but also a strategy of embodiment that exposes the convoluted relationships that undergird the continued maintenance of such structures.

The seriousness of intent and outcome attendant on such performances demands that we also question the impersonator's popularly conceptualized motives and effects. Oftentimes, impersonation is understood as a frivolous act, one meant to entertain by virtue of demonstrating the fraught pleasures of both *acting as* a public figure but not actually *being* that person. Indeed, impersonation is often understood to be a kind of performance taken up specifically to entertain others. It seems no coincidence that Asian American acts of impersonation have traversed the seeming disjunction between the serious and the comic. A performance designed to gauge and negotiate the multifarious permissions and injunctions that structure subject formation, impersonation grants its practitioners the ability to turn sober endeavors into jokes and vice versa.

Jane Gallop recognizes impersonation as a "double structure" that requires us to take it "at one and the same time both as a joke and as serious" (5). Seeing Elvis impersonation and female impersonators as emblematic of how impersonation holds in tension the comic and the critical, Gallop's acknowledgement of impersonation's ambivalent effects helps us to think about the nature of the "double realization" that makes the tensions "less painfully contradictory" (17). Asian American impersonators have understood the nature of that relationship to audience expectation, particularly with respect to their enactments of stereotype. Even more critically, Asian American acts of impersonation have highlighted the difficulty of resisting imposture's stereotypical pose—even as they acknowledge the importance of having fun (and being able to make fun of themselves) to the larger project of re-working the imposing cultural constructions that seek to over-determine the practice and expression of Asian American identities. To a great extent, Asian American performances of self via the public performance of stereotype have worked to entertain in ambivalent ways: to a mainstream audience they assuage anxieties about the fixity of otherwise problematically unreadable Asian American identities while they also operate as an "inside joke" that can both expose differences in a pan-ethnic coalition and further cement affiliations within the same coalition.[9] I see impersonation and its nature as a performance of dual allegiance as an extremely effective vehicle for articulating such double aims and thus an invaluable site for critical investigation.

While all performance may be said to be of dual allegiance, impersonation makes the duality of its ontology manifest. To perform without exposing the slight but key fissures that crack the façade of the perfect original is to become something else entirely. Significantly, while many Asian American acts of impersonation begin in a context of necessity—they are not undertaken for pleasurable reasons but because livelihood, citizenship, identity, and survival are dependent upon their careful enactment—impersonation also can contain a pleasurable component that characterizes it in some contemporary contexts. To borrow Sau-ling Wong's important formulation of a key paradigm for understanding Asian American literary and cultural production, impersonation thus often manifests an *extravagant* nature whose excesses and self-reflexivity make it a practice whereby spectacular criticisms can emerge from the politics of the everyday.

Clearly, inherent in Schwartz's disquisition on the distinctions between imposture and impersonation exists the awareness that impersonation can be performed with a seriousness of purpose that affects not only the performer but we who constitute the impersonator's audience; why else is the issue of betrayal in question? Studying Asian American acts of impersonation makes apparent how such performances are always deployed with more than one audience in mind. In addition to questions of audience, the nature of the identities being impersonated demands our attention. Unlike the performances Schwartz and Gallop interrogate, the acts of impersonation *Double Agency* emphasizes are usually not ones wherein the public identity being assumed is a recognizable public identity belonging to someone else. Instead, this project seeks to explore the usefulness of impersonation as a way of investigating the contexts and strategies by which Asian Americans have been subject to and embrace Asian Americanness as a viable category of identity. Thus, if we assume Asian American impersonation to be a specific act that involves the assumption of a public identity that does not necessarily belong to "someone else" but that has been assigned to and subsequently adopted by the performer in question in order to articulate an identity comprehensible to the public, the manifest possibilities of how impersonation and identity are not only related but in some sense mutually constitutive become key sites for thinking through the complicated process of performing into being Asian Americanness.

Laura Browder argues in her study of the "slippery characters" who have utilized autobiography to invent for themselves a new identity that ethnic impersonation has not only been a practice "peculiarly suited to American national mythologies" but has been, in some key sense, a performance fundamental to "revis[ing] the basis for a national sense of self" (2, 6).[10] In my examination of Asian American impersonation, the function and practice of impersonation take on an even more "slippery" character. Impersonation and imposture, even as their distinctions are acknowledged, become confused and confusing. Unlike the performances Browder discusses, the Asian American acts I investigate here are not perpetrated primarily in order for their subjects to assume new ethnic identities and thus new opportunities.[11] This kind of act is one that both Browder and Gotanda's character Vincent Chang would term impersonation but that, according to the distinctions I have already outlined, might be considered more representative of imposture. Vincent, who changed his name from Shigeo Nakada after World War II in order to find work as an actor, gives rise to remembering this one, emblematic moment as foundational for thinking about the ways in which imposture does not so much become impersonation as part of some evolutionary process of Asian American identity formation but rather gestures to the simultaneous performance of identity and not-identity that become foregrounded in the re-enactment of a stereotypical role that is both desired and disavowed. In this way, Vincent's transformation exemplifies the synchronic practice of both acts and, even more significantly, raises the question of how such doubled performance works to grant cultural legitimacy even as it questions the legitimacy of certain cultural contexts. This demands a consideration of how impersonation works when it is performed not in order to assume another, more desirable or "known" public identity but when it is undertaken in order to perform into existence a public identity that has already been used to label you. Even more bluntly, how do our ideas about the acts and subjects of impersonation change when we see the contexts of such performance as a critical avenue by which those whose identities have been marked as "Asian American" are not only questioned but, in some very real sense, always in question? Impersonation is thus an act of doubled intent: it performs and challenges identity at the same time.

By focusing on impersonation as a way of understanding the pleasures and problems of identity formation, I limn in an Asian American context a specific set of responses to some central U.S. discourses of race and power. As evidence of how subject formation is impacted by hegemonic discourses compelling particular kinds of behavior for "good" minority subjects, impersonation bears some similarity to the African American practice of passing. According to Pamela Caughie, while passing is a practice that is generally implicated in a racist social organization, "the phenomenon is so very American in the anxieties it arouses and in the behaviors that define it" (20). What is "so very American" about passing is, as Caughie suggests, the centrality of racial history and politics in the makeup of contemporary identity issues that continue to remember in some ghostly way the markers of identity that our postmodern society would like to move beyond.[12] Like passing, impersonation is a performance in multiple registers: it can be undertaken as a way of disrupting pre-existing categories of identity even as it maintains identity as a powerful way of understanding subjectivity.

In the work on passing undertaken by African Americanist critics, integral to understanding the ways in which such a practice operates to "turn what [is] conceived of as a natural opposition into a societal one" (Fabi 5), namely racial hierarchies and dichotomies, the notion of "crossing the [color] line" not only becomes the locus of passing's effect but also constitutes the very conditions of passing's definition as a performance of racial imposture. Gayle Wald suggests that racial passing reflects "subjects' desires to control the terms of their racial definition, rather than be subject to the definitions of white supremacy" (6). In this particular kind of challenge to the "definitions of white supremacy," racial passing as a practice that questions pre-existing constructions of race and the naturalization of race as a social construction depends upon a subject performing both "blackness" and "whiteness" in order to demonstrate the ways in which the "color line," while not stable in its placement, maintains the authority of a racialized social order. Passing is thus an act of boundary crossing that is performed in order to reveal both a desire to "fix" race into essential categories as well as the impossibility of fixing race in such static ways. Passing's challenge to racial categories and the assault it poses to race itself as a primary category through which to understand identity and subjectivity co-exist with the potentially problematic ways in which the desire to pass seems to "require [the] valorization of racial discourse (if not necessarily of 'whiteness' or 'blackness' itself)" (Wald 7). This dilemma—what I would term the impasse of passing—shares with impersonation a concern regarding the circumscribed conditions under which strategies of resistance for minority subjects emerge. As Wald reminds us, passing narratives usefully instruct us about how "it is in the nature of any 'strategy' that we do not get to choose either it or the circumstances in which its desirability is manifested" (187). As organic strategies of simultaneously resisting and acknowledging how racial ideology and race as a category of identity mark the subjectivity and identity of what Juda Bennett terms "the passing figure" and what I am naming the impersonator, both passing and impersonation wrestle not only with the tactic of how to perform as well as undermine racial constructions but also with the implications and contexts of such performances as they are affected by specific cultural, historical, and political circumstances. Thus, it is important to remark upon the ways in which passing and impersonation are shared practices that also must be differentiated in particular ways in order to address the distinct positions African Americans and Asian Americans occupy in national discussions of race and racial difference.

While passing and its operation in an African American context is a useful comparative model for thinking about Asian American acts of impersonation, the difference between these two paradigms derives from the particular ways in which Asian Americans have been deployed in and by the U.S. American imaginary to function as markers of inassimilable difference of a specific sort. Although "blackness" in the U.S. imaginary has historically served to mark the outer limits of difference itself, a function that emerges with increasing clarity in the practice of denoting various ethnic groups such as the Irish as "black" until such time as the conditions of their incorporation into a national body seems more possible and appropriate, Asianness has quite consistently denoted a difference of such magnitude that it cannot be incorporated into the national body-politic—or, at the very least, such incorporation is always suspect in some way.[13]

Thus, one of the defining characteristics of the *public identity* Asian Americans have been assigned is that of perpetual foreignness. As critics have noted, the terms "Asian" and "American" have often been perceived to be incompatible, a perception whose cultural rootedness and currency is undergirded by an entire network of historical, legal, and social practice. The disjunction inherent in the idea of the mutual irreconcilability of East and West, Asian and American, marks a fundamental reason why impersonation proves such a provocative trope for the understanding of Asian American identity formation.[14] The sense of alienation from self, the very visceral dimension of embodied being that is co-dependent upon the notion of a publicly constituted identity that you must find ways of making your own even as it claims you for itself, in uncanny ways evinces the paradox that makes impersonation a powerful, compelling, and necessary political act.

With the pervasive ideas of Asian Americans as somehow never being able to be "American" enough, the very nature of Asian American identity might be thought of as *one that requires one to impersonate fundamentally oneself.* These particular ideas of Asian Americans being alien to U.S. American identity—stemming, in part, from "the historical racialization of Asian-origin immigrants as nonwhite 'aliens ineligible to citizenship'" (Lowe 20)—are accompanied by the related stereotypes of Asians as "sneaky," "secretive," and "inscrutable." Such characterizations coalesce into the figure of the Asian American as spy or alien, a figure whose foreign allegiances make it not only possible but probable that his/her claims to American-ness are suspect or, in other words, impostured.[15]

This conceptualization of Asian Americans as somehow more prone than other visibly identified minority groups to imposture and to threatening the sanctity of national belonging through a *pretense* of docility and obedience (the legacy of an enduring combination of two pervasive cultural ideas of Asian Americans as both representative of "the model minority" and "the yellow peril") depends upon a notion of Asian Americanness as somehow fundamentally fraudulent. Even when seen as successful examples of the possibilities of assimilation, members of a "model minority" whose status as "honorary whites" grants them opportunities to overcome the prejudicial and exclusionary barriers confronted by other minority groups in the United States, Asian Americans are subject to the overweening perception that they are somehow "illegitimate Americans" (Tuan 39).[16] Such perceptions constitute Asian Americans as frauds who pretend to American identity by performing, with an intent to deceive, the rights and responsibilities of citizenship.[17] *Double Agency* argues for differentiating impersonation from performances of imposture and of passing in order to expose the rhetorical and narrative blind spots that make such ontological definitions so problematic for Asian Americans and undertakes a more systematic interrogation of the ways in which the performance of Asian American identities both relates to and challenges the dynamics by which American identities are constructed in the first place. By differentiating imposture from impersonation through characterizing imposture as the seamless performance of an adopted public identity that is understood to belong to someone else and considering impersonation as an act that makes apparent, in particular contexts, its own origins and confounds the issues of betrayal that are so seemingly clear in calling out imposture, this study attempts to delineate a praxis through which Asian American identities can be performed into being and agency claimed.

In juxtaposing models of passing in an African American context with the paradigm of impersonation being developed to discuss Asian American identity formation and aesthetic practice, I theorize impersonation as an act that shares passing's problematization of race and its essentialization. However, while the two performances share an interest in interrogating the fluidity of race, a politics of impersonation does so not by crossing the color line but by investigating the partiality of racial performance inherent *within* the very notion of Asian American identity itself. More specifically, what marks my delineation of impersonation as a performative strategy that is distinct from the practice of passing is its emphasis on the ways in which such a politics depends not on attempting to perform a "normative" identity—for the African American subject, "whiteness"—but through the very performance of Asian Americanness itself. As *Double Agency* argues, embedded within the performance of Asian Americanness exists the awareness of the ways in which such an identity has, from its earliest moments in U.S. legal and social history, been constituted as an oxymoron but comprises the conflicted reality that those who have been ascribed this identity must nonetheless embody, confront, and adapt to their own ends.[18]

Recently, Traise Yamamoto has elaborated upon "masking" as a trope for understanding the ways in which Japanese American women negotiate the dynamics of self-authorship.[19] I enact a related project here: investigating the contours and complexities of performances that both circumscribe and condition Asian American acts of impersonation. By concerning itself with how impersonation works—thematically, formally, and politically—in a broadly conceptualized field of texts, *Double Agency* hopes to make its critical endeavor self-reflexive even as it invests heavily in both the practicality and possibility of identity as an organizing concept through which academic inquiries can be made, literary representation enacted, and social change effected. The currency of poststructuralism and its privileging of fragmentation, indeterminacy, and multiplicity conceptualizes identity not as the concrete foundation of self but as a set of "identity-effects." While critics like Lisa Lowe have mobilized such ideas very successfully in addressing the realities of the racialized subject, it remains important to note how such approaches to the issue of identity "should involve recognizing the ways in which dominant culture subjects rely on a granted, assumed coherency that may then be both bracketed and deconstructed. For subjects marked by race, or by gender and race, fragmentation is very often the condition in which they already find themselves by simple virtue of being situated in a culture that does not grant them subjecthood, or grants them only contingent subjectivity" (T. Yamamoto 74–75). Yamamoto's sensitivity to the different conditions under which dominant culture subjects and marginalized subjects construct their identities via discontinuous notions of difference elaborates upon Susan Koshy's injunction that we do not necessarily discard the fiction of Asian American identity even as we resist its totalizing tendencies: as Yamamoto rightly suggests, it is paramount that we reconceptualize difference "as that which both 'undermines the very idea of identity' and as that which 'does not annul identity. It is beyond and alongside identity'" (79). This doubled project—of both undermining and yet not annulling identity—is one manifestation of the double agency of impersonation that this project seeks to examine.

History and a Politics of Impersonation

Impersonation operates critically in contemporary Asian American literature in large part because it has been so formative as a practice by which Asian immigrants transformed themselves into Asian Americans and, concomitantly, contested dominant notions of how Asian Americans should perform within the cultural, social, and political landscapes of the United States. I'd like to sketch several specific historical acts of impersonation and, by briefly reading such performances as they have been represented in literary and cultural production, suggest how charges of imposture and acts of impersonation—performances whose discrete meanings oftentimes blurred in rather confusing but significant ways—function to create Asian Americans as "double agents" who work both to establish their own claims to a U.S. American identity and to critique the American institutions that have designated them as "aliens" whose incorporation into the body politic is thus always already suspect.

There are a number of historical contexts within which the network of understanding and practices that I am terming a politics of impersonation might be examined. Providing an exhaustive inventory of such contexts is not possible and also not the priority of this project, which seeks to delineate how impersonation as a strategic method of articulating Asian Americans as subjects and agents operates in twentieth-century Asian American literary and cultural production. The grounding for such a project might seem willful and arbitrary; it is certainly partial and limited in scope. However, I will delimit two contexts that were particularly helpful to me in generating my ideas about impersonation—the existence of "paper sons" and "paper daughters" in a Chinese American context and the practice of bringing picture brides to the United States via the *shashin-kekkon* system of photo-marriage—in order to extrapolate from them a more concrete framework for understanding how and why it is so critical to examine the importance of acts of impersonation to the existence and maintenance of Asian Americanness in the United States. After using these two contexts to foreground some of the contours of impersonation as a conceptual paradigm for thinking about Asian American literature, I will address Susan Koshy's influential argument about the limitations of Asian American literary studies as a field of inquiry and suggest how a concept such as impersonation provides a way to account for the "multiple, conflicted, and emergent formations of Asian American literature" (470) by emphasizing its impossible origins. Such an argumentative framework will, in part, furnish some of the scaffolding necessary for perceiving the enduring presence of impersonation as not simply a thematic presence or narrative through which to consider Asian American experiences but a hermeneutics through which representation and aesthetics continue to inform contemporary Asian American literary production. It will also outline the ways in which acts of impersonation have helped us both to imagine the possibilities of Asian American literatures and to perform self-consciously the limitations and contradictions of the literary and cultural enterprises of Asian America.

"Paper sons" (and daughters) emerged during a critical opportunity in the history of Asian America to practice impersonation as a strategic response for the articulation of subjectivity. By thinking about the foundational implications of such acts, we can imagine—as many paper families did—a critical process of interrogation by which not only identity comes into question but also the social structures that determine how such formulations are deemed acceptable. Chinese sojourners comprised the first major wave of Asian immigration into the United States. As their stories demonstrate, the immigration restrictions and exclusions governing their entry into the country produced an elaborate family of paper children whose claims to citizenship were predicated on a series of interconnected performances of family obligation and identity. As historian Roger Daniels records, while individual Chinese are reported in Pennsylvania as early as 1785, Chinese immigration to the United States began in earnest with the California gold rush of 1849 and ended with the passage of the Chinese Exclusion Act of 1882. Approximately 300,000 Chinese were recorded entering the country during those thirty-three years. After the passage of the Chinese Exclusion Act, Chinese immigration dropped significantly and opportunities to immigrate, particularly for the laboring class, were sharply restricted.[20] Given these circumstances, Chinese men were faced with living out their lives in segregated Chinatowns and resigned themselves either to being separated from the families they left behind in China or to living the rest of their lives as "bachelor-uncles." In this context, practices of imposture began to abound and would eventually evolve into a network of practices that comprise the groundwork for what I have termed a politics of impersonation.

In order to subvert restrictive immigration policies, many in the Chinese American community sought out "paper" identities that would provide them opportunities to expand their personal and communal opportunities. Since the law allowed Chinese merchants the privilege of bringing their families to the United States, a number of laundrymen, restaurant owners and laborers attempted to present themselves as "paper merchants" to authorities. Such deception could only succeed with the establishment of entire networks of partner relationships these impostors set up with businesses in their communities. Similarly, after an earthquake and a series of fires in San Francisco in 1906 destroyed the town hall and virtually all of the municipal records of the city, Chinese settlers capitalized upon this catastrophe to create immigration and citizenship opportunities for an entire new generation by virtue of the paper son industry. This practice, which took advantage of the law and its stipulation that children of Americans were automatically citizens of the United States, even if they were born in a foreign country, depended upon forging documents, identities, and family alliances in order for incoming immigrants to claim citizenship status. While such practices might seem to be strictly acts of imposture—attempts to deceive by relinquishing one identity in order to assume another—I would submit that for a number of different reasons they contribute to the repertoire of impersonation by challenging the distinctions of "real" and "false" that imposture does not really challenge. Significantly, the registers of performance that impersonation more adequately realizes than imposture concern not only the complication of issues of betrayal and visibility, as my earlier discussion articulates, but also the attenuations of multiple identities that do not disperse agency into radical postmodern play but continue to recognize the viability of the coherent, political subject. In order to illustrate this, I will turn briefly to two texts—the memoirs of Tung Pok Chin and Fae Myenne Ng's novel *Bone*.

Tung Pok Chin's *Paper Son: One Man's Story* (2000) examines the experience of Chinese immigrants who made themselves American citizens by virtue of imposture that slips into a kind of impersonation. A memoir written by an actual paper son, Chin's story is valuable for illuminating the process by which so many Chinese immigrants performed into reality their identities as Chinese Americans—performances that questioned U.S. legal definitions of who could become a citizen as well as stable definitions of the "original" identities with which these men began. Chin, who entered the United States in 1934, immigrated to the United States after buying for himself an identity paper naming him as a single man. Integral to understanding Chin's story is his past as an adopted son, his struggles to claim his multiple identities, and his acknowledgement of the contexts and practices that transformed his acts of imposture into ones of impersonation.

Paper Son outlines the rather straightforward imposture required by the obstacles U.S. immigration law posed to Chinese immigrants seeking to enter the country. Purchasing an identity paper for $2000, Chin memorized a series of "facts"—"my paper name, my paper father's name, my paper mother's name, my age, their ages, my place of birth, their places of birth, their occupations, and so on" (12)—that would enable him to verify to U.S. authorities his identity and thus gain him U.S. citizenship. However, the dynamics by which Chin and others lived out their lives as paper children reflect the ways in which Chinese American identities emerged from a complex series of practices and effects that I am terming a *politics of impersonation*. As Chin's own experience reveals, the public/private, visible/invisible distinctions raised by Crane and Schwartz are complicated in the Chinese American context: despite always representing himself as Tung Pok Chin in "official, governmental way(s)," Chin admits that "in the Chinese community we freely revealed ourselves and our past because we all knew how most of us got here . . . We felt we were among family and we could be ourselves again, all sticking together in a foreign land" (71).

Chin's rhetoric—"we could be ourselves again"—seems to suggest a rather uncritical understanding of his own paper son identity as impostured act in the same ways understood by the U.S. government, whose continued vigilance in determining the authenticity of Chinese American identities extended to the 1950s and a Cold War program of surveillance and confession that encouraged paper sons to confess themselves as impostors in exchange for a probationary period of appraisal and re-application for citizenship. However, a consideration of the social and cultural contexts for Chin's history and his decision to continue identifying as Tung Pok Chin, even as he clearly maintains that he both is and isn't such a character, helps us to see the ways in which the relatively simple imposture that Chin began enacting as a paper son gradually metamorphosizes into a more complicated network of impersonative practices. As Chin's example demonstrates, the issue of self-consciousness becomes key to understanding both the interpretive problems and the performative possibilities impersonation provides. The doubled audience with whom Chin is engaged, like his fellow impersonators, proves critical to thinking through the ways in which differentiating Asian American impersonation from the charges of imposture is of necessity confounding: Chin's act is simultaneously imposture to a mainstream U.S. audience even as it is impersonation within the Chinese American community. And, even more significantly, the distinctions between these different acts operate simultaneously given the multiple contexts for Chin's performances of self. This simultaneity speaks to one of the premises of *Double Agency*: the doubled performance undertaken by Chin and his fellow impersonators illuminates the ways in which such synchronicity produces differences in meaning, function, and effect that have usually been interpreted as a desire to betray but must also be read as acts of faith in the power of performance to produce viable (and flexible) paradigms of self-fashioning.

In addition to the effectiveness of Chin's memoir in helping us understand the general contours of the paper son experience, his particular attention to his adopted status even before he becomes a paper son and the real obligations such impersonated familial relationships require demand that our attention be focused on the other nuances of his performance that impersonation makes manifest. Significantly, Chin relates to us that even before he purchases his paper son identity in order to enter the United States, he was sold in China to a couple to be their son. Chin's history as someone who was kidnapped by a warlord and sold to a barren couple as their "son" raises the interesting question of what makes one identity more "authentic" than another. In many ways, Chin perceives his "real" name—Lai Bing Chan—as no different from his "paper" name. Thus, Chin considers the U.S. government's interest in getting him to confess to his "real identity" during the 1950s to be misguided. Clearly, paper sons like Chin did not attempt to pass within the Chinese American community and thus were doubly affiliated with both paper and "real" families. However, over time—and given the equally significant fact that the identification of one paper son's imposture would jeopardize an entire paper family—the bonds and obligations of paper families manifested an undeniable realness that was no less powerful for being initially assumed. Thus, when Chin's wife's "real" nephew arrives in the United States and discovers the hardship of life and considers returning to Hong Kong, Chin cautions that his decision concerning his own status cannot be made in isolation but must instead be determined within the context of the paper family to whom he is indebted. "In a confession you will totally destroy not only Hom Suey Wah's livelihood by exposing his paper status, but you will destroy the lives of your other 'uncles' as well. Remember, Uncle Hom has six paper brothers. They have done you absolutely no wrong" (63).

Similarly, Fae Myenne Ng's novel *Bone* (1993) emphasizes the ways in which paper identities are taken up, not as impostured performances, but as impersonative possibilities that create very real networks of obligation and familial responsibility. The story of what happens to one Chinatown family after the middle daughter commits suicide, *Bone* is narrated by Leila, the oldest daughter of Mah and Leon. Preoccupied by the question of what makes family endure—blood, paper, obligation, pain, and promise—Leila knows that while Leon is "not my real father . . . he's the one who's been there for me. Like he always told me, it's time that makes a family, not just blood" (3). This is a lesson she learns not just from her own relationship with Leon but from understanding his past as a paper son and watching the ties he formed with his fellow paper brothers. Unlike "You Thin[, who] changed back to his real name as soon as he could . . . Leon never did. Leon liked to repeat what he told You Thin: 'In this country, paper is more precious than blood' " (9). Keeping his paper name and building a life upon that name reflects Leon's decision to establish himself as an impersonator who holds in visible tension his public and private identities and, in the process, problematizes the (in)visible distinctions that demarcate one from the other. Like Chin, Leon never hides the fact that he is a paper son from those in the Chinese community; like Chin, both Leon and later Leila are aware of the ways in which impersonation derives its power from an ability to confound the distinctions between the fake and the real. Thus, Leila acknowledges in the process of looking for Leon's affidavit of identification that the truth lies somewhere between what is on paper and what has been performed for her. Indeed, *Bone* makes its commentary about the power of familial obligations and possibilities dependent upon the fact that we always know who Leon is and is not supposed to be, a paradox that stems from the ways in which his identity, impostured in some ways but very much the concrete foundation for Leila's sense of self, depends upon an impersonative notion of how identities are anchored in fluid performances and widely divergent interpretive communities.

Following impersonation's historical traces can result in dead ends, unexpected outcomes, and the sense of impossible origins. We never discover Leon's "real" name even as we come to understand that Leon Leong both is and isn't Leon Leong. Significantly, such mysteries force us to engage with the paradoxical nature of impersonation as an act of faith *and* of skepticism. As we learn from the paper sons and daughters of the exclusion era, their impersonations of identity and family relationships reveal a very situated sense of obligation as well as of exploitation; the cynicism undergirding the slot system whereby a person could claim an identity not his or her own in order to enter the United States illegally existed alongside notions of filiality and kinship that became real by virtue of their pretense. Such complex interconnections bespeak one important aspect of impersonation in its subsequent use and deployment in contemporary Asian America: the legacy of impersonation as a necessary act of posturing has also become, for many Asian Americans, the concrete foundation upon which a politics of identity as impersonation becomes accessible and real.

Another historical context for understanding how impersonation emerges as a trope for thinking about Asian Americanness might be the existence of the picture bride system that constituted a significant method through which Asian American marriages were negotiated and executed in the late-nineteenth and early twentieth centuries.[21] In texts like Marie Hara's short story "Honeymoon Hotel, 1895" (1994) and Kayo Hatta's 1995 film *Picture Bride*, we see the issue of deception perpetrated through photographic mis-representation foregrounded and the consequences of such acts explored. Both Hara's story and Hatta's film deploy the case of impostured identity as a trope through which to examine the emergence of a grounded, Japanese American presence in Hawai'i. In Hara's story, the protagonist—Sono—arrives in Hawaii to discover that her husband "looked too old!" since "the photograph she kept in her kimono depicted a smooth-shaven young man" while "the Yamamoto person who stood at the desk appeared to be at least forty years old and bearded heavily" (10). Similarly, in *Picture Bride*, Riyo Nakamura arrives in Hawai'i only to find herself married to Matsuji, a man who has "gambled" their future happiness on her ability to forgive his deception in sending her a photo of himself as a much younger man. In each of these texts, an act of imposture as facilitated by the photograph's ability to capture an image and literally freeze time heralds the opening of the stories to follow.

Critically, while the deceptions being perpetrated by Yamamoto and Matsuji are important to Sono and Riyo—Sono expresses a reserved but distinct sense of disappointment while Riyo openly expresses her anger at being deceived and repeatedly resists Matsuji's efforts to consummate the marriage—the texts generated by Hara and Hatta helpfully illuminate two important aspects of the argument I've been delineating. Both works suggest that the situations the characters find themselves in demand that imposture's logic of discarded and assumed identity be revised to account for the complicated dynamics by which *all* identities, not just the ones being claimed, are in negotiation and contestation in order to produce the possibility of the construction of another, Asian American identity. By emphasizing one aspect of impersonation that I have thus far stressed—a performance of identity wherein one doesn't attempt to pass one's self off as someone else but that exposes an aspect of (in this case) Japanese American identity that is being constructed via the restrictive nature of the U.S. contexts within which such an identity is of necessity formed—Hara and Hatta lay the groundwork for constructing these beginning moments of deception and fraud as mutual and mutually constitutive.[22] *Picture Bride* reveals how Riyo herself, although faithful to the likeness as represented by her wedding portrait, also has a secret: her decision to accept Matsuji's offer of marriage and immigrate to Hawai'i is motivated, in part, by her desire to leave "the ghosts of the past" behind and avoid the stigma attached to her as the daughter of parents who died of tuberculosis.

As the relationship between Riyo and Matsuji deepens, we see the way in which Matsuji's act of impersonating his *younger* self needs to be interpreted as something more than a moment of personal deception. Indeed, Matsuji's impersonation produces a commentary about and critique of the racial and economic conditions to which he is subjected as a Japanese plantation worker. In one pivotal scene when the tensions between Filipino and Japanese workers are highlighted, a young Filipino laborer protesting the difference in treatment Filipinos and Japanese receive yells in frustration: "Do I have to be as old as him [Matsuji] before I can afford to send away for a young wife like [Riyo]!" As the film makes clear, Matsuji's impersonation of his younger self opens up a space from which the oppressive conditions under which Asian Americans provide the "hana-hana" (work) that sustains the plantation economy can be both illuminated and criticized. In the process of such a doubled practice, impersonation contributes to the possibility of constructing an alternative narrative, one of romantic and political possibility, to the one suggested by imposture's betrayal.

Yoji Yamaguchi's novel *Face of a Stranger* (1995) takes up this trope of an impostured performance that gestures beyond itself to highlight the ways in which impersonation contributes to social and political critique. *Face* explicitly thematizes impersonation as an artistic and conceptual framework through which to evaluate the potential and problems of Asian American identity formation. Yamaguchi's novel investigates the narrative thread that Hara and Hatta choose *not* to foreground in their stories: that of deception and betrayal that the picture bride system fostered when women were lured to the United States with the promise of marriage and then discovered themselves either married to men who most certainly were not the ones in the pictures they received or forced into prostitution to serve the majority-male Asian labor population.[23] Quite importantly, *Face*'s plot developments depend upon an original act of imposture: a handsome and dissolute young man, Takashi Arai, agrees to sell his photographic likeness to an old man, Kori, who tells Arai that he intends to use the photo in order to woo and to win for himself a young picture bride. What seems to Arai a gesture of limited consequence for three people turns into a situation where many women are deceived by his picture, promised husbands of great beauty only to find themselves either married to homely men or, even worse, brought to America in order to serve as prostitutes in ghettoized Asian communities.

As Yamaguchi's farcical novel makes clear, the masquerade and confusion about identities in *Face* result from—and are extreme examples of—the illusory promises America makes to potential immigrants. Although Arai feels some twinges of guilt in his (somewhat unwitting) part in deceiving so many women, he also concludes that, like them, he too has been fooled by the allure of the American dream:

KITARE, NIHONJIN!
COME MERCHANTS! AMERICA IS A VERITABLE HUMAN PARADISE, THE ICHI-BAN MINE IN THE WORLD! GOLD, SILVER, AND GEMS ARE SCATTERED IN HER STREET!
Now that was a pretty picture. But it didn't depict him stooped over picking lettuce under a scorching sun, or working as a houseboy for two churlish, dwarflike spinsters, the Warren twins Joan and Jane, and their irascible dog. This was the life Takashi found awaiting him in this veritable human paradise. Why should he feel bad for these picture brides who were just as gullible as him? (10)

Thus, *Face* utilizes the trope of the unlike(ly) photograph in order to comment on the social, political, and economic contexts within which Asian American immigrants labored. By making evident the ways in which the exchange of Arai's picture heralds more than individual acts of imposture but rather, signals to the proliferating contexts that undercut the "pretty picture" of the United States that is equally misleading for immigrants, Yamaguchi develops in his novel a politics of impersonation as a critical practice, a method through which social and political critique can been mounted. To that end, *Face* emphasizes the dizzying proliferation of acts that are called into question by Arai's over-circulated photo.

In constructing a politics of impersonation, *Face* features a motley cast of characters—all of whose acts contribute to the developing notion of identity as constructed and impersonation as an act that not only offers a way of performing into being Asian American identity but also concomitantly performs into being an insistent regard for the importance of institutional critique. Kikue, the prostitute who masterminds a plot to get revenge on Takashi, must survive the conditions of her own experience as a woman who is not only fooled regarding her promised husband, but told that she is "nobody but who [her pimp] say[s] that you are . . . [because] that girl—I can't even remember her name now—no longer exists" (22). What does it mean to impersonate, then, into being her identity when the original referent for who she is—"that girl"—is not recognized with any legitimacy or as having any authority? Other situations deployed in the novel continue to wrestle with this notion of authority, seeking to show how impersonation causes the re-evaluation of the very structures of authority and (de)legitimation that seek to overdetermine Asian American identity in the first place. Thus, Takashi's experience as someone who is dubbed "Charlie" by his employers not simply because " 'Arai' and even plain old 'Takashi' proved too difficult for their thick *hakujin* tongues" but because "his predecessor was also named 'Charlie,' as were all the Issei houseboys who worked for the Warrens" (32) is reversed to great effect: we learn that he works for two sisters who are identical twins and his difficulties in distinguishing one from another is highlighted throughout the novel by referring to each woman as either "Joan (or Jane)" or "Jane (or Joan)."

As we see from the examples given here, while impersonation cannot always be distinguished very satisfactorily from imposture, the possibilities of attending to those moments when such acts can be differentiated—moments in which categories of identity and affiliation are called into question—can help us not only to trace alternative histories and narratives but also to produce a space in which agency is not capitulated and identity becomes a sustaining fiction that makes apparent both the possibilities and problems of strategically necessary performances. Such moments operate according to what José Esteban Muñoz terms a practice of "disidentification," a mode of dealing with dominant ideology that neither "opts to assimilate within such a structure nor strictly opposes it" but rather "tries to transform a cultural logic from within, always laboring to enact permanent structural change while at the same time valuing the importance of local or everyday struggles of resistance" (11–12).[24]

Impersonation's Uncomfortable Fit

There are unique aspects of the Chinese American and Japanese American experiences I outline here but as Roger Daniels suggests, "from a legal and legislative point of view, of course, Asian Americans have shared a common status: all were 'aliens ineligible to citizenship' " (67). This enduring conception of Asian Americans as somehow perpetually alien forces us to think about the implications of what it means, both for notions of Asian Americanness and U.S. American identities, if Asian Americans are always already constructed as pretenders to the very idea of an "American" identity. Impersonation, with its attention to challenging such constructions from within the category of Asian American identity itself, has proven a particularly effective strategy for launching political, social, and institutional critique. Thus, even as I have outlined two ethnic-specific contexts from which I am deriving some insights about impersonation as an *Asian American* response to the injunctions and demands placed on certain subjects, I now turn to a third context and concern: the pan-ethnic nature of Asian American identity as it has been formulated by the identity movements of the 1970s and institutionalized by the field of Asian American literary studies. I do this in order to make the case for impersonation as a paradigm that derives its contours and application from both the perceived disjunction between "Asian" and "American" and the discontinuities inherent within a specifically pan-ethnic notion of identity that continues to be operative for many contemporary Asian Americans and to exert critical suasion in determining the shape of the academic discipline. In the process of making this argument, I advocate the usefulness of the concept as a way of addressing the concerns within the field of how to balance a need for identity politics and coalition-building without disavowing or repressing the very real instability of the category of Asian Americanness that has proven so critical in the establishment of Asian American studies as a discipline and an institutional presence in higher education. The "uncomfortable fit" between the diverse realities of Asian America and any theoretical conceptualization offered for how to speak about and to such disjunctions in a cohesive way is clearly one aspect of what a politics of impersonation allows us both to acknowledge and negotiate. By refusing the seamless performance, the unremarkable virtuosity of imposture, impersonation demands that we attend to performative gaps in order to consider how we cannot not perform certain identities even as we also cannot perform such identities without being self-reflexive about the consequences of such performances.

In "The Fiction of Asian American Literature" (1996), Susan Koshy delineates a compelling critique of Asian American literary studies, maintaining that the "validity [of Asian American literature] as an ordering rubric" (467) is deeply problematic. According to Koshy, despite the limitations of the category of inquiry—limitations that include an unarticulated representational logic, a perpetuation of outmoded paradigms of coalitional identity, and an ungrounded celebration of plurality at the expense of addressing the disjunctions inherent within the field—Asian Americanists strategically continue to defer providing concepts that will help theorize the "inner contradictions, . . . representational inconsistencies and dilemmas" characterizing contemporary Asian American literature. Koshy's incisive evaluation of Asian American literary studies asserts that critics need to recognize the inadequacies of the term "Asian American" even as we acknowledge it to be an indispensable formulation—in her words, "a rubric that we cannot not use" (491). In order to accomplish these seemingly contradictory goals, it is critical that new conceptual frameworks for articulating this paradoxical formation of Asian Americanness be provided. Impersonation, with its emphasis on visibly performing both the alterity inherent within Asian American identity formations as well as the ways in which Asian American subjects are constructed as alter subjects within the Euro-American imagination, advances a notion which we can use both to recuperate and to interrogate "Asian American" as the identity marker by which we understand the tangled affiliations that disparate Asian-origin groups in the United States have with each other.[25]

One significant aspect of the double agency enacted by impersonation treated in this project concerns the question of allegiance and its relationship to the multiple constituencies that claim Asian Americanness and which Asian America claims for itself. For example, in his collection of essays *The Accidental Asian: Notes of a Native Speaker* (1998), Eric Liu repeatedly emphasizes his tenuous but undeniable relationship with Asian American identity. Although he claims a relationship to Asian Americanness (they are "twin siblings, separated at birth but endowed with uncanny foreknowledge of each other's motives"), he also registers "mutual feelings" of disagreement, frustration and disappointment that mark the fact that "[w]e react to the same world in very different ways" (58). This relationship of both distance and proximity is one of the hallmarks of impersonation and Liu experiences it firsthand while acting as a "special guest" on a cable news show about the controversial cover of the *National Review* depicting President Clinton, Hillary Rodham Clinton, and Vice President Gore in yellowface. For this performance, Liu, who claims not to be "deeply offended" by the cover, understands that he is to play "the Asian spokesman, ever vigilant against affronts to my race" (61).

Significantly, Liu's quip about his distance from the role he undertakes— "I am not an Asian American activist; I just play one on TV" (63)—belies the complicated nature of the impersonation that he enacts while on that program. Although Liu begins by seeing the role of Asian American activist as precisely that—a role—he discovers in the course of the heated exchange that "[a]lmost by chance, it seemed, I'd become a righteous, vocal Asian American. All it had taken was a stage and a villain" (62). Although Liu's losing himself in the role he was ostensibly performing bespeaks one of the dangers of impersonation—that it becomes an act of imposture that erases the self-reflexivity and performative gaps that impersonation uses to draw attention both to the performer as well as the nature of the performance itself—the way in which he textually rehearses the shifting allegiances that his performance makes manifest produces this instance as one that shows how impersonation works to reveal the complex dynamics by which Asian American identity operates as both defensive strategy and performative possibility. For as Liu acknowledges, both "stage" and "villain" make the role so tempting and so dangerous. This emphasis on the performed nature of Asian Americanness, a performance that has the power to make itself invisible to the performer even as it challenges its own sustainability outside the "theater" of the public gaze, is recognized by many writers other than Liu in their investigations of impersonation as a strategy by which to interrogate and utilize identity. Certainly, this recognition results in the prominent figuration of the actor in the texts examined in *Double Agency*'s third chapter, an instance where Asian American playwrights make use of the figure of the actor to dramatize the implications and possibilities of how to configure Asian American identity in relationship to the performances, both public and private, of stereotype.

Impersonation is a performative strategy taken up by Asian Americans who may claim, like Liu, that the roles they play are always an uncomfortable fit. Nowhere is this discomfort more recognizable than with the performance of stereotypes—those roles by which Asian Americans find their identities overdetermined. As the next two chapters detail, the stereotype is a role that demands to be impersonated if one is to perform it as a way of claiming it as constitutive but also as constituted. In the following discussion of Fu Manchu, stereotype is revealed as a sort of originary imposture whose performative power can be addressed through impersonation as hermeneutic act. Only by truly examining the nuances of stereotype can Asian American subjects (and critics) then enact the double agency of impersonation articulated in this chapter, an ambivalent performance that nonetheless offers a recuperative space within which identities are claimed and political agency articulated.

Dissecting the "Devil Doctor": Stereotype and Sensationalism in Sax Rohmer's Fu Manchu

In the introduction to *The Big Aiiieeeee!* (1991), Jeffrey Paul Chan, Frank Chin, Lawson Fusao Inada, and Shawn Wong attempt to counter what they see as a dangerous propensity: the emphasis of "belief over . . . fact, and the fake over the real, until the stereotype has completely displaced history in the white sensibility" (xiii). This assessment of stereotype, which is motivated by a concern about the emasculation of Asian American men in "mainstream" American culture, identifies Fu Manchu as the "worst" image in the "white liberal American" imagination, a figure who surpasses an "effeminate closet queen like Charlie Chan" to become a full-blown "homosexual menace" (xiii).[1] The anxiety these critics articulate involves not only the perception of stereotype but also the detection of its boundaries, a process requiring the vigilant policing of parameters to demarcate the good from the bad and "the real" from "the fake." While Chan and his fellow editors voice a desire for "authenticity"—constituted as "history," "fact," and "the real"—the vehemence with which they make such distinctions marks the impossibility of ascertaining such differentiations. As Daniel Kim asserts, the "intent to establish a neat binary between 'how we are seen' and 'how we are' . . . is always turning against itself" (275). The fear of perception becoming "the real" demands a retraining of how to see, an insistence on ferreting out the "fakes" among us.

Chan et al. essentially charge that Fu Manchu is a "fake" who perverts

Asian American masculine expression. Significantly, Fu Manchu's "fakeness" raises the issue of how stereotype is not only an important context for but also, in some unsettling ways, inextricably tied to the "authenticity" of Asian American identity formation. Although the "Devil Doctor" constitutes a problematic image for Asian Americans, his vexed textual and visual representation must be interrogated more systematically if his sway over the public imagination is to be addressed. Doubtless, Sax Rohmer's Fu Manchu books catered to the racist and sensationalistic proclivities of their intended audience. While the racism and formulaic nature of the books seem to render nuanced criticisms of them absurd, I propose in this chapter a reevaluation of Dr. Fu Manchu and, by extension, a critique of the stereotype that he has come to represent for Asian Americans. Recognizing stereotype's capacity to be ideologically ambivalent in its formation if not always in deployment is critical as Asian Americans seek to counter the representational legacy of stereotypes that have been produced about them by non-Asians.

Homi K. Bhabha reminds us that "[t]he stereotype is a complex, ambivalent, contradictory mode of representation, as anxious as it is assertive, and demands not only that we extend our critical and political objectives but that we change the object of analysis itself" (70). According to Bhabha, an integral part of "chang[ing] the object of analysis" involves "construct[ing the stereotype's] regime of truth, not . . . subject[ing] its representations to a normalizing judgment" (67). In that vein, this chapter seeks to strategize stereotype by reading against its surface and probing for the fissures and contradictions that are always embedded in such representation. By focusing on Rohmer's original depictions of Fu Manchu—particularly his construction of Fu Manchu as a creolized character, his investigation of imperial desire even as he succumbs to it, and his exploitation and critique of museological practice—I hope to expose the crucial blindnesses of Rohmer's white protagonists, his contemporary reading audiences, and Asian American literary critics who have decried Fu Manchu as "nothing more" than a stereotype. I begin by emphasizing the impact of music hall performance on Rohmer's depiction of "Chineseness" and "authenticity." I then demonstrate how this visible masquerade of "authentic Chineseness" depends upon both the reluctance of Rohmer's white protagonists to see Fu Manchu as a hybrid figure and Rohmer's strategic use of conventional representations of Otherness. I conclude with a critique of Rohmer's staging of Fu Manchu as a racial exhibit by delineating the process by which hybridity becomes fetishized as freakishness and by exposing how museological practice informs the series' structure and its ideological ambivalence.

Central to this chapter's governing logic is an exhortation to move beyond labeling Fu Manchu as an impostor by offering a set of readings attuned to the ways in which impersonation can operate as hermeneutic practice. More precisely, I propose that we think about how we might read the acts of imposture perpetrated by Rohmer's literary figure (and Rohmer himself) through the lens of impersonation as a *metacritical* strategy that emphasizes the interrelated dimensions of "the real" and "the fake" even as it promulgates a critical framework characterized by self-reflexive ambivalence in its deployment. As I indicated in chapter 1, critical insights derived from Asian American acts of impersonation can paradoxically vivify dominant American society's manifold acts of racial and cultural imposture—a paradox this chapter makes manifest. Reading the stereotype of Asian villainy in this way sets the stage for my discussion in subsequent chapters of the intricate ways in which contemporary Asian American authors undermine stereotype through acts of (literary) impersonation, thereby suggesting impersonation's urgency as a paradigm for Asian American literary and cultural studies.

Introducing the Mysterious Dr. Fu Manchu

As the story goes, deep in the forests of colonial Burma, Sir Denis Nayland Smith narrowly escapes the poisoned tip of an arrow and steals his first glimpse of "the most malign and formidable personality existing in the known world" (Rohmer, *Insidious* 15). Although Scotland Yard's finest operative was ostensibly the protagonist of one of the most widely read series of books published in the twentieth century, he was not the series' chief attraction: instead, that role was reserved for the man he characterized as "the yellow peril incarnate," known to millions as Dr. Fu Manchu. Fu Manchu's status as a transnational popular icon granted him a material presence that would dictate the series' evolving politics.[2] While the early novels pit Smith's "British" intelligence against the "Chinese cunning" of Dr. Fu Manchu, later books re-frame their conflict in more expansive geographical and cultural terms. Reflecting the emergence of the United States as a world power, many of the post-1933 books pair Smith with young American partners, thereby enacting an ethnocentric transfer of not only global responsibility, but also the burden of representation.[3] Benedict Anderson has convincingly demonstrated how print culture works to establish the formation of communities across time and space. Although Anderson discusses the emergence of an "imagined community" in the context of nationalism, the Fu Manchu stories created an Anglo-American alliance between England and the United States, cementing them into a cohesive Western unit in the battle against the Eastern forces commanded by the "Devil Doctor."[4] The "alliance" has proven formidable: the series' popularity in both countries has established Fu Manchu as one of the most enduring stereotypes of Asian villainy.[5]

In his study of Chinese American images in American fiction, William Wu grants Fu Manchu the status of "archetypal Asian villain" in the American consciousness because of the character's warm reception by the American reading public. Rohmer's textual accommodations to his American audience included making his younger protagonists American, setting several of the later novels in New York, and writing a book about Fu Manchu's attempt to take over the American presidency. Consequently, "[t]he Fu Manchu character [was] the first Asian role of prominence in modern literature to have a large American readership" (Wu 164). Don Hutchinson writes that the Fu Manchu novels "were, if anything, even more popular in the U.S. than they were in Britain" (xxviii). In fact, Rohmer's exploitation of Yellow Peril fears proved so compelling to American audiences that when the series ended after the first three books with the Doctor's apparent demise at the end of *The Hand of Fu Manchu* (1917), readers of *Collier's* pressured the magazine to commission the revival of both the series and its lead character.[6] Despite his British origins, Fu Manchu was quickly adopted into American popular culture, appearing in television, newspaper comics, movies, and pulp fiction.[7]

West vs. East: A Study in Mythic Opposition

The series pits Sir Denis Nayland Smith against the diabolical genius of Dr. Fu Manchu, the head of a secret organization aiming to wrest world control away from the West. At its most basic level, their adventure is a tale of conflict cast in racialized terms. Smith, who initiates his struggle against Fu

Manchu as a Burmese colonial official, literally represents the British empire.[8] According to Smith's rhetoric, the British empire stands for race as well as nation: he cautions his partner Petrie, a medical practitioner who narrates the first three novels, "I have traveled from Burma not in the interests of the British Government merely, but in the interests of the entire white race, and I honestly believe—though I pray I may be wrong—that its survival depends largely upon the success of my mission" (Rohmer, *Insidious* 6). Just as Smith metonymically figures both the British empire and the "White" race, Fu Manchu and the organization he represents are the Yellow Peril, a threat to (inter)national security figured in racial terms. In the most famous description of the Doctor, Smith tells Petrie to

> [i]magine a person, tall, lean and feline, high-shouldered, with a brow like Shakespeare and a face like Satan, a close-shaven skull, and long, magnetic eyes of the true cat-green. Invest him with all the cruel cunning of an entire Eastern race, accumulated in one giant intellect, with all the resources of science past and present, with all the resources, if you will, of a wealthy government . . . . Imagine that awful being, and you have a mental picture of Dr. Fu-Manchu, the yellow peril incarnate in one man. (Rohmer, *Insidious* 17)[9]

Figured in these terms, the story is an old one. It is the fight between Self and Other, the West and the rest, a political conflict cast in mythic terms of opposition. Yet, while such clear distinctions lend themselves well to the genre Rohmer was writing, they were not always appreciated by Rohmer's critics. According to Christopher Frayling, "Rohmer's books have always had bad Press . . . it be[ing] a critical commonplace to categorize [them] as the lowest form of racist propaganda, a humourless version of the mid-Victorian penny dreadfuls" (66).[10] Such criticisms reflect the tendency John Cawelti identifies in his study of formula fiction to brand the generic conventions of formula stories as inferior to "more serious" literature.[11] Focusing largely on the series' sensationalist and racist properties, critics of Rohmer's writing have generally overlooked the ways in which the texts complicate received conventions of racial representation in early twentieth-century popular literature. As we shall see, Rohmer's writing often problematizes the clear distinction between "good" and "bad" that scholars perceive to be the defining characteristic of popular fiction (Watson 109).

"The devilish doctor is the reason why . . ."

Much of Fu Manchu's popularity as a character did seem to depend upon the exaggerated struggle between "good" and "bad" that his conflict with Smith symbolized. To that end, his countless appearances in other contexts, command performances capitalizing on his "evil" nature, gradually distorted Rohmer's original characterizations of the Doctor. Fu Manchu's name usually conjures up images of the feminized, long-clawed, bearded visage of the character's popular reincarnation in other media. Rohmer's own writing style, tailored toward the melodramatic and repetitive, abetted this transformation by giving the public several reductive labels for the Doctor. Ironically, the man who believed himself the reincarnation of a Nile dweller as well as a Caribbean pirate would watch the popular imagination reincarnate his creation, sometimes to such an extent that he deemed it unrecognizable.[12]

During the course of the novels, Rohmer himself resurrected Fu Manchu several times, thereby enhancing his awesome appeal.[13] Despite popular assumptions about his "sinister," "Satanic" and "loathsome" character, Fu Manchu did not remain the mysterious, wholly evil personality that Smith and Petrie first encountered. Unlike the mass media representations of the Doctor, the reincarnations of Fu Manchu in Rohmer's later texts tended to develop and complicate the simple villainy Fu Manchu evinced in Rohmer's earlier books. Originally depicted as the head of a "yellow octopus . . . whose tentacles were dacoity, thuggee, modes of death, secret and swift," Dr. Fu Manchu's sense of honor and Smith's increasing reliance on the inviolability of his word recast him as the undeniably majestic "Emperor of Lawbreakers." As the series evolved, Smith's repeated characterizations of Fu Manchu as Satan provided a dark counterpoint to later assessments of the Doctor's appearance. Time transmuted the Satanic visage into "a most wonderful face" that was "aged, yet ageless" (Rohmer, *Bride* 112). Changing political situations caused younger protagonists to read different qualities into the Doctor's countenance. In *The Drums of Fu Manchu* (1939), the Doctor attempts to prevent the eruption of a second World War by threatening to kill any government leaders who agitate against international stability. As a result, Smith and Fu Manchu find themselves working toward the shared goal of world peace, a situation reflected in protagonist Bart Kerrigan's impression of the Doctor:

[His face] might have been the face of an emperor. I found myself thinking of Zenghis Khan [sic]. Intellectually, the brow was phenomenal, the dignity of the lined features might have belonged to a Pharaoh, but the soul of the great Chinese doctor lay in his eyes. Never had I seen before, and never have I seen again, such power in a man's eyes as lay in those of Dr. Fu Manchu. (Rohmer, *Drums* 107)

This description echoes the observations of Alan Sterling, the protagonist who falls in love with Fu Manchu's chosen bride and who thinks that the Doctor's "wonderful face . . . might once have been beautiful" (Rohmer, *Trail* 97). Eventually, even Fu Manchu's association with the unrelenting evil symbolized by the Devil mellowed into a reminder that Satan was once "Lucifer, Son of the Morning: an angel, but a fallen angel" (Rohmer, *Trail* 97).

Smith, doomed to forever being the same hyperactive criminal investigator introduced in the first book, could not compete with the Doctor's mesmerizing evolution. During the course of almost a half century, Fu Manchu undergoes a host of transformations: from a representative dispatched by a secret organization to "pave the way" into a leader of the Si-fan, the most powerful secret organization in the world; from an unmitigated force of evil intent on the destruction of Western civilization into a powerful ally in the fight against Communism; from a diabolical enemy into a god-like being whose abilities to transcend the laws of time and man set him "above good and evil"; from a master criminal into a "mighty instrument of vengeance" aimed at warmongers; and from the harbinger of death into "the supreme physician." Speaking for contemporary readers, Alan Brien, in an article criticizing Rohmer for being a "dedicated righty," concludes that "the devilish Doctor is the reason why we can still read Rohmer, one of those great good-bad writers" (32).

Staging Race

Rohmer's flair for creating such a memorable character can be traced to his theatrical background and the lessons it taught him concerning the conjunction of race and "authenticity" in popular representation. Christopher Frayling has argued that "many of the incidents, characters, and stylistic trademarks of the first three Fu Manchu stories . . . are strongly reminiscent of the music hall world in which Rohmer was mixing" (67).[14] Although the horror and thrills of Rohmer's suspense novels are not readily associated with the song and dance of the music hall, the music hall set the stage in crucial ways for the formation of the Fu Manchu novels. As "imperial theatre," the incredible popularity of the music hall denoted a pervasive theatrical interest in melodrama and the staging of cultural and racial difference (MacKenzie 41). In addition to escapist musicals set in the Orient, the music hall of Rohmer's time also hosted variety shows billing rival magicians Ching Ling Foo (who marketed himself as "Court Conjurer to the Empress of China") and Chung Ling Soo (characterized as "a rare bit of old China"). The representational issues at the heart of Chung Ling Soo's stage show appeared only at the moment of his death: after being shot in the chest while performing his popular DEFYING THE BULLETS act in 1918, surgeons discovered that Soo, despite using interpreters and Chinese assistants for over ten years, was actually a Euro-American named William E. Robinson. Robinson's death exposed the complex issue of "authenticity" that authorized performances such as his.

The idea of performing authentic "Chineseness" on the music hall stage was a product of the "institutional culture of the gaze" operating at the end of the nineteenth century to represent the unknown in prescripted ways (Moy 8).[15] As Chung Ling Soo's act demonstrated, the authenticity afforded by the visual very often turned the performance into the real. Rohmer's experience working with music hall performers known for doing vaudevillian sketches of Chinamen might be seen as an apprenticeship of sorts in racial stereotyping: when he became a fiction writer, Rohmer had no qualms about appropriating "Chineseness" in creating his villain.[16] After seeing the popularity that "Chinese" magicians and vaudevillian sketches of Chinamen enjoyed on stage, he knew exactly how to manipulate race as a signifier of the exotic and unfamiliar. Fu Manchu, with his long silk robes, mandarin cap, and opium pipe, fulfilled Euro-American expectations of what it meant to be Chinese by exploiting the kind of representational practices exposed by Robinson's death. As yellowface performance made clear, performances of race were very often racial masquerade, a farce having more to do with the desires of the performer and audience rather than the desires of those being staged.

Significantly, Rohmer demonstrates a keen awareness of the ways in which his racial representations depend upon notions of a plausibly "(in)-authentic" Other. In *The Trail of Fu Manchu* (1934), Rohmer's depiction of the novelist Mrs. Crossland makes clear his self-consciousness concerning the orientalizing nature of much of his own work: "Mrs. Crossland's reputation and financial success rested upon her inaccurate pictures of desert life: of the loves of sheiks and their Western mistresses" (197). Focusing on the "pseudo-Orientalism" of Mrs. Crossland's work, the commentary in *Trail* reveals a self-reflexive understanding of the exploitative nature of Rohmer's own racial representations. Rohmer knew that he was not revealing "authentic" aspects of what he was ostensibly depicting. As he acknowledged, "I made my name on Fu Manchu because I know nothing about the Chinese!" (van Ash 72).[17] Fu Manchu's skill with disguises and his ability to reverse racial masquerade by passing as a European doctor or professor—talents that often render him invisible to those pursuing him—foreground the ways in which the white protagonists, unlike Rohmer himself, refuse to see beyond their conventions of racial representation.

The blindnesses exemplified by Rohmer's white protagonists are structurally reinforced by the manichaeisms permeating the texts. The battles waged are mythic, "starkly contrasting white and black, good and evil, superiority and inferiority, civilization and savagery, intelligence and emotion, rationality and sensuality, self and Other, subject and object" (JanMohamed 63).[18] Such conflict, although easily read as a naive racism, marks a complex series of "perverse identifications" and "crucial exclusions" that both threaten and reinforce ideas of national culture and racial purity (Shohat and Stam 20, 14). The cultural hybridity that inevitably attends imperial interests constitutes one such "crucial exclusion," an integral aspect of imperial culture that is often marked by a calculated lack of scrutiny. In *The Native Races of the Empire* (1924), part of a twelve-volume series directed at giving "a complete survey of the history, resources, and activities of the [British] Empire looked at as a whole," Sir Godfrey Lagden argues that the book's aim precludes an "account of the classes known [as] Half-castes" (iii; xv). As Lagden's justification notes, "Half-castes" are "known in every possession," an undeniable reality of imperial rule.

"Half-castes in every possession"

Perhaps the most famous "half-caste" ever to make an appearance in the Fu Manchu series was the first: Karamaneh, the Arab woman who captured Petrie's heart with her "predilection, characteristically Oriental," for him.

Petrie paints her as an enchantress of mixed parentage: "With the skin of a perfect blonde, she had eyes and lashes as black as a Creole's which, together with her full red lips, told me that this beautiful stranger . . . was not a child of our northern shores" (Rohmer, *Insidious* 13). Early descriptions focus on Oriental features that lend her "a beauty of a kind that was a key to the most extravagant rhapsodies of Eastern poets" (Rohmer, *Insidious* 176). Her delicate loveliness masks the skill with which she implements Fu Manchu's daring schemes. She is the first assault on the "truth" which Smith commits himself to upholding: "East and West may not intermingle" (Rohmer, *Insidious* 120). Smith, disappointed by an unspecified love affair while in the East, never loses his conviction in this "undeniable" truth. Petrie, on the other hand, revises his philosophy to accommodate his romantic interests. When Karamaneh becomes too "exquisite" to be resisted, Petrie's previous distinctions of what is East and West become meaningless, if only momentarily: "Her eyes held a challenge wholly Oriental in its appeal: her lips, even in repose, were a taunt. And, herein, East is West and West is East" (Rohmer, *Insidious* 176).

Significantly, Karamaneh's active part in the adventure soon ceases. After marrying Petrie and retiring to Cairo, Kara, as she is renamed, becomes progressively more passive. Whereas she was once capable of swinging on wires, racing across moors, and perpetrating crimes in various disguises, her marriage to Petrie renders her weak, nervous, and unable (or at least not allowed) to do things by herself. Smith and his later partners make much of her happiness as Petrie's wife but in so doing, they relegate her voice to the background. Despite the surface rhetoric of the books, which juxtapose her slavery to Fu Manchu with the freedom enjoyed by English and American women, Kara's Anglicization does not make her more free; rather, she is trapped by her fear of being alone, controlled by Petrie's demand that she "conquer . . . the barbaric impulses that sometimes flamed up within her" (Rohmer, *Hand* 85). By the fourth book of the series, *Daughter of Fu Manchu* (1931), the erasure of her "Oriental" attributes—not to mention her name—signifies Kara's successful assimilation: "In *Mrs. Petrie's* complex character there was a marked streak of Oriental mysticism—*although from her appearance [one] should never have suspected Eastern blood*" (210, emphasis mine). Karamaneh's incorporation into British colonial society exemplifies an attack on imperial structures of representation that has been (predictably) overcome through the subgenre of (inter)racial romance. However, Fu Manchu is not so easily reincorporated.

Fu Manchu's "fiendish armory" of "natural" weapons, both human and animal, bolsters his threatening presence. Color as an unproblematized signifier seems to indicate racial, ideological, and political alignments. By association, Fu Manchu links himself to the brown and black men he employs to help him win control of the world. Brown-skinned Burmese dacoits who signal the commencement of his crimes with their "low, wailing cr[ies]" are later joined by Indian thugs, Middle Eastern *phansigars* (religious stranglers), and African assassins.[19] In the overt discourse dictated by manichaean allegory, clear distinctions demarcate white from non-white. Consequently, Fu Manchu's alignment with the darker side of the equation reinforces his "discoloration," positioning him against the whiteness—and by extension, moral superiority—claimed by Western imperial desire.

Despite such clearly delineated positioning, a repeated emphasis on Fu Manchu's honor and integrity sets the stage for a specular affiliation with the Euro-American community against which he is ostensibly posed. At times, Rohmer constitutes him as a mirror image, perhaps inverted and/or distorted, of Smith, a relationship of similarity which works to undercut Fu Manchu's connection with darker peoples. The repeated assertions of political, cultural, and racial oppositions between Fu Manchu and Smith obscure their similarities. The "febrile glitter" of Smith's eyes mirrors the "viridescence" of the Doctor's "reptilian gaze." Petrie's description of Smith as "a great, gaunt cat" yokes together two of the signature characteristics ascribed to the Doctor: his "gaunt" frame and "cat-like gait." Smith's customary "staccato" style of speech lapses, in moments of extreme stress or provocation, into the "sibilance" that marks the speech of Fu Manchu.[20] While these similarities between Smith and Fu Manchu problematize clear distinctions of difference, the inversions and distortions registered between Fu Manchu and Smith are revised and given wider implications in *President Fu Manchu* (1936). Professor Morgenstahl, Fu Manchu's unwilling accomplice, spends every waking hour trying to sculpt a life-sized bust of the Doctor from a tiny picture which turns out to be a "three-cent Daniel Webster stamp, dated 1932, gummed upside down upon a piece of cardboard, then framed by the paper in which a pear-shaped opening had been cut" (Rohmer, *President* 238–39). The framing of the stamp renders one surprising fact "unmistakable: inverted and framed in this way, the Daniel Webster stamp presented a caricature, but a recognizable caricature, of Dr. Fu Manchu!" (Rohmer, *President* 239). Rohmer's depiction of the Doctor as Webster's inverted distortion capitalizes on as well as challenges the science of phrenology. While the use of inversion and distortion seems to reinforce the racial and attendant moral differences between Webster and Fu Manchu, their similarly large foreheads problematize the racial distinctions made by phrenological science. According to Orson and Lorenzo Fowler, characterized by Reginald Horseman as "[t]he oracles of practical phrenology in the United States" during the mid-nineteenth century,

> The European race (including their descendants in America) possess a much larger endowment of these organs [the frontal and coronal portions of the head], and also of their corresponding faculties [intellect and morality], than any other portion of the human species. Hence their intellectual and moral superiority over all other races of men. (qtd. in Horseman 143)

By inverting Webster's prominent forehead into the Doctor's "Shakespearean" brow, Rohmer not only refigures the basic precepts of phrenology; he also calls to attention Fu Manchu as a threat figured in both internal as well as external terms.[21] The evolution of the Si-fan into an organization boasting members among high-level Western politicians as well as Eastern leaders refigures racialized fears into political concerns exceeding racial boundaries. Morgenstahl's need to invert the Daniel Webster stamp in order to see the face of the Doctor metaphorizes Fu Manchu's evolution from a clearly and easily recognizable foreign threat to imperial interests into one embedded within the very structure of what empire desires to protect. The Other which is projected, rejected, and held at arm's length is also, paradoxically, the one whose incorporation nurtures imperial growth.

Physically, Fu Manchu could very well fall into Lagden's "Half-caste" classification, although his political and ideological leanings mark him as an outsider and a threat to the hegemony exercised by British and American imperialisms. Fu Manchu *cannot* be purely Chinese, despite Smith's conjecture that he descends from "a certain very old Kiangsu family" (Rohmer, *Insidious* 174). His height (over 6 feet), his eye-color (green) and his hair (which is described as "sparse and neutral colored") make it clear that Fu Manchu claims partial Caucasian ancestry. Fu Manchu is obviously a product of racial mixing but significantly, none of the characters in the series, despite repeated and closely detailed physical descriptions that are so uncharacteristic of Chinese ancestry, ever sees him as anything other than purely Chinese. The doubled discourse of empire encourages single-minded categorization even as it introduces hybrid formulations. To extend Homi K. Bhabha's discussion on colonial discourse to include imperialism, the idea of "fixity" constitutes an important feature of the "ideological construction of otherness"(66).[22] Bhabha contends that "[f]ixity as the sign of cultural/historical/racial difference . . . is a paradoxical mode of representation: it connotes rigidity and an unchanging order as well as disorder, degeneracy and daemonic repetition" (66). "Fixing" the Other, making its "degeneracy" the mark of unwavering difference, becomes a way of satiating the desire to enact binaristic choices, a mentality typified by Rohmer's white protagonists despite shifting allegiances created by interracial romance and politics.[23]

A Way of Not Seeing

In creating such an interesting discrepancy between Fu Manchu's appearance and how he is seen, Rohmer makes visible one of the ways in which Orientalism works. Although the characters train their dissecting gaze on Fu Manchu, their attitude reflects a carefully cultivated "way of not seeing" that works by designating cultural "others" in such a way that they can be easily dismissed as always already "[O]ther" (Thompson 69). Fah Lo Suee, Fu Manchu's daughter, is definitely Eurasian. However, the books postulate her destiny as racially overdetermined by her part-Chinese ancestry. This classificatory practice runs throughout the series. Smith and his cohorts immediately regard as suspicious characters who have any kind of Oriental background.[24] This practice remains uncountered until the final book, *Emperor Fu Manchu* (1959), which introduces male and female protagonists Tony McKay and Jeannie Cameron-Gordon, both one-quarter Chinese and unimpeachable allies in the fight against Fu Manchu.[25] The deliberate refusal to see any affinity between Self and Other comprises an important part of an entire system of classification and representation crucial to imperial definitions of Self; as Edward Said asserts, "[w]ithout examining Orientalism as a discourse[,] one cannot possibly understand the enormously systematic

discipline by which European culture was able to manage—and even produce—the Orient politically, sociologically, militarily, ideologically, scientif-
ically, and imaginatively" (3). As such, Orientalism automatically signals two
levels of discourse, one of which depends upon the systematic refusal to acknowledge the complexity and undeniable impact which the other wields.

This "refusal to see" plays itself out in the two levels of rhetoric structuring the Fu Manchu novels. Smith and to a partial extent the narrators vo-
calize the surface disquisition. Smith's racist assertions, many of which are
initially adopted or sporadically ventriloquized by other protagonists, lay the
basis for the xenophobic attitudes that have caused critical dismissal of the
series. However, a closer examination of the descriptive language of several
narrative protagonists reveals that while most of the narrators *consciously*
subscribe to Smith's view of Fu Manchu, their impressions of the Doctor often register deviances which can be read as opposing and/or subverting the
controlling discourse of empire represented by Smith.

One of the key sites of subversion to imperial discourse(s) of representation—a subversion whose potential presence rests deeply hidden within the
"subconscious logic" of imperialism—involves the relation hybridity bears
to purity (JanMohamed 63). Although imperial interests rendered hybridity
an ineradicable part of empire, a negative view of cultural and racial mixing
continued to dominate the images produced by imperial machineries of representation. Ella Shohat and Robert Stam acknowledge hybridity as a
"power-laden and asymmetrical" relationship: "historically, assimilation by
the 'native' into a European culture was celebrated as part of the civilizing
mission [while] assimilation in the opposite direction was derided as 'going
native,' a reversion to savagery" (43). In the Fu Manchu books, this "asymmetrical" relationship between hybridity and empire, which either seeks to
co-opt hybridity through the amalgamating redemptions offered by assimilation or completely denigrate it by an alignment with the "savage," is cir-
cumvented and given new permutations in the figure of the Doctor.

Beyond the biological/physical, Fu Manchu is also a culturally hybrid
character. Despite the political and ideological concerns which posit him as
"Other," he exists as a singular product of both Eastern and Western discourses. He simultaneously embodies Chinese cruelty, the logical product of
a society which kills its girl children, and Western scientific accomplish-
ment. His knowledge, partially cultivated while the most outstanding stu-

dent at at least three distinguished European and American universities, pushes science and medicine to unimagined levels of achievement. His ability to take elements from both East and West and mold them into new products and new visions dismantles an understanding of cultural identity as the outcome of an overdetermined binaristic choice. Fu Manchu never feels constrained by the "either/or" option articulated by Shohat and Stam. He is a "native" who moves among Euro-American society, both as himself (he possesses the mysterious title of "Marquis") as well as in disguise (quite often he appears as some European professor or doctor), and excels at its most civilized tasks. However, Western identity never subsumes him: he resists the "assimilation" which such performances often dictate. His ability to see beyond cultural and racial borders makes him threatening to Western hegemony since he has no compunction in harnessing whatever cultural elements, taken from both sides, he can use. This mentality is reflected in his decisions to employ half-caste servants for high-profile positions in the Si-fan; embodied in his daughter Fah Lo Suee, whom he conceived upon a Russian mother; and expressed in his choice of Fleurette as his Empress-bride, a woman chosen for her "pedigree on both sides," chosen because "[s]he has [both] Eastern and Western blood" (Rohmer, *Bride* 160).

A measure of Fu Manchu's threat to the political and social economy of empire rests in his ability to envision new coalitions between East and West. Although he begins the series as a representative intent on "paving the way" for a powerful, unnamed shadow organization and later progresses into empire building on a large scale, his eventual preoccupation with preventing war and combating Communism finds him willing to forge an alliance with Smith. Fu Manchu offers his services in their common goal of maintaining a peaceful world: "I ask you to join me now—for my enemies are your enemies" (*Drums* 33). Smith and those he represents refuse to entertain any notion of alliance although Fu Manchu's aim "must enlist the sympathy of any sane man" (Rohmer, *Drums* 30).

Smith's denial disavows his own history as a man formed by both East and West. Although he toils tirelessly in the interests of British and American imperialisms and is awarded a baronetcy for "saving the Empire" from the fatal infection posed by the "insidious breath of the East," he feels more comfortable in Burma than in London. Smith informs Petrie that "although I can stand tropical heat, curiously enough the heat of London gets me down almost immediately" (Rohmer, *Return* 133). He feels out of place in Britain, a displacement underscored by his immediate departures after each case. As readers, we are never privy to his time in the East (unless he is actively in pursuit of the Doctor) and his life before confronting Fu Manchu in Burma remains a mystery. These blanknesses typify his refusal to see the influence of his Eastern experience on his own character formation, even though such experience allows him the occupation in which he finds his truest expression: Fu Manchu's nemesis. Only the necessary construction of the East as the "insidious enemy" allows Smith to posit a self-image of the West as "clean efficiency"; paradoxically, such a construction is authorized by Smith's own exposure to the East, marked by the fact that only he can match Fu Manchu's ability to perform racial masquerade convincingly.

The antagonisms posed by the Doctor's presence constitute themselves in two distinct ways: the surface rhetoric posits him as a danger to the world because of his imperial ambition and his unscrupulous methods while the more compelling threat, his ability to break down the binaristic categories critical to the maintenance of an us/them dichotomy, remains largely unspoken. At the end of *The Trail of Fu Manchu* (1934), this threat becomes a reality, if only for a moment. Petrie, blackmailed by fears for his daughter's safety, commits himself to preparing the *elixir vitae* that Fu Manchu must have to survive. Despite the initial use of force to requisition his help, Petrie discovers that once at Fu Manchu's bedside, he, unlike Smith, cannot see this "Emperor of Lawbreakers" as merely a criminal. As Petrie "battl[es] with the most difficult case ever entrusted to him" and "hop[es for] . . . success [to] crown his hours of effort," he finds himself believing in the man characterized as "Satan incarnate":

> For one insane moment, the glamour of the Si-fan swamped commonsense. Petrie found himself questioning his own ideals; challenging standards which he believed to be true. Definitely, the world was awry; perhaps it was possible that this amazing man . . . had a plan to adjust the scheme of things 'nearer to the heart's desire.' . . . Perhaps the redemption of mankind, the readjustment of poise, could only be brought about by a remorseless, steely intellect such as that of Dr. Fu Manchu. Perhaps he was a fool to fight against the Si-fan. . . . Perhaps the Si-fan was right and the Western world wrong! (217–18)

The Doctor's recovery quickly represses Petrie's fleeting identification with him. Re-aligned with Smith at the end of the novel, Petrie envisions Fu Manchu's "phenomenal return to vitality" as a foreboding omen, filling the world with "blood and violence; a ghastly picture of death and destruction" (219).

There are other moments in the series when the rhetoric against Fu Manchu breaks down in similar ways; they are also resolved somewhat unconvincingly. All of the narrative protagonists, especially those who love the half-castes in Fu Manchu's employ, fight against moments of sympathy with the Doctor by reciting his misdeeds in a litany of protection. Romantic relationships provide fleeting and unstable opportunities for cross-cultural as well as cross-racial understanding. Protagonists regard such moments as submission to the Doctor's dominion. When Bart Kerrigan attempts to persuade Ardatha—a former servant of the Doctor who has, predictably, fallen in love with him—of the unrighteous methods of the Si-fan, he casts his objections in moral terms: "Do you understand what this society stands for? Do you know that they employ stranglers, garroters, poisoners, cutthroats, that they trade in assassination?" (*Drums* 51). Ardatha refutes his easy judgments, her impassioned reply calling into question his assumptions of Western innocence and Eastern guilt: "And your Christian rulers, your rulers of the West—yes? What do *they* do? If the Si-fan kills a man, that man is an active enemy. But when your Western murderers kill they kill men, women and children—hundreds—thousands who never harmed them—who never sought to harm anybody. My whole family . . . was wiped from life in one bombing raid" (51).

In response to her attack, Kerrigan's security in the rightness of his position falters: "I felt the platform of my argument slipping from beneath my feet. This was the sophistry of Fu Manchu! Yet I hadn't the wit to answer her" (51). Categorizing her argument as "sophistry," Kerrigan abruptly terminates their discussion. His decision echoes the discomfort of previous narrative protagonists who have fallen in love with women already involved with Fu Manchu. Alan Sterling, an earlier narrator, never fully convinces Fleurette of Fu Manchu's evil, even admitting that his "conception of her as a victim of the powerful and evil man who sought to destroy white civilization was entirely self-created" (*Bride* 213). Kerrigan's inability to override Ardatha's argument signals his impotence in the face of her logic, an impotence rendered doubly debilitating in light of his romantic pursuit of her. And ultimately, the romantic pursuit saves Kerrigan and the other men from really questioning their value systems. The destabilizing effect of their attraction to Eastern women allows them to "explain away" their rhetorical and argumentative inadequacies to Fu Manchu's "sophistry" by ascribing their illogic to weaknesses of the flesh. Such a convenient resolution lacks persuasive force for the reader who perceives the pregnant pauses in the texts.

The exchanges overtly recognized and valued in the books are material. Smith appropriates various scientific formulas and technological inventions used by Fu Manchu, making "science . . . richer for our . . . brush with the enemy" (*Insidious* 22). From the Doctor, Smith acquires poisons, life-giving elixirs, particle-dissolving rays, interpersonal communication devices, and a wide exposure to hitherto unknown creatures, both natural and unnatural. This notion of the "unnatural"—a characteristic that, according to Smith and the texts' surface logic, Fu Manchu, his half-caste servants, and his most dangerous inventions manifest—masks even as it gestures toward the fear of hybridized contact undergirding the modernity of the world Rohmer reflected and contributed to his books.

"Primitive" In(ter)ventions

Fu Manchu's scientific and technological endeavors manifest his negotiation of hybrid formulations most fully. Contrary to Smith's ideological objections to his projects, cast primarily in moral terms, Fu Manchu does not view his explorations of new combinations of elements found in the natural world as ugly or sordid. For him, engineering hybridity productively harnesses the exciting potentials of nature. The Si-fan, a transnational, trans-racial organization including members from both "East" and "West," reflects such a philosophy. As an inventor, Dr. Fu Manchu fuses "primitive" elements with "modern" advancements to create new technologies that defy penetration by Smith. In *Island of Fu Manchu* (1940), the Doctor uses one of his "inventions" to deliver a message to Bart Kerrigan, the novel's protagonist. A curious contraption, it inspires "revulsion" in Kerrigan, who views it as a "dreadful exhibit." What Kerrigan sees is a human head, "that of a bearded old man, reduced by the mysterious art of Peruvian head-hunters to a size no greater than that of an average orange[,] . . . mounted and set in a carved mahogany box having a perfectly fitting glass cover" (Rohmer, *Island* 96). Its "repellent" appearance stems partially from the primitivism it seems to celebrate. As Marianna Torgovnick writes in *Gone Primitive* (1990), primitivism is the name we assign the darker aspects of ourselves, the label we use to distance our "untamed selves" from our images of self (8). By its projection of "id forces—libidinous, irrational, violent, [and] dangerous" onto other peoples as a way of demarcating difference, it continually tropes "Otherness" by figuring it as exotic and degraded (Torgovnick 8).

Kerrigan recoils from the shriveled head and the "native work" on the box encasing it because they seem emblematic of the wide gulf between him and the Doctor. Ironically, when "a low, obscene whispering" begins to emanate from the head, the differences structuring Kerrigan's world begin to blur, devouring carefully wrought distinctions between Self and Other:

> 'So it befell—so it befell . . .' The whispering was in English! 'Ica I was called—Ica . . . Chief was I of all the Quechua of Callao. But the Jibaros came: my women were taken, my house was fired, my head struck off. We were peaceful folk. But the head-hunters swept down upon us. Thought still lived in my skull, even when it was packed with burning sand . . . My brain boiled, yet I knew that I was Ica, chief of the Quechua of Callao . . .' (Rohmer, *Island* 106)

This narrative of violence and dismemberment seemingly corroborates the expectations of primitivism aroused in both Kerrigan and the reader as they gaze at the display, frozen with fascination at the sight of the decapitated head. Nevertheless, Ica's head, framed by its glass case, problematizes even as it foregrounds Western notions of primitivism.

While Ica's story reinforces Kerrigan's horror and disgust, it also partially negates his preconception of the primitive as completely Other and vice versa. Kerrigan's surprise at the whispering *in English* foregrounds his own horrified consumption of the shriveled head, a consumption highlighted by the museum display case within which the head rests. While the *Jibaros* who destroy Ica's home might refer to either the peasantry or to the Jívaros, a tribe of Indians known for their skill in shrinking heads, Ica's narrative invokes a sequence of colonial relationships that are no less "primitive" than the examples of native violence it explicitly articulates. Quechuans, linked to the Inca Empire through a marital alliance between Viracocha Inca and the daughter of the chief of Anta, lent their language to Incan bureaucracy and government, thereby cementing the expansion of the Incan empire. Calling up the violence of both Incan and Spanish imperialisms, Ica's fragmented tale ruptures the clear boundaries between Self and Other by accenting the violent legacy and the absent presence of Spanish colonialism on native peoples.

Yoking together "primitive" and "civilized," the "undeveloped" with the futuristic, Fu Manchu's hybrid experiments—and ultimately, even Fu Manchu himself—re-image racial and cultural categories only to have imperial structures of representation reabsorb their disruptive potential through the fetishization of freakishness. In *Fu Manchu's Bride* (1933), the Doctor cultivates a "freakish" Tsetse fly capable of spreading a "hybrid germ" combining sleeping sickness and plague. At once meticulously honorable as well as cunningly cruel, Fu Manchu's power stems from the fact that there is nothing about him considered normal. He can claim to be the world's greatest intelligence. His green eyes are covered with a thin film which reminds Petrie of the *"membranas nictitans"* possessed by birds. His skull is of a prodigious (and nearly unbelievable) size, a physical detail considered abnormal for a Mongoloid. As the texts illustrate, the discomfort Smith feels about the disruptive potential of Fu Manchu's hybrid formulations is one that can be assuaged by fetishizing hybridity as freakishness.

Different Performances, Performing Difference

According to historian Richard Altick, freakishness inspired a "common curiosity [that] erased social distinctions: the quality and the rabble, the cultivated and the ignorant mingled to see the latest marvel" (36). The "marvels" they paused and paid to wonder at included a variety of visual deviants, the more deformed or grotesque the better. At Bartholomew Fair (the biggest and longest lived of London fairs), William Wordsworth observed that

> All moveables of wonder, from all parts,
> Are here—Albinos, painted Indians, Dwarfs,
> The Horse of knowledge, and the learned Pig,
> The Stone-eater, the man that swallows fire,

Giants, Ventriloquists, the invisible Girl,
The Bust that speaks and moves its goggling eyes,
The Wax-work, Clock-work, all the marvellous craft
Of modern Merlins, Wild Beasts, Puppet-shows,
All out-o'-the-way, far-fetched, perverted things,
All freaks of nature, all Promethian thoughts
Of man; his dulness, madness, and their feats
All jumbled up together to make up
This parliament of Monsters. (Wordsworth ll. 679–91)

Clearly, what constitutes freakishness includes physical deformity, exoticism, unbelievable "skills" and "talents," a certain amount of illusion (and gullibility), and the demonstration of technology so new that it borders on the "magical." To read Wordsworth's graphic list of what fairgoers paid to gawk at is, after taking into consideration the changed sensibilities effected by the "progress" of a century, to have an idea of what kind of display Rohmer offered his readers in the Fu Manchu books. Most of the creatures used or created by the Doctor, and even the Doctor himself, possess freakish characteristics. Consistently identified by the enormous size of his skull, the descriptions of Fu Manchu's head, tempered by the "dignity" and "majesty" of his expression, are nonetheless reminiscent of the hydrocephalic children popularly displayed for public viewing during late-nineteenth-century freak shows. The conception of the Doctor as "freakish" also made sense in the context created by the traveling exhibition featuring Chang and Eng, the Siamese twins whose presentation to both British and American publics "further contributed to the institutionalization of Chinese racial representation as appropriate for museum or freak show display" (Moy 13).

Each of the books in the series introduces at least one new exotic or deformed specimen to the reading public. From the Zayat Kiss delivered by the giant scolopendra centipede imported from Burma to three-and-a-half-inch-high Negritos hailing from West Africa; from the *Cynocephalus hamadryas,* a sacred baboon with "an unreasoning malignity towards [men]" to the shriveled but still-talking head of a Peruvian Indian chief; from Hassan the white Negro to Zazima the Panamanian Dwarf, Fu Manchu—courtesy of Rohmer's vivid imagination—provided a veritable freak show for his audiences. Altick writes that "the March of Intellect had not progressed so far as to deprive countless . . . visitors of their credulity and their appetite for human wonders, whether natural or contrived—armless artists, hydrocephalic children, fat or pigfaced ladies, spotted men and women, and so on" (253). Rohmer's immersion in the music halls had prepared him to take advantage of the visual as spectacle. In an increasingly modern and alienating world, the spectacle of Otherness performed by freak shows and their later cousins forged a sense of community in the face of what could be seen as the truly alien.

Although the freak shows of the nineteenth century gradually disappeared from public view, the popular fascination they catered to did not simply evaporate. Rather, the curiosities and human differences they exploited for the purposes of show were adopted by a variety of other institutions. The latter half of the nineteenth century saw the rise of anthropology and ethnology as scientific discourses. What was previously gaped at as exotic was now closely studied in the name of science and progress. Science legitimated the public desire for spectacle and the display of difference, and made it respectable. Zoos, museums, and international exhibitions provided increasingly scientific forums for the study of exotica, along with their more ostensible programs of educating and enlightening their patrons. A close look at the presentational structure of the novels makes Rohmer's deliberate appropriation of popular interest in a burgeoning museological culture startlingly clear.

As exhibits like Ica's mummified head demonstrate, Rohmer exploits a quasi-scientific desire to see, in one panoramic sweep, a wide range of the foreign. Thanks to the Doctor's ability to penetrate the deepest jungles of Asia, Africa, and the Middle East, Rohmer's audiences enjoyed the thrill of "seeing" sights and people without leaving the comfort of their homes. While the surface rhetoric of the books condemns Fu Manchu for attempting to build a Chinese empire, the Doctor's techniques of collection and demonstration actually mirror *Western* imperial practice. Like the "human showcases" featured at International Exhibitions, Fu Manchu's scientific companions are "specimens" who have been collected and processed into an imperial project; each scientist is placed in his "natural environment" and observed while "performing" in his established area of expertise. What made Fu Manchu's "human showcase" so repellent to audiences were considerations that should have been equally at play in the collection and display of native peoples. Rohmer exposes Fu Manchu as the ultimate man of empire and such exposure horrified readers, who discovered the ability of the Other to be as imperialist, as Western, as themselves. The inversion of empire presented by the Doctor not only reveals the limits of a fully articulated critique against his design, a pattern of imperial acquisition already forged by the Western nations hypocritically condemning his project, but also emphasizes a threatening mimicry of Western imperial agency.

However, Fu Manchu is not the only one to take advantage of visual display in the interests of empire. Rohmer's books undermine many of the critiques against imperial representation that he embeds within them. While specific elements of the Fu Manchu novels critique, sometimes unconsciously, the gaze of empire as it had been trained against other peoples, the books also exploit the curiosity and fears creating that imperial gaze. Ultimately, the texts functioned as justification for British and American discrimination against the Chinese.

As such, Rohmer often treats Fu Manchu himself as an exhibit. Like Afong Moy, a " 'Chinese Lady' . . . offered to the public gaze at the American Museum in New York City," Fu Manchu's performances take place in settings that conform to public expectations of "Chineseness" (Moy 12). Moy's "performance" of ethnicity relied upon an elaborate set decorated with chinoiserie: James Moy notes that the "simple foreignness of Afong Moy was deemed sufficient novelty to warrant her display" (12). Rohmer's textual presentation of Fu Manchu borrows heavily from public displays of Chineseness exemplified by "exhibits" like Afong Moy, where much of what was considered representative of the Chinese emerged from the display of material objects. Rohmer's depiction of the Doctor emphasizes those aspects of the Doctor's setting that would provide the "authenticity" expected by his reading public. As such, the Doctor usually dresses in a "long yellow silk robe," wears a "black mandarin cap with a coral bead," and smokes opium from a "jade pipe"—all while in a room decorated with "lacquer furniture" and other appropriately "authentic" chinoiserie.

Rohmer carefully deploys exotic elements in the familiar framework of British and American social structures. Although some of the novels take place in exotic locales, most of them maintain contact with territorial landscapes with which readers could identify; as such, London and New York figure prominently in the series. The contrast of the familiar with the exotic provides a frame, a setting for each of the unfamiliar places—and by extension, the most recent specimens—promised in each new installment of the Fu Manchu drama. Rohmer's writing embodies the impact of the visual by articulating it within the context of an enormous exhibition. Responsible for staging as well as enacting the exhibit, Fu Manchu amazes his audience with a dizzying array of new species of men, animals and plants. In these texts and performances, authority resides not only in the spectacular nature of the display but also in its capacity to extend the visual to the visceral. As such, the displays are ordered not so much for educational value as for their ability to produce a reaction in the reader. The horror engendered by the displays proliferates from the displacement of specimens from their perceived "natural environments." Kerrigan's horror at Ica's glass-encased head derives, in part, from its removal from a museum setting and displacement onto a landscape that foregrounds his own specular consumption of the head. Similarly, much of the terror inspired by the Doctor's "fiendish armory" of scorpions and poisonous flowers derives from its (mis)placement in the "sanitary" environment of the metropolis.

The formulaic nature of the books reinforces the image of a carefully constructed museum of wonders. As the most important exhibit in this museum, it is the "authenticity" of Fu Manchu's performance that inspires readers' confidence in the rest of the exhibits. The framing provided by metropolis and the careful deployment of current events lend credibility to the wonders populating Rohmer's fantasy museum. The series constructs the museum slowly, careful to take visitors through already familiar parts of the display before introducing new and stranger sights. Just as museum exhibits gradually took on thematic organization, the rooms in Rohmer's museum of wonders annexed various parts of the world and turned them into displays that both edified and frightened Rohmer's patrons: Limehouse, New York's Chinatown, Haiti, Communist China, the French Riviera, Persia, Venice— all of these places became rooms in a textual edifice dedicated to the specular consumption of racial and cultural difference.

⌐

At the end of Fu Manchu movies, his voice is always heard threatening his return.[26] His longevity as a character, and his various incarnations in popular culture, suggest that he has had a lot to say about Western desire and the contexts of Asian American representation. Fu Manchu demands an investigation into the complicated ideological issues of representation that produce the anxiety and desire characteristic of stereotype as a discursive formation. As my discussion has suggested, reading Fu Manchu as a stereotype reflective of a racist agency must involve more than denigrating the negative images he embodies. I do not argue against acknowledging the dangerous ramifications of stereotype, or lose sight of racism's use of stereotype to persecute Otherness; rather, I suggest moving beyond denunciations of racist agency to explore the powerful ways in which that expression works to structure the representational frameworks that Asian Americans have necessarily had to engage. To that end, I have tried in this chapter to look at Fu Manchu as stereotype in the most productive sense by using insights derived from impersonation as metacritical strategy. Such a strategy helps us to recognize the complicated nature of Rohmer's deployment of the Doctor and all its intended and unintended ambivalences—a necessary step toward deconstructing the power of stereotypical representation.

THREE

De/Posing Stereotype on the Asian American Stage

> To be natural . . . is such a difficult pose to keep up.
>
> *An Ideal Husband*, Oscar Wilde

> God who has made me in His own likeness. In His Own Image in His Own Resemblance, in His Own Copy, In His Own Counterfeit Presentment, In His Duplicate, in His Own Reproduction, in His Cast, in His Carbon, His Image and His Mirror. Pleasure in the image pleasure in the copy pleasure in the projection of likeness pleasure in the repetition. Acquiesce, to the correspondance [sic].
>
> *Dictee*, Theresa Hak Kyung Cha

Stereotype has a style all its own.

Its ability to represent that which we fear as well as that which we would desire marks its divided nature. To cite Craig Owens's elegant formulation of stereotype's hold, it "confers on the individual the dream of a double postulation: [the] dream of identity / dream of otherness" ("Medusa" 193).[1] While Asian American artists working to oppose stereotype might dream of its utter destruction, the likelihood and even the desirability of such obliteration comes under question as they wrestle with the ways in which stereotype and identity are mutually constitutive, bound together by a shared desire for articulation and coherency in the project of producing a viable subjecthood. The effort to compose into existence a recognizable configuration of identity by which one might be known lies at the heart of both the construction and the deconstruction of stereotype.

Exposing stereotype can be an extraordinarily painful and difficult process, especially when those who are being stereotyped are confronted by the multifarious ways in which the necessary role-playing such exposure demands comes to suggest the boundaries and limits of what identity might mean for an entire population. In many ways, the "agony of the stereotype" creates "reflexive creatures" who, in agitating against its dimensions, still find themselves limited by its demands (Chin, "Come All Ye . . ." 9). Sheng-mei Ma finds the overlaps between stereotype and identity a particularly fruitful site of critical investigation; he argues that although it is popularly assumed that Orientalism and Asian American identity are oppositional to each other in both desire and effect, it would be more productive to consider the ways in which they are "strange bedfellows," both conjoined in what he terms a "deathly embrace" that ultimately results in the atrophying of ethnic identity (xi, xxiii). Ma's insistence on rethinking the political poses and outcomes of oppositionality gestures to the complicated dynamics that make the deconstruction of stereotype such a seemingly impossible project. Since stereotype is, by nature, oppositional, opposing stereotype requires more than counteracting it with antithetical representations—a move that merely redeploys the logical structures by which stereotype works in the first place.[2]

Deposing stereotype through its performance on the Asian American stage, this chapter demonstrates, is a collective enterprise and one that requires multiple strategies that take advantage of stereotype's performative nature and respond to its penchant for stylization in a visual register. Stereotype's theatrical exertions are counterposed by Asian American playwrights in a variety of ways: through a recontextualization that forces the audience to visualize in a double register that refuses the fixity that visual stylization connotes; through the transposition of roles so as to reveal the partial allegiance to identity itself as a performed role; through the hyperbolic pleasures of camp performance designed to exceed the limitations imposed by stereotype; and through a systematic over-explication, both visual and auditory, designed to challenge the acts of literacy that comprise the foundations for our readings of racial identity. While each of these tactics is effective in identifying the troubling ramifications of stereotypical performance on both the actor and the spectator, stereotypes remain visibly present and continue to exert suasion despite theatrical efforts to undermine their performative power. This chapter argues that the act of impersonating stereotype through its staged performance entails *embracing stereotype's effectiveness in staging the conditions by which a collective, pan-ethnic coalition is performed into being synchronically with the more troubling aspects of stereotype.* The end result is not the elimination of stereotype's specter but a recalibration of its performative power so that it might be used as an aid, one of many, in the endeavor to constitute Asian American selves—through acts of im-personation—as subjects.

Critical to this project of self-constitution is a reconsideration of the imbricated relationship between stereotype and identity. If, as Emily Apter suggests, stereotype might be considered to be character's "degraded cousin" and that "the very notion of character . . . is a fixing in flux," then "[c]haracter itself emerges as stereotype in drag, ethnically, socially, and culturally . . . imitative" (23). Apter's provocative reformulation of both character and stereotype suggests that identity—that which stereotype is often posed against and against which stereotype's authority is called into question— might be most usefully conceptualized as itself constituted through an act of impersonation. And as an act of impersonation (an act that manifests a doubled allegiance through its rejection of virtuosity and its emphasis on the conditions of its own emergence), identity becomes the vexed site from which stereotype isn't so much *countered* as it is *given greater depth.* Accordingly, the parameters of any discussion regarding stereotype and identity must include the relative positioning of both as *performatively equivalent options.* Considering stereotype as a performance that is, on any level, equivalent to identity can produce, to be sure, great anxiety. After all, on what grounds might stereotype be undermined if there is no recourse to the position of moral and cultural authority (as exemplified by Frank Chin's vigilant policing of "the real" and "the fake") and no automatic privileging of the epistemological authority of experience?

While the subjects of stereotype have performed and re-performed stereotypes in a concerted effort to "recycle them as powerful and seductive sites of self-creation" (Muñoz 4), the conflicted process of such a reformulation manifests itself in a variety of responses. As Karen Shimakawa demonstrates in *National Abjection: The Asian American Body Onstage* (2002), one tactic employed by many Asian American playwrights seeks to "distinguish, in Chin's terms, the 'fake' stereotypes of Asian Americanness from the actual experiences, traditions, and achievements of 'real' Asian Americans. Plays employing this strategy juxtapose those representations positioning Asian Americanness-as-abject (racially, culturally, sexually, and nationally aberrant)

against representations of 'real' Asian Americans who personify the diamet-
rically opposing antistereotype" (99–100).[3] As Shimakawa goes on to argue,
this strategy of representing antistereotype derives its effectiveness from its
ability to offer for view "alternative ways of seeing Asian American bodies
and lives"; however, it can also inadvertently reify the very binary structures
of representation upon which stereotype depends by not challenging the
real/fake distinctions framing the discussion in the first place.

Thus, one of the most intriguing results of conceptualizing identity as
"stereotype in drag" is a refocusing of attention—not necessarily away from
stereotype but certainly on identity and the ways in which it, too, needs to
be (re)considered in ways that problematize binary schemas. In this regard,
José Esteban Muñoz compellingly argues that "the use-value of any narrative
of identity that reduces subjectivity to either a social constructivist model or
what has been called an essentialist understanding of the self is especially exhausted" (5). Offering a notion of identity as a "process that takes place at
the point of collision of perspectives that some critics and theorists have understood as essentialist and constructivist," Muñoz "locates the enacting of
self at precisely the point where the discourses of essentialism and construc-
tivism short-circuit" (6). Impersonation gives name to particular aspects of
self-constitution performed by the enacting subject that Muñoz identifies.
In what follows, I conceptualize identity as a performance that emerges as a
moment of negotiation, one that, via impersonation, manifests itself in ways
that challenge the prescribed representational roles available to the performing subject even as its very visibility as an *imperfectly* performed act marks its
operation as social criticism. Further, I advocate the need for reading strategies and performance tactics that enable us to identify as double agents those
who are bound to a problematic representational history but equally bound
to re-staging that history to make an intervention that re-scripts the possibilities of what we might perform into being in the future.

Such reinscription helps to contextualize some of the difficulties encountered in the deconstruction of stereotype as well as to bring to attention
questions regarding the simultaneous claims and antagonisms that identity
and stereotype—often thought to be oppositional if not, at least, mutually
incompatible—exert on both subjects and performers. Thus, the conflicted,
sometimes co-extensive relationships between the performance of stereotype

and the performative impositions of identity must be delineated in order to expose the (im)postures of stereotype, the contingencies of identity, and the ways in which impersonation proffers Asian Americans a strategy by which they perform into visibility both of these possibilities—often synchronically. While stereotype must not only be acknowledged but also *inhabited* before it can be undermined or displaced, impersonation's simultaneous enactment of both distance and proximity reveals how the issues of ownership as well as subversion are complicated by the possibility of doubled agency being performed on behalf of both the performer and the audience.[4]

A number of Asian American playwrights have, individually, taken up the challenges such redirection produces; collectively, Asian American theater in the last fifteen years has staged repeated acts of impersonation in an effort to delineate a set of strategies by which Asian Americanness assumes both expected and unexpected forms. To that end, they (and some of the characters they create) perform into visibility Homi Bhabha's injunction to "shift from the ready recognition of images as positive or negative to an understanding of the *processes of subjectification* made possible (and plausible) through stereotypical discourse" (67; emphasis original). As Jacques Lacan cautions, "Whenever we are dealing with imitation, we should be very careful not to think too quickly of the other who is being imitated. To imitate is no doubt to reproduce an image. But at bottom, it is, for the subject, to be inserted in a function whose exercise grasps it" (qtd. in Owens 190). In examining a diverse set of dramatic pieces—Elizabeth Wong's one-woman playlet "China Doll" (1996); David Henry Hwang's Broadway hit *M. Butterfly* (1989); Philip Kan Gotanda's Asian American theater staple *Yankee Dawg You Die* (1991); and Diana Son's collective performance piece "R.A.W. ('Cause I'm a Woman)" (1996)—this chapter assesses the limitations inherent in any re-performance of stereotypes but also attends to the potentially promising aspects of what it means to acknowledge the significance of being "inserted in a function whose exercise grasps it." I suggest here that by considering how impersonation helps us to focus on the shared terrains animating the performance of stereotype *and* of identity, we might usefully consider the ways in which stereotypical performance becomes the common ground upon which Asian Americanness as coalitional identity and political mobilization is performed into possibility.

Act One: Com/Posing Stereotype

Since the "fixity" of stereotype, as Bhabha has noted, is predicated upon incessant repetition—it "vacillates between what is always 'in place,' already
known, and something that must be anxiously repeated" (66)—stereotype's
very nature as that which demands continual imitation produces opportunities for resistance and confrontation. Bhabha understands this practice as
mimicry, the "representation of a difference that is itself a process of disavowal" (86). As previously outlined in chapter 1, impersonation both em-
braces the resistant possibilities of Bhabha's notion of mimicry—its formulation of the "not quite" in order to open up alternative spaces for
identity-formation and subversion—and encourages an attention to the
process by which the performative dimensions of Asian American identity
are constituted via a dynamic exchange between Asian America's competing
definitions of itself.

In order to consider the ways in which stereotype assumes form through
visual stylization, we might return briefly to Sax Rohmer's work and focus in
particular on a character who, in addition to Fu Manchu himself, has attained an infamous level of notoriety and cultural currency. Rohmer's representation of Fu Manchu's beautiful Eurasian daughter Fah Lo Suee, the prototypical "Dragon Lady" whose vampiric sexuality threatens both the men
she woos and the cultural stability of racial distinctions, enacts the ways in
which stereotype depends upon a certain kind of fixity for its effectiveness.
In *The Daughter of Fu Manchu* (1931), Fah Lo Suee attempts to resurrect the
power of the Si-Fan after Fu Manchu's reported demise. The novel begins
with the "living death" of Sir Lionel Barton while he is excavating a tomb in
Egypt.[5] The immobilization of Barton, who has been drugged into a state of
catalepsy, sets the stage for Fah Lo Suee's entrance. Her identity is kept secret for the first half of the novel and the mystery of who she is occupies narrator Shan Greville's attention. Such attention manifests itself in a series of
detailed descriptions whose consistency of imagery is striking:

> Her hair was entirely concealed beneath a jeweled headdress. She wore jew-
> els on her slim, bare arms. A heavy girdle which glittered with precious
> stones supported a grotesquely elaborate robe, sewn thickly with emeralds.
> From proudly raised chin to slight, curving hips she resembled an ivory
> statue of some Indian goddess. (142)

Greville's description of Fah Lo Suee likens her to a statue of Kali, the Hindu goddess of destruction, and his perceptions of her danger and beauty are crystallized through repeated allusions to her stillness: "She employed scarcely any gesture. Her breathing could not be visually detected. That slender body retained its ivory illusion" (143).

Images of Fah Lo Suee's immobilized body occur repeatedly in the text and the distinction between the "ivory illusion" that she represents and the voracious interest that Greville's descriptions expose constitutes the paradox at the heart of stereotype: "the stereotype requires, for its successful signification, a continual and repetitive chain . . . . the *same old* stories of the Negro's animality, the Coolie's inscrutability or the stupidity of the Irish *must* be told (compulsively) again and afresh, and are differently gratifying and terrifying each time" (Bhabha, "Other Question" 77; emphasis original). Accordingly, Rohmer re-stages Fah Lo Suee's next appearance in the theatrical terms of stereotype, terms that capitalize on the fascination her immobilized body generates. When she attempts to thwart her father's impending marriage in *Fu Manchu's Bride* (1933), he orders two "powerfully built negresses" to tie her so that she may be whipped.[6] Tantalizing the reader with a stylized image of "an ivory body hanging by the wrists" (235), the composition of this scene presents stereotype as a gesture that is "not a blow that is interrupted" but "certainly something done in order to be arrested and suspended" (Lacan, qtd. in Owens, "Medusa" 192). Thus, Fah Lo Suee's representation enacts the paradoxical nature of stereotype and reveals the stylistic process by which it assumes presence.

Craig Owens asserts that this formulation of stereotype as that which "transforms action into gesture" (192) depends upon a complicated negotiation of both fixity and fluidity. Accordingly, stereotype itself should be understood as a paradoxical pose, one "enjoy[ing] an unlimited social mobility that must nevertheless remain fixed in order to procure the generalized social immobility which is its dream" (195). Owens's characterization of stereotype also acknowledges its inherently performative nature, its dramatic investments in pretense, disguise, and the spectacular representation of identity as a fixed enactment. The issue of pretense embodied by the notion of the stereotype as pose "suggests [that] what is ultimately at stake in the placement or presentation that constitutes 'posing' is the artifice or fictionality of 'position,' understood simultaneously as a social and spatial location of embodiment" (Cohen 40).

These issues of artifice and fictionality have been of great concern to Asian American writers. And yet the allure of stereotype and the difficulties it poses for those who have been subjected to it are that those distinctions between reality and illusion that it concretizes are not always readily distinguishable. Indeed, as I argued in chapter 1 and demonstrated through my reading of Fu Manchu in the last chapter, laying out a series of provisional characterizations of each of these enactments—"real" and "fake," imposture and impersonation—exposes the convoluted dynamics between these different kinds of performances. Significantly, the key to making such an inventory effective as a critical hermeneutic strategy is to understand the ways in which all of these performances work in *enmeshed* ways so as to reveal the intricacies of Asian American response and effect. Thus, understanding stereotype as a pose dependent upon as well as potentially deconstructed by impersonation, which operates as both performative act and critical endeavor, helps us to understand the vexed relationship between "the real" and "the fake" that Frank Chin and others have demanded we recognize.

Impersonation as a particular mode of performance resists reifying binary distinctions between the real and the performative. Unlike imposture, which "relies on acting and seeming genuine" (Crane x), impersonation asserts its own fictionality even as its success is predicated upon an illusion of "the real." Although it pretends to a certain sort of mastery over "the real," its effectiveness depends upon an act of repetition that *rejects virtuosity*.[7] Jane Gallop understands impersonation as a "double structure—'both serious and comic'" and this doubleness, which Asian American playwrights have deployed in an effort to redouble back against the doubleness of stereotype, is one that breaks down traditional oppositions of authenticity and pretense enacted in performance. Asian American dramatists who choose to use impersonation as a strategy against stereotype often effect their serious endeavors via the "comic" practices of parody, specifically camp and drag—a strategy utilized to great effect, as we will see, in Gotanda's *Yankee Dawg You Die*.

The performative dimension of stereotype makes it particularly apt for representation on the stage. As a type of "histrionic perception" (J. Lee 90), stereotype's relationship to theatrical expression is a fundamental one: clearly, the problematic relationship between stereotype and identity derives from the ways in which they both stake claims on embodiment. Thus, Asian American dramatists have had to re-stage stereotype's hold on the body in order to challenge stereotype's cultural authority before they can explore the more productive possibilities of seeing stereotype and identity as mutually constitutive enterprises. The rest of this chapter shows how Asian American theater offers a repertoire of possible responses in the process of such re-staging, a repertoire that draws on the doubled logic of impersonation as a performance of allegiance and resistance, in order to complicate the questions concerning identity and identification posed by stereotype.

I argue that these playwrights are all interested in strategizing against the impositions of stereotype, exposing stereotype's constructed nature by problematizing the distinctions between "the real" and "the fake" that it supposedly embodies. Their attempts to undermine the authority of stereotype theatrically demonstrate a nuanced understanding of the intimate relationship stereotype bears to identity. Admittedly such an understanding runs the risk of re-imposing stereotypes. However, it also effectively exposes the issues of mastery and desire at the heart of stereotype in order to deconstruct stereotype's mastery, if not its pervasiveness. While these playwrights' efforts to de/pose stereotype result in different measures of success, their dramatic texts reveal the importance of addressing stereotype as a performance that can be re-imagined through acts of impersonation. The provisionality of impersonation as an act that creates opportunities for identification as well as alienation accounts for the need to acknowledge stereotype's partial function in shaping character and identity, even as it provides a way of deconstructing those very categories of identity that might otherwise prove immobilizing.

Act Two: Re/Posing Stereotype

Elizabeth Wong's short performance piece "China Doll" unveils the constructed nature of the pose and attends to the ways in which the stylized pose of "Chineseness" foregrounds the process by which identity becomes codified. Focusing on the figure of Chinese-American actress Anna May Wong, the piece explores how the performance of race is predicated upon a certain stylization of the body that achieves its effects through a type of imposture—yellowface performance—and illustrates the dangers by which virtuosity as the logic of imposture can seduce even the actor attempting to impersonate the roles being played. The play's premise is ironic: Anna May Wong, known for her movie performances as the faithless slave girl and Fu Manchu's treacherous daughter, must instruct a young white actress on how to play the stereotype of the "[p]retty China doll" (313) who is also the "wily, possessive, vindictive, and manipulative . . . dragon lady" (315). As Anna May breaks down her performance into a discrete set of poses for the white actress to emulate, showing her how to swoon, how to embody "a fantasy" that bespeaks "sandalwood and jasmine[,] . . . the promise of faraway places" and how to "die a little each time" (313), the process by which stereotype pretends to a certain reality is highlighted.

Anna May learns to her dismay that Miss Harrington's training requires distinguishing between stereotype and those it supposedly represents. The rehearsal of a scene in which the Chinese slave girl betrays her mistress to the enemy becomes an occasion for the staging of such distinctions: "Don't squint. Darling, look, darling, no. Your eyes must look shifty—without being shifty. Don't you know we Chinese are a devious underhanded race[?] *(Pause)* Don't agree with me, dear! That was a joke" (313). Although the representation of the "Chinese girl in the arms of a white man" is exposed as problematic precisely because its performance dictates a disempowering identity for Asian American women who "are never real" (313), the play also acknowledges the seductiveness of such pretense.

Thus, even as Anna May rebels against the impositions of what she is not only asked to perform but to perpetuate as a code of racial performance, she is quick to assert authority over the poses that Miss Harrington finds so difficult to enact:

> ANNA Now, you see darling how it 'tis. My arms like so. My legs like so. . . . And when your leading man sweeps you up and gathers you in his arms, you die a little. Like so. Just a small turn of the head. . . . Now let's see you do it.
> *(She retrieves a thermos, pours tea into a cup. A pained expression comes over her face as the actress attempts an imitation.)*
> No! No, no, no darling.
> *(ANNA steps back into the light.)*
> Well, it's interesting. But no. Look, this is how you look.
> *(She takes an awkward pose.)*
> We don't want that. No self-respecting Chinese girl thrusts out her breasts. (313)

Anna May's disgust with the stylization of the Chinese female body as one that is impossible for her to perform without "d[ying] a little each time" exists alongside her small pleasure in being able to assert an authority based on what a "self-respecting Chinese girl" is "really" like. Staged in this manner, stereotype as a stylized performance of race is exposed as an artificial construction that nonetheless lays claim to an "authenticity" that can seduce *both* performer and audience.[8]

Wong's play re/poses stereotype in a number of different ways. In addition to deconstructing the pose through the ironic performance of the China doll, Wong also seeks in this piece to historicize the conditions under which actors like Anna May Wong performed. As the play unfolds, Anna May's desire to play roles that are not stereotypical or at least more positive in their representations of Asians is refused by movie executives who would rather cast white women in such roles.[9] The lack of opportunities afforded Anna May as an actress are detailed in her history of playing the same part over and over again. As the real Anna May Wong asserted in an interview with the London press: "I was killed in virtually every picture in which I appeared. Pathetic dying seemed to be the thing I did best" (qtd. in See 225).

Theatrically, the piece is staged as either a one-woman show or an ensemble piece with all the other characters—Miss Harrington, Anna May's father, an interpreter, a limousine driver, and movie producers Irving Thalberg and Samuel Goldwyn—performed silently. Although Wong allows the option of staging these other characters, she specifies in her production notes that "These characters are on stage throughout, *frozen as if they were dolls on display.* Their faces are white; the stage is white; the world is white" (312; emphasis mine). Although the play re-stages the limitations imposed on Anna May as an actress, it also reassigns the impositions of "doll" status by rendering all of the other characters silent and still. Significantly, such staging reverses the immobility of stereotype; it is the Asian American woman who controls, physically, the theatrical space while the other (white) bodies on stage are paralyzed and displayed in much the same manner as the "China doll" and "Dragon Lady" stereotypes position Asian and Asian American women. Whether performed with or without the other characters, Anna May is the center of the play, a theatrical re-staging that addresses her history of playing characters who either die or are relegated to the peripheries of the narrative at the end of the movie.

Finally, "China Doll" poses stereotype as a form of racial drag that does not necessarily depend upon a performer's race in order to critique notions of "authenticity" and "the real." The practice of hiring white actors to perform the roles of Asians is the occasion for Anna May's tutelage. Her frustration with Miss Harrington expresses itself repeatedly as a critique against the impostures of yellowface performance, which attempts to substitute a grotesque illusion for real Asian American bodies: "If you persist as you do, your yellow goop will rub off, your eye prostheses will stick to your leading man's nose, and the camera will see a white girl in bad makeup" (313). Although yellowface, revealed as a cheap stage trick, is castigated as a shameful practice, the play advances the more provocative notion that the "realness" of race does not necessarily guarantee against performing racial drag. For racial performance to accede to "a more supple . . . authority" (Karamcheti 145), we must conceptualize racial drag as a type of performance that is not contingent on the racial identity of the performer. In other words, Anna May Wong's performance of yellowface must be acknowledged alongside that performed by Miss Harrington and the similarities between their shared performances recognized as well as the differences. The constructedness of performance inherent in this doubled idea of racial drag, which exposes a dangerous temptation to claim authenticity even as it foregrounds the fictionality of racial representation, articulates a possible way of strategically impersonating stereotype.

Act Three: Trans/Posing Stereotype

The issue of identity as something that emerges as stereotype-in-drag and that can be mobilized as either performative and/or political strategy is also taken up by David Henry Hwang in his Broadway hit *M. Butterfly*. Inspired by an actual relationship between a French diplomat and his Chinese mistress, Hwang's play examines the possibility of an Asian actor exploiting the allure of stereotype by performing it as a type of racial drag of the kind Karamcheti describes. Hwang notes in the "Afterword" to his play that "I . . . concluded that the diplomat must have fallen in love, not with a person, but with a fantasy stereotype. I also inferred that, to the extent the Chinese spy encouraged these misperceptions, he must have played up to and exploited this image of the Oriental woman as demure and submissive" (93). The exploitation of the fantasy that stereotype embodies constitutes one possible strategy of resistance to stereotype, albeit one fraught with anxiety and limited by its homage to the virtuosity of such re-performance. As

Hwang's play demonstrates, the fantasy of the stereotype can seduce both actor and intended audience, and exploitation of a desire for stereotype can easily turn into the production of stereotypical desire.

Like "China Doll," *M. Butterfly* examines the cultural stereotypes that undergird the performance of Asian American identities. However, unlike Wong's play, Hwang's drama utilizes the more spectacular strategies of Brechtian disruption to critique stereotype's functions and effects. While "China Doll" is concerned with the "real" Anna May Wong and the ways in which her performative options as an actress were circumscribed by the material reality of stereotype as concretized in codes of racial performance, Hwang's play—despite being inspired by a "real" situation—isn't concerned at all with notions of the "real" that exist beyond stereotype.[10] All of the minor characters of *M. Butterfly* are drawn as stock characters and the two major characters, Rene Gallimard and Song Liling, are shown to be constructed entirely as vehicles of stereotypical desire. Indeed, Hwang admits that his initial interest in the figure of the Asian woman as Butterfly did not stem from any first-hand knowledge of Puccini's famous 1904 opera and that his fascination with the story derives from the subsequent circulation of Puccini's heroine as a cipher for Asian femininity: "I knew Butterfly only as a cultural stereotype; speaking of an Asian woman, we would sometimes say, 'She's pulling a Butterfly,' which meant playing the submissive number" (95).

As Colleen Lye has noted, the charge of "pulling a Butterfly" clearly reveals the Butterfly metaphor as a "term of reproach used by Asian American men against Asian American women" (262). With reversals and inversions (of gender, sexuality, culture, racial identification, and power positions) as his primary modes of critique, Hwang presents *M. Butterfly* as a "deconstructivist" version of the Butterfly story. The play aims to demonstrate the "perfect explicab[ility]" of what seems an "impossible story": a twenty year affair between Gallimard, a French diplomat, and his Chinese mistress, Song, who turns out not only to be a spy, but also a man. In reworking the racial and gender implications of "pulling a butterfly" by having *both* Gallimard and Song play differently inflected versions of "the submissive Oriental number," Hwang offers another reproach—this time against the "wealth of sexist and racist clichés" promulgated by Puccini's operatic tragedy and the dissemination of cultural and sexual stereotypes that can be traced to the "archetypal East-West romance" it articulates.

Reflecting Hwang's interest in deploying Brechtian techniques of disruption, the text's structure as "a play within a play within a play" foregrounds the importance of framing to the play's meaning and forces the audience to confront the implications of having each character performing more than one role—and of having two characters perform, with different inflections, the same role.[11] Hwang's decision to begin the play with his protagonist—already branded as a spy and a fool—in prison foregrounds Gallimard's *re-production* of the Puccini opera and suggests that while dramatic roles may inspire a character's identification and loyalty, they are constructions that are not entirely congruent with the live bodies enacting them. This issue of in/congruency with relation to the re-performance of stereotype is critical to both the play's meaning and structure. Indeed, in/congruency figures prominently in the criticism surrounding the performance of Song and the act of impersonation and unmasking around which the entire play pivots: Song's transformation from female to male during the production's intermission. As Hwang stipulates in his notes to the Dramatists' edition of the script, Song's role should not only be played by a male actor but the drag performance that so seduces Gallimard should also be one that doesn't actually fool the audience: "They [the audience] are to believe that Gallimard was seduced by a man disguised as a woman" (Hwang 1989, 89).[12]

Within the text, there are many overt theatrical gestures whose meaning stems from the incongruency between bodies and roles—an incongruency that speaks to the rejection of virtuosity that marks impersonation as a particular kind of enactment. Gallimard's desire to become the protagonist Pinkerton of Puccini's opera is parodied by his own identification of and with the "hero, the man for whom [Butterfly] gives up everything, [. . . as] not very good-looking, not too bright, and pretty much a wimp" (10). Hwang employs Brechtian double-role casting and role reversal to foreground further the disjunctions and conflations between actor and performance, stereotype and identity. After the first scene between Gallimard/Pinkerton and Marc/Sharpless, Gallimard announces to the audience: "In the preceding scene, I played Pinkerton, the womanizing cad, and my friend Marc from school . . . *(Marc bows grandly for our benefit)* played

Sharpless, the sensitive soul of reason. In life, however, our positions were usually—no, always—reversed" (11). The irony of such reversals works in concert with the other unseamless performances delivered in the play as well as foreshadows the production's final role reversal between Gallimard and Song.[13]

This combination of role reversal and double casting calls attention to the process of representation.[14] As the audience, we become aware of how the actor never completely conflates with the character she or he is playing and as a result, our own role in the production involves negotiating the multiple perspectives being staged and played out. Brecht termed such defamiliarizing techniques, culled from his observations of Chinese acting, "alienation effects" and theorizes the use of the "A-effect" in dismantling a simple audience identification with the characters of the play by making audience acceptance or rejection of the character's actions a conscious, rather than subconscious, operation (Brecht 91).

The role reversals staged early in this re-production of Puccini's opera provide the context for understanding the later transposition of roles between Gallimard and Song staged in *M. Butterfly*. As the ambiguity of the play's title suggests, the role of Butterfly is performed by both Song and Gallimard and through the transposition of the roles of Butterfly and Pinkerton, Hwang demonstrates the illusions that stereotype exploits. Although Gallimard initially identifies as Pinkerton, the "cad" who inspires the love and devotion of Butterfly despite his unworthiness, he discovers that the issues of power and control that structure his fascination with the "perfect woman" are much more complicated than even he can imagine. Consequently, the position of dominance that he assumes for himself is deconstructed by the realization that he also plays the Butterfly figure and that Song, accordingly, is also able to manipulate the Pinkerton role. The relationship between Song and Gallimard is structured by the roles they perform and Butterfly and Pinkerton are shown to exist only in relation to each other. While Hwang's decision to transpose actors and roles calls into question the authority of any performance, it also manifests a logic that keeps stereotypes in circulation. When Gallimard identifies himself as Butterfly and commits suicide at the end of the play, the figure of Butterfly as a powerful cultural fantasy remains solidly in place.

As a play about the dominance and control of stereotype, *M. Butterfly* deconstructs the pose of the Butterfly only to reconstruct it again. In the end, Gallimard is still invested in the fantasy of the perfect woman and the stereotype of the submissive Butterfly is not so much eradicated as given new life. This result can be ascribed to the play's rejection of the Brechtian strategies that worked so brilliantly in the first half of the play to expose stereotypical desire by re-presenting it through acts of impersonation—ones that highlight the citationality of performance itself and make visible the dangers of virtuosity celebrated by imposture. The play's unwillingness to commit to the impersonation of stereotype results in a return to the kind of realism that motivates Gallimard's stereotypical desire for Oriental women in the first place. Thus, Gallimard commits suicide rather than witness the destruction of his "vision of the Orient" and its

> slender women in chong sams and kimonos who die for the love of unworthy foreign devils. Who are born and raised to be the perfect women. Who take whatever punishment we give them, and bounce back, strengthened by love, unconditionally. (95)

His death and Song's earlier ejection from the stage render any hope of understanding between the two characters an impossibility. *M. Butterfly* leaves its audience disturbed by the power of stereotype and crucially aware of the need to reposition itself in relation to it. Yet, Hwang's failure to provide insight into Song's feelings and motivations leaves the audience ultimately unsure about how such a repositioning might play itself *out*.[15]

Act Four: Out-Posing Stereotype

Philip Kan Gotanda's *Yankee Dawg You Die* is also structured by an awareness of how stereotypes—the "Jap" soldier, the loyal servant, the "bucktoothed, groveling waiter," the North Vietnamese general, the "Chinaman gook," the "oriental houseboy"—dictate a history of Asian American representation that must be wrestled with and owned so as to create new roles for Asian Americans. Starring Vincent Chang, an older actor known for his history of playing stereotypical roles, and Bradley Yamashita, a young actor who prides himself on not sacrificing his Asian American political consciousness in order to succeed as an actor, *Yankee Dawg You Die* explores the dilemmas of performing identities that have emerged, perhaps can only emerge, from a history of stereotypical performances. The play's staging of stereotype is complicated by a number of contradictory impulses, which are emblematized by the play's ironic conclusion in which Bradley accepts a stereotypical role while Vincent decides to turn down a lucrative part in order to work on an Asian American independent feature. Such a conclusion symbolizes the difficulties of deconstructing stereotype but also, I believe, works in conjunction with Gotanda's use of camp as a strategy for out-posing the pose of stereotype to "show the levels at which opposition can be both contestatory and complicit, and yet still constitute a subversion that matters" (Kondo 11).

The play opens with the portrayal of Sergeant Moto, a "Jap" soldier who acts in *"an exaggerated, stereotypic—almost cartoonish—manner"* (6). Performed by Vincent, Moto's monologue reveals the ways in which stereotype distorts perception. Despite graduating from UCLA, Moto is perceived as a "Jap" and cannot make himself understood. Moto's frustration with his listeners' (deliberate) confusion of his pronunciation of "thirty-four" as "dirty floor" is articulated at the end of his monologue when he asks, "What the hell is wrong with you? Why can't you hear what I'm saying? Why can't you see me as I really am?" (6). By repeating this monologue three times in the play, Gotanda foregrounds the possibility of re-signifying stereotype by "reviewing" what stereotype enacts. Significantly, when Sergeant Moto's performance is repeated at the end of the play, what begins as a "cartoonish" rendition of stereotype becomes a performance of *"great passion"* (50). By first acknowledging how stereotype helps to form identity and then re-staging stereotype using its own performative repertoire of exaggeration and grotesqueness, *Yankee Dawg You Die* argues for the possibility of out-posing the poses of stereotype.

Gotanda has been criticized, along with Hwang, for the ways in which he replaces stereotypes with characters who are so "disfigured" by "the long-standing history of the stereotype" that they "self-destruct at the very moment of their representation" (Moy 124–25). However, he has also been recognized for his awareness of how the "pleasure of recognition of the Asian body in the playing of stereotypes is one that often confuses the reading of stereotypes strictly as racial oppression" (J. Lee 97). When Bradley criticizes Vincent for his willingness to "do any old stereotypic role just to pay the bills" (26) and identifies those performances as the cause of "all that self-hate" (25), his desire to blame Vincent for the social disempowerment of Asian Americans is predicated upon seeing the stereotype solely in terms of "racial oppression." This desire is complicated, however, by Gotanda's decision to feature Vincent and Bradley re-performing stereotypes together throughout *Yankee Dawg You Die.*

In response to Bradley's accusation that he is a "Chinese Stepinfetchit," Vincent contextualizes his own performances and insists upon a recognition of how his choices, like those of Anna May Wong, were limited by a lack of opportunity:

> VINCENT: You think you're better than I, don't you? Somehow special, above it all. The new generation. With all your fancy politics about this Asian American new-way-of-thinking and seven long years of paying your dues at Asian Project Theater or whatever it is. You don't know shit, my friend. You don't know the meaning of paying your dues in this business. . . . You want to know the truth? I'm glad I did it and I'm not ashamed, I wanted to do it. . . . At least an oriental was on screen acting, being seen. We existed. (24–25)

Vincent's speech articulates the difficulties faced by an earlier generation of Asian American actors, a situation that Wong also examines in "China Doll." However, Vincent admits to an emotion while playing stereotype that is surprising: gladness. Josephine Lee argues that this emotion signifies the "complex identification" implicit in the performance of stereotype: "Even though the role of the stereotype is familiar and detestable, the casting of the Asian body is enough to ensure a kind of welcome disruption, an illicit pleasure that sets up a key tension between stereotype and performer" (101). Although Lee's recognition of the possibilities of an "illicit pleasure" in Vincent's performances is invaluable in helping us reconsider the possibilities of how to approach stereotype, her assessment echoes Vincent's assertion that such performances are heroic because they made Asian Americans visible if not admirable.

While this assertion identifies an important context for understanding the history of Asian American performances of stereotype, it de-emphasizes the more troubling, and perhaps more politically significant, ramifications of Vincent's pleasure. Specifically, identifying such pleasure as only one of "disruption" of a particular field of perception denies the complicated relationship that binds stereotype to identity. Vincent's insistence on re-enacting his stereotypical performances for Bradley indicates the ways in which his life story *is constructed, perhaps can only be narrated, through his film roles.* Rather than seeing stereotype as a performance that exists in contradistinction to the performance of identity, Vincent's pleasure and his insistence on re-performing stereotype both for and with Bradley indicate an awareness of how his identity has been formed through stereotype. For Vincent, enacting stereotype reflects both agency and its lack. He is both the performing subject and the object being performed, and the result, "being seen," is one way of claiming a (provisional) identity. Such an act of impersonation suggests the ways in which identity and stereotype, while not interchangeable, are in some respects mutually constitutive. Owens articulates this paradoxical process in his treatise on posing: "the subject in the scopic field, insofar as it is the subject of desire, is neither seer nor seen; *it makes itself seen.* The subject poses as an object *in order to be a subject*" (215; emphasis original).

The implications of such an understanding are later addressed by a show about Martin Luther King that Vincent watches on television. When surrounded by nightriders, "[King] felt something inside he never felt before—impotent, like the slave, willing to go along, almost wanting to comply. After that, he realized he had to fight not only the white man on the outside, but that feeling, the slave inside of him. It is so easy to slip into being the 'ching-chong-chinaman'" (44). As Vincent understands, the pleasures of performance can easily translate into a debilitating identification with stereotype. In order to avoid being the "ching-chong-chinaman," Vincent must develop a way of impersonating the stereotype that allows him both to identify with and distance himself from what he is enacting. As Rhonda Blair's litotic formulation of this mode of contrary performance argues, impersonation enables an actor to be "both outside of the character and in it— a not-me/not-not-me" (303). Blair's concept of the not-me/not-not-me encapsulates the fundamental structure by which impersonation creates a space of critical mimesis that challenges authenticity even as it pays homage to it.

As critic Indira Karamcheti has suggested, tactics mobilized by those who resist oppressive representation are not a result of choice and must always be considered as both strategic and symptomatic: "they are strategies for seizing control of the machinery of representation but also always symptoms of powerlessness . . . as well as power" (Karamcheti 145). Clearly, impersonations of stereotype must acknowledge stereotype's constitutive powers as well as enact a certain distance from its poses. The pleasures of how to enact this type of impersonation are explored in more detail when Bradley and Vincent perform together. Despite Bradley's disgust with Vincent's enjoyment in reenacting stereotypes, he joins Vincent in all of these scenes and, most significantly, also experiences the pleasure of such performances. When Vincent convinces Bradley to help him reenact "Charlie Chop Suey's love song to Mei Ling," Bradley's initial feelings of discomfort are replaced by a developing involvement in their mutual re-staging. As they *"whirl around the stage"* with Vincent *"singing and tap-dancing"* and Bradley *"singing in a high-pitched falsetto,"* both actors get *"more and more involved, acting out more and more outrageous stereotypes"* (21; italics in original). Although Bradley *"starts to realize what he's doing"* and accuses Vincent of being a Chinese Stepinfetchit, his enjoyment of their collaboration is undeniable. The pleasure of their histrionic performance of stereotype is extended in a later bar scene, when Bradley encourages Vincent to recite the line "Yankee Dawg You Die" in increasingly exaggerated "Hollywood Orientalese."

Significantly, these moments of mutual pleasure and collaboration between Vincent and Bradley reveal the political possibilities of the characters' shared investment in and exposure to a history of stereotypical representation. When Vincent and Bradley first meet at a party, their differences are made manifest in a series of verbal exchanges that illustrate how, despite their shared Asian heritage, they are limited in how they might communicate with each other. Vincent's vocabulary—"Oriental," "low-budget movie"—offends Bradley, who introduces him to a more politically correct terminology: "It's Asian, not oriental. *(Vincent still doesn't follow. Bradley, embarrassed, tries to explain.)* Asian, oriental. Black, negro. Woman, girl. Gay, homosexual . . . Asian, oriental" (8). These initial exchanges are important for the ways in which they illuminate the divide—both generational and political—separating the two men and become critical to understanding how the problematic representational history of stereotype that each wrestles with also becomes the shared vocabulary that the two might use to engage each other. Thus, Gotanda repeatedly stages moments throughout *Yankee Dawg You Die* that show Vincent and Bradley re-performing stereotypical roles, roles that are revealed to be oppressive but also pleasurable and effective in creating bridges between such two different actors and personalities.

In each of these scenes, Gotanda marshals camp as a performative strategy. According to Pamela Robertson, camp is uniquely able to reveal "the porousness of pleasure, its locally overlapping features of passivity and activity, affirmation and critique" (16). As a result, camp can help to reconceptualize "resistance and subversion to account for the way in which . . . simultaneous pleasures of alienation and absorption refuse simplistic categories of dominant-versus-resistant readings" (17). By taking a certain agency from the campy performance of stereotype, Vincent and Bradley create alternative ways of appropriating Asian American identities for themselves. The formation of a coalitional Asian American identity that can account for both Vincent's conservativeness and Bradley's political consciousness is demonstrated in their workshop production of "Godzilla . . . Aahk!"

An Asian American drama by Robinson Kan, "Godzilla . . . Aahk!" provides Bradley and Vincent with yet another opportunity to forge a connection with each other through the hyperbolic performance of stereotype. The production insists upon the campiness of their earlier re-enactments; Godzilla, played by Vincent in costume, is characterized as "a giant zucchini gone to seed. A huge capsized pickle with legs" (33) and his only cry, "Aahk!," is uttered with the same exuberance of Vincent's "Yankee Dawg You Die" delivery. Bradley plays a "reporter out of the fifties" whose narration, nonetheless, reflects a much more contemporary ironic sensibility: he reports that despite rampaging across the Bay Bridge, Godzilla "pays no toll. Cars screech, children cry, mothers with babies scream. The men don't. They're 'manly.' Godzilla!" (33).

The production reappropriates Godzilla for Asian Americans, casting him as a hero to a young boy who has been called a "dirty Jap" by a classmate. As the production progresses, Bradley and Vincent take turns narrating the action and playing the different roles of Godzilla, the reporter, and the little boy, often simultaneously. Like Hwang, Gotanda employs the Brechtian strategy of multiple role casting in his production-within-a-production. By foregrounding the possibility of multiple impersonations, multiple layers of identity and stereotype, Gotanda stages critical distance between performer and role even as he illuminates the process by which such roles create alternative identities for, and new coalitions between, Bradley and Vincent. Although there is a fear of becoming the stereotype, the insistence on overplaying the already exaggerated nature of stereotype enables both actors to recognize stereotype's impact on identity formation in order to create more palatable roles. At the end of the play, Vincent accepts a part in an Asian American film that reflects his own childhood experiences. While Vincent's new opportunities denote a compelling transformation, Gotanda is careful to demonstrate the difficulty of leaving stereotypical representation behind as Bradley finds himself accepting the roles he once criticized Vincent for performing. Theatrically, *Yankee Dawg You Die*'s effective mobilization of camp in order to out-pose stereotype suffers from its very effectiveness. This contradiction signals the paradox at the heart of camp as a performative strategy: "Camp depends upon our simultaneously recognizing stereotypes as stereotypes to distance ourselves from them and at the same time recognizing, and loving, the hold and power those stereotypes have over us. It is always a guilty pleasure" (Robertson 142). Gotanda's play demonstrates that the guilty pleasures of camp performance are, indeed, dangerous and problematic . . . but also acknowledges how they can become the partial foundations on which some of the coalitional frameworks of Asian American identity might be erected and maintained. This attention to coalition is fundamental to understanding the performative nature of Asian American identity, which in some ways must always be performed into existence through acts of impersonation.

Act Five: De/Posing Stereotype

All of the dramatic texts discussed thus far have sought to de/pose stereotype by having Asian American bodies impersonate them on-stage. Josephine Lee argues that the presence of "the literal Asian body" challenges stereotype because it "threatens to exceed its caricatured role and its assigned function as projection" (97). While Diana Son's ensemble performance piece "R.A.W. ('Cause I'm a Woman)" challenges stereotypes by dismantling their poses, her confrontational play encourages Asian American women to refuse the enactment of stereotype even as it stages the ways in which stereotypes often frame the perception and expression of Asian American female identity. Where the above texts treat variously the allure of stereotype, Son dramatizes the *impositions* of stereotype. The refusal of her characters to be limited by the artistic and ideological force of received stereotypes dictates the play's structure, its development, and its style of representation. Significantly,

Son—like Gotanda—ultimately acknowledges the ways in which the reductive limitations imposed by stereotype can be re-framed as the common
ground from which an effective coalitional Asian American identity and
praxis can be generated.

"R.A.W." stands for "raunchy Asian women" and as the title denotes, the
performance piece deals with the stereotypes of Asian American women as
exotic, submissive, and sexually adventurous creatures. Featuring four
women who are identified by number rather than by name, the play addresses stereotype's power to invoke a particular kind of performance by uti-
lizing a multi-media format to refocus the eye. The women of "R.A.W." are
victims of stereotype, forced to deal with multiple misperceptions about
Asian and Asian American female sexuality. Although Son chooses to name
these misperceptions, she refuses them the pleasure of embodiment, decid-
ing instead to direct the spectator's eye away from the sight of Asian American female bodies re-performing such roles. As such, the first half of the play
compels a critical inspection of the men who are motivated by stereotypes of
the women; the men's lines remain unspoken, projected on slides, and the
women who respond to these lines are allowed to deconstruct them without
first having to embody the desires they articulate.

The first series of slides projects a number of popular pick-up lines that
men use on Asian and Asian American women. The opening scene, "a
crowded room, in a smoky place, in a bar with no light," sets the stage for "a
man" to approach and say:

> *Slide: I've never been with an Oriental woman before.*
> 3: And I try to give him the benefit of the doubt.
> 4: I think "been with" that comes from "to be."
> 1: He wants to be with me.
> 2: He wants to know me.
> 3: He wants to fuck me.
> 4: He wants to see if my clit is sideways.
> 2: He wants to make me moan in ancient languages.
> 1: He wants me to bark like a Lhasa Apso.
> 3: He wants to wow me with the size of his non-Asian dick. (292)

The slides, in addition to the women's interrogation of the stereotypical desires motivating the statements, are an effective way of addressing the stereotypical perceptions of Asian and Asian American women while not requir-

ing that they be re-enacted. Son's production notes insist that "the slides should not be substituted with an actual man's voice" because "[a] live actor can be tempted to interpret the man's character, to give him an attitude" (291). Aware of the power of the body in performance, Son's use of slides refuses to grant the male speakers the potential power of impersonation even as she offers the women an opportunity to de/pose the stereotypes invoked by the lines.

Without having to embody the stereotypes first, the four women of "R.A.W." can confront and resist the magnetism of stereotypical desire. This response is performed as a litany of refusal, each woman contributing to a collective rejection of stereotype's demands:

> I will not give you a massage. / I will not scrub your back. / I will not cook exotic meals using animal parts that aren't normally eaten. / I will not *not* get on top. / I will not be your Soon Yi. / I will not kill myself to save your son. / I will not light your cigarette afterwards. / I will not let you come without me. / I will not be your china doll. / I will not be a virgin. / I will not call you papasan. / I will not worship you. / I will not be your fetish. (293)

At this point in the play, the women speak chorally, one response blending into another. The ensemble nature of their performance, which acknowledges the ways in which stereotype constructs group identity, co-opts the power of collectivity in order to refute the impositions of stereotype.

The play's structure is also dictated by the process of de/posing stereotype. Although the performance piece recognizes the power of stereotype to determine Asian American identity and response by beginning with the women performing their parts without distinguishing them from one another, it also models a process for de/posing stereotype by allowing each of the women to begin claiming an individual identity as the play progresses. "R.A.W." reveals that the similarities binding these women to one another exist in relation to their disparate histories and locations. A woman whose mother encourages her not to eat kimchee so that her breath will be fresh for kissing her first boyfriend Paul, a "purebred whiteboy"; a second woman who is "not beautiful outside" but whose "heart is the home of great love" (294); another who insists on her lesbian sexuality even though others wonder "[w]hy would a cute Asian girl have to be queer?" (295); and a final woman who dates an Asian American man only to discover that she cannot understand him when he tells her *"sarang hae,"* that he loves her—all of the women in "R.A.W." refute the dominant perceptions of stereotype by telling their very different, uniquely individual, stories.

By asserting their individuality, the four women of Son's text refuse to be limited by the poses stereotype allows them. Their differences in the face of the *"same old"* stories Bhabha speaks of effectively undermine the immobilization by which stereotype imprisons. The performances of these women constitute one final act of impersonation: an "im-personation" that, unmodified, "is *appearing as a person"* (Gallop 9; emphasis original). Although Son mobilizes these women as individuals, she also recognizes the potential that coalitional identity offers. The ending of "R.A.W." reflects such a recognition. The women, once again, come together in an ensemble performance, although this time their contributions are informed by the distinctive identities they articulate in the middle section of the play:

> 3: And I will eat kimchee and kiss you right afterwards.
> 2: And I will let you love me inside and out.
> 4: And I will stick my tongue down your throat because we *are* more than friends.
> 1: And I will spend sweaty hours speaking a language that we both understand.
> 3: And I will give you the benefit of the doubt.
> 2: And I will let you know me.
> 4: And I will have ideas of my own.
> 1: And I just may give you the blowjob of your life, I mean it depends on the ones you've had before.
> 3: And I will love.
> 2: And be loved.
>   ......
> That's all. (296)

⤷

Karen Shimakawa argues that critical mimesis—a mode of performance that invokes "the deauthorizing power of imitation" (103) in an effort to turn a form of subordination into an affirmative strategy of subversion—has been a particularly favored mode on the Asian American stage, strategically deployed in order to counter the processes of exclusion by which Asian Americans are constituted as subjects in U.S. American culture.[16] My use of impersonation as both hermeneutic and performative tactic acknowledges the significance of Shimakawa's argument; however, the assessments produced by impersonation as a theoretical approach yield results that differ in emphasis from her conclusion about the consequences of invoking stereotype performatively. Even as Shimakawa concludes that the emancipatory play of such performances is always limited in some way, an assessment that the readings in this chapter support, I read the *nature* of such limitation in different ways through the lens of impersonation. Impersonation, as these texts and authors demonstrate, helps us to understand how the process of de/posing stereotype is indeed always *in process,* a reflection of the twinned project of creating a self through and in response to the vexed representational history of Asian America. To consider the limitations inherent in the acts of de/posing stereotypes is also to attend to the limitations in any performance of identity itself. And, as Gotanda and Son reveal in their dramatic works, the possibilities that such shared recognition produces are ones that can lead to seeing beyond the simple victimization of Asian Americans as the injured objects of stereotype to acknowledging the political effects of coalition-building on subject-formation, a recognition that can only emerge when, as Lisa Lowe suggests, we begin "basing the identity on politics rather than the politics on identity" (75). The acts of impersonation staged by contemporary Asian American dramatists identify stereotype as a pose that, to be deposed, must first be reposed and out-posed with an attention to the pleasures and problems that such performances inevitably produce for the Asian American subject.

PART II

Double Agents, Double Agency

Bodily Negotiations: The Politics of Performance in Hualing Nieh's *Mulberry and Peach*

If the first part of *Double Agency* is preoccupied with differentiating acts of imposture from acts of impersonation, particularly as such enactments center on issues of stereotype and authenticity, the second section of the book focuses on Asian American acts of impersonation that move beyond the reiteration of stereotype. In this chapter and the two that follow, I emphasize how Asian American characters im-personate themselves as subjects who resist the ways in which their identities as Asian/Americans are legally and socially over-determined. As such, the focus of each chapter in this section is on tracking the process of how characters who have been marginalized—as illegal aliens, as crazy immigrants, as invisible members of U.S. American society—perform into being viable roles that grant them both space to maneuver and the ability to resist singular interpretation. Significantly, the second half of this book illuminates the ways in which the domestic critiques enacted by Asian American literature, critiques which continue to operate as key sites of impersonation as critical practice, must be understood in relation to meta-national dynamics that function as part of larger, global economies of subject-formation and cultural production. Such an emphasis stresses the possibility of enacting simultaneous critique via an understanding of impersonation as both literary and critical practice—one that insists upon the critic, too, as double agent. In other words, what I propose in the second unit is that critics of Asian American literature train themselves, like the characters and authors I treat here, to see and act in multiple registers by considering the mutually formative dimensions of the literature's "national" and "transnational" valences.

Additionally, I concentrate on the double agency of characters and authors who, through their acts of impersonation, focus our attention on the always already constructed identities that are thrust upon Asian Americans as well as on the necessity of taking on those roles in order to subvert them in the very moment of their performance. To that end, this chapter addresses issues of subject-formation and performance by dilating on the site of the Asian/American body; in the process, I suggest that approaching Hualing Nieh's *Mulberry and Peach: Two Women of China* (1988) via the critical lens of impersonation and assessing the performative dimensions of the text produce new readings about the functions and effects of Nieh's protagonists and new opportunities for thinking about Nieh's novel as itself subject to the problems and possibilities of literary impersonation. Impersonation is thematized in this text by the figure of two women whose personalities are caught in the same body, a circumstance that subjects them to intense scrutiny by a U.S. immigration official but also subjects to our critical scrutiny the processes by which Asian American subjects are constructed and legitimated. As I will demonstrate, the figuration of Mulberry and Peach as distinct identities who struggle to share and to claim a single body encourages us to consider the body as a generative site of inquiry, one that makes (in)visible the mutually constitutive dimensions of identity and performance as well as the potentially disastrous effects of assuming a public identity. Critical to my argument here is a re-consideration of schizophrenia as an act of impersonation. While I acknowledge Mulberry and Peach as multiple personalities who by medical definition suffer from a pathological condition, this chapter suggests a more complex reading of what such a condition can signify by revealing the ways in which Nieh's re-working of schizophrenia within a context of its performative possibilities challenges the distinctions between sanity and insanity that work to police identity formation and that affect Mulberry and Peach both as women and illegal immigrants. By focusing on the performative dimensions of both embodied experience and textual metamorphosis with regard to Nieh's novel, I not only illuminate impersonation as a strategy of embodiment that exposes the convoluted relationships undergirding the legal and political structures that determine Asian American identity but also suggest the ways in which impersonation operates as a hermeneutics by which we can make apparent the diverse critical investments that have been brought to bear on the novel.

I.

In this matter of the visible, everything is a trap.
Four Fundamental Concepts of Psycho-Analysis, Jacques Lacan

The body is neither a purely natural given nor is it merely a textual metaphor; it is a privileged operator for the transcoding of these other areas.
The Politics and Poetics of Transgression, Peter Stallybrass and Allon White

The body defies its own appearance, constantly referring to, escaping, or embodying multiple modes of cultural production and social control. Far from existing simply as a biological or material entity, the body transcends corporeality to become what Susan Bordo calls a "medium of culture" (13). The body operates simultaneously as spatial topography as well as textual metaphor; within the confines of the body, not only are social formations constructed and subjectivities constituted, but systems of ideology are inscribed and reinforced. The body, singularly arresting in its anatomical representation of identity, deceives the eye with its simple lines and presence of solidity. Flesh, covered by the thinnest veneer of skin and materially substantive to the touch, hides a highly constructed network of blood, bones and organs, a network which, despite its seeming naturalness, is rendered meaningful only by the cultural systems of belief that invest it with the possibilities for semiotic generativity. Despite its surface display, the body is never just a body. Rather, it alternately acts as a surface for the inscription or a space for the embodiment of social, cultural, and political articulations. As Elizabeth Dempster writes in her discussion of the dancer's body, "ideologies are systematically deposited and constructed on an anatomical place, i.e. in the neuromusculature of the . . . body, and a precise reading of this body can only proceed if the reader/spectator's gaze is not deflected by, but penetrates beneath, the brilliance of the body's surface" (37).[1]

Originally written in Chinese, *Mulberry and Peach: Two Women of China* by Hualing Nieh stages the body to reveal the ways in which it is never just a corporeal object, but always an arena for inscription and contestation. A difficult narrative to summarize, *Mulberry and Peach* tells the story of Mulberry, a Chinese woman who, while enduring a series of traumatic confinements and escapes in China, Taiwan and the United States, develops another personality: Peach. Moving from one geographic location to another, Mulberry suffers a series of tragedies: at sixteen, she runs away with her lesbian friend only to be trapped in a Yangtze River gorge when their boat is stranded upon rocks; she travels alone to Beijing to marry her betrothed and finds the city under siege by the Communists, her husband-to-be more concerned with her lost virginity than with her desires; while in Taiwan, she and her family are fugitives who are forced to live hidden in an attic because her husband Chia-kang is guilty of embezzling money; and finally, in America, she exists as an illegal alien, hounded by immigration officials about her identity, and pregnant with the child of a married man. Mulberry's struggles to maintain a sense of self-control and self-coherence in the face of national, cultural, and emotional upheaval result in Peach's increasing command of the body both women inhabit.

The novel begins with Peach in control of the body. She tells an INS agent that not only is she *not* Mulberry but also that his interest in Mulberry's past relationships—with her husband Chia-kang and her daughter Sang-wa as well as with a series of lovers (Lao-Shih, the Refugee Student, Uncle-Ts'ai, and I-po)—will not aid him in discovering the "truth" of who Mulberry is. Without acknowledging the distinctions between Peach and Mulberry, it proves impossible to "know" Mulberry. Because the agent insists on confusing the two women, Peach decides to travel west and the narrative is related through a series of her letters and Mulberry's journal entries that she sends the immigration official to convince him that she and Mulberry are very different people. The geographical, temporal and textual dislocations of Nieh's novel foreground the existence of two distinct identities vying for expression within the confines of a single body. *Mulberry and Peach* explores the problems of the female body as it exists within the context of larger cultural and political bodies, dramatizing the ways in which the construction of the body as corporeal entity is problematized by the multiple guises available to it. The body as inhabited by Mulberry and/or Peach is never singular in its epistemological expression. Haunted by *two* women who cannot both be visible at the same time, their body is, alternately or simultaneously, a woman's body, an outlaw/fugitive body, an exiled/alien body, and a documented/undocumented body. The body thus becomes the staging ground for how impersonation is enacted corporeally in the face of pressure to produce singularity; in other words, the divisions registered within the body inhabited by Mulberry and Peach make manifest the pressures placed on Asian/American subjects to produce themselves according to a logic of correspondence that, "in seeking to simplify complex forms of identification and disidentification, blinds us both to the precise politics of separation, and, concomitantly, to their grounds for interpenetration" (Palumbo-Liu, *Asian/American* 308).

In Nieh's text, the body, rather than being an object that represents or defines what we understand as identity, subjectivity, or consciousness, instead serves as contested ground for the playing out of various performative possibilities. The staging and enactment of the body as it is cohabited by the identities of Mulberry and Peach produce a drama that not only questions the fantasy of psychological wholeness but also problematizes the notion of a singular correspondence between the body as a visual signifier and identity. Judith Butler suggests that the disjunctive space between these two ideas of the body operates as a result of the performative demands of embodiment:

> [t]he body is not a self-identical or merely factic materiality; it is a materiality that bears meaning, if nothing else, and the manner of this bearing is fundamentally dramatic . . . One is not simply a body, but, in some very key sense, one does [performs] one's body differently from one's contemporaries and from one's embodied predecessors and successors as well. ("Performative Acts" 272)

The embodiment of which Butler speaks is always shadowed by the different bodily performances of others. By literalizing the shadow that haunts the body, Nieh foregrounds the ways in which the body as a visible marker of identity is a fiction that compels complicity. In *Mulberry and Peach,* the body acts as a site where, in Elin Diamond's words, "the romanticism of identity" is first offered to the spectator as a performative possibility and then refused as a viable alternative. Hualing Nieh's staging of the body, which becomes a split signifier that both masks and exposes the ways in which the "identities" of Mulberry and Peach are the result of different performative acts of self-constitution and self-definition, also speaks to the ways in which the larger, politicized terrain inhabited by these women refuses to recognize or is unable to demarcate how they have been rendered indistinguishable from the body that defines them.

Rendered an icon for female essence, definitions of women's bodies have served to separate women from men while conflating female identity with corporeality. Butler describes the process of female reduction to bodily form as one predicated upon the imperative of masculine disembodiment:

> masculine disembodiment is only possible on the condition that women occupy their bodies as their essential and enslaving identities . . . by defining women as 'Other,' men are able through the shortcut of definition to dispose of their bodies, to make themselves other than their bodies . . . and to make their bodies other than themselves. From this belief that the body is Other, it is not a far leap to the conclusion that others *are* their bodies, while the masculine "I" is the noncorporeal soul. The body rendered as Other—the body repressed or denied and, then, projected—re-emerges for this "I" as the view of other as essentially body. Hence, women become the Other; they come to embody corporeality itself. ("Variations" 133)

The female body thus becomes equatable with female identity, a marker of difference that is extremely powerful in its seeming naturalness. Characterized by Trinh Minh-ha as "the most visible difference between men and women," the body is "the only one to offer a secure ground for those who seek the permanent, the feminine 'nature' and 'essence,' remain[ing] thereby the safest basis for racist and sexist ideologies" (100). Constructed and then read as an organic depiction of the female, the body lends itself to the notion of it being a finished and reliable representational object. As an object, the body means what it *appears* to mean, stripped of any abilities to generate ideological control. However, the power of the body lies precisely in the masking of its power to act as a text that, according to the Barthesian distinction between *work* and *text,* is both "meaning-generating and meaning-subverting" (Johnson 40).

Although the concept of textuality is usually understood to be particularly applicable to writing *(l'écriture)* and other communication mediated through chirographic mediums as opposed to more corporeal methods of communication, the distinction between bodies and texts rests upon the ways in which bodies are perceived to be less constructed than texts. However, the differences between orders of communication and semiosis—one founded on a model of performance and necessitating the unmediated access of speaker and listener, the other predicated on the graphically mediated relationship between reader and writer—are ultimately collapsible.

In "Bodies and Texts," Harry Berger designates these hypothetically separate modes of interaction "the order of the body" and "the order of the text." In the first mode, "all messages—nonverbal as well as verbal—are transmitted through the channel of the body and its extensions, while in the second, all messages are abstracted from the body and reconstructed in graphic media so they can pass through written channels" (147). However, despite the apparent differences between these two orders of body and text, Berger concludes that since different interpreters produce different texts by virtue of reading which becomes a kind of writing, even if it is not literally inscribed, the world becomes a text and this understanding of text as "not a thing but as a function . . . the value we give to whatever we treat as an object of interpretation, and subject to the fate of reading" subverts the polarity between the two orders (150). As such, "the historical emergence of the order of texts merely exteriorizes the repressed inner 'truth' of the order of the body [and while] the grammatocentrist claims that the world constituted by the signifying practices of the body is a text, a product of interpretation," such a move from text to body obscures the interpretive power and textuality of the embodied text by constituting it as natural and representative of a pre-existing reality (151). Those "texts" that remain unwritten and embedded in the body undergo a process of detextualization that works to mask their textuality. With regard to the signification produced by the body, detextualization obscures the ways in which the body is constructed and imbued with ideological meaning by displacing it from its collective "human source" and attributing it to "nature" or "cosmos" (152). As a result, the signifying practices of the body become what Berger terms "citational texts," nonliterate texts and acts that "perform the author-function and prevent against interpretation by closing down on unbound meaning" (155). Thus, collapsing the theoretical distinctions between the order of the body and the order of the text helps make apprehensible the ways in which systems of articulation are always playing themselves out between textualizing and detextualizing processes. And it is precisely the shift between textualization and detextualization that an act of impersonation can make manifest as it performs into visibility identity as a process of social construction and the contestation that the correspondence between body and identity often obscures. A discursive formation even as it offers up the materialities of muscle, bone, blood and skin, the body in Nieh's novel attains meaning insofar as it operates as a venue for Mulberry and Peach to stage acts of impersonation that claim for each woman an identity that isn't recognized by the state. The body is exposed, via the two women's acts of impersonation and embodiment, as a field of negotiation between the ideological and the material, the personal and the political, the imagined and the possible.

II.

> Writing the body, then, is both *constative* and performative. It signifies those bodily territories that have been kept under seal; it figures the body. But, writing the body is also a performative utterance.
> "The Politics of Writing (the) Body," Arleen B. Dallery

Nieh's novel foregrounds notions of performance structurally as well as thematically. The disjointed narrative unfolds through a series of letters and notebooks that Peach sends to the INS agent while on her westward journey. Peach does not provide a coherent story and the work required to piece together the fragments of Mulberry's diaries foregrounds the performative aspects of what we, as readers/spectators, must acknowledge as integral to meaning-formation in the text. The text itself becomes a body of dramatic possibilities and as such, the structure of Nieh's novel consistently draws attention to its use of theatrical apparatus: each scene is introduced, each character assigned a role. Significantly, the "theatrical" trappings of the text—a listing of "dramatis personae" and setting at the opening of each chapter—were considered necessary for making the book accessible to an English-speaking audience and only added when the book was first published in English by Beacon Press. The act of translation—both cultural and linguistic—as itself a performance predicated upon the demands, desires, and limitations of an audience bolsters the text's thematic preoccupation with the performative possibilities of female bodies.[2] According to Sau-ling C. Wong in her article on the differences between Asian and Asian American interpretations of the novel, the subtitle and character lists added to the English translation of the book result in "the questions of fidelity and equivalence usually obtaining with translations [being] raised exponentially" (133). Significantly, such incorporations foreground the meta-textual performance of Nieh herself and the ways in which the novel has been viewed as an act of literary impersonation.

The concept of role as a part meant to be played and not necessarily equivalent to the identity of the character playing it is crucial in the construction of character and the relationship between the body and identity in *Mulberry and Peach*. The juxtaposition of the main text of each chapter with the "roles" to be played by each character that are presented at the beginning of each of the four parts of the novel gestures toward the Brechtian theatrical practice of foregrounding the process of representation. The double-role casting of Mulberry and Peach within the same body as well as the characterization of several roles as "representative" of larger cultural forces (i.e. "Refugee Student," "The Old Man" and "Peach Flower Woman") work to develop an awareness of how actors can never be completely conflated with the characters they represent.[3] In differentiating the performance enacted by the body from a corresponding identity, the Brechtian consistently focuses attention upon the constitutive nature of what is mediated through the body. As such, the gaps and tensions that remain between each actor and her/his "role" reveal the processes by which representation must always be understood as a performative construction. In this way, the identities staged and played out in *Mulberry and Peach* refuse to remain completely embedded within the bodies dramatizing them. Rather, they rest uncomfortably under the skin, unable to find representative material expression through the bodies they inhabit.

Even as Mulberry and Peach are performed within the confines of a single female body, Nieh's text stresses the ways in which the female body is constructed by and functions within the political body of the nation-state. As Sidonie Smith has articulated in *Subjectivity, Identity and the Body* (1993), "the cultural meaning assigned to the material body permeates the body politic through the metaphorization of the social through the bodily" (129). Its materiality providing the raw substance from which the social environment is constructed, the "facile movement from the body to the body politic makes the invocation of the body for the purposes of the social a discursive commonplace" (Smith 129). Acting as the background for the contest between Mulberry and Peach, each identity waging a fierce battle for recognition and bodily expression, the looming presence of the body politic strategizes against the individualistic struggles of both women.

The novel's allegorical nature, its geographical scope, and the complicated cultural positioning of Nieh herself all work to problematize the multiple critical lenses through which the novel may be read.[4] Sau-ling C. Wong demonstrates how acts of criticism depend upon cultural and ideological orientations: whether read as modern Chinese literature, part of the literature of exile, a feminist work, or an Asian American text, *Mulberry and Peach* "must be recognized as an unstable textual complex that traverses multiple national, political, linguistic, and cultural borders" (133). Wong's provocative examination of the often competing critical practices differentiating Sinocentric readings of Mulberry as a figure of the diasporic Chinese from Asian American readings that challenge assumptions of any prior privilege assigned to the "Chinese" aspects of the novel demands a critical acknowledgment of the difficulties in discussing any aspect of the novel without situating it in a specific historical and cultural context. Even more, as Wong's recounting of the vexed publication history of Nieh's novel suggests, *Mulberry and Peach* cannot, like the women it features, be thought of as a single entity.[5] Rather, the novel—given the many incarnations (serialization, translations, editions), excisions, and addenda to which it has been subject— might itself be understood to be performing multiple acts of impersonation. Just as the characters whom I have identified as impersonators make the historical conditions of their performances of identity evident, so too do *Mulberry and Peach*'s various incarnations speak to Nieh's response to the various historical circumstances that have rendered the novel alternatively celebrated and banned. Sensitivity to the text's multiple incarnations requires us to resist re-performing the restrictions and judgments perpetrated by the novel's government agent against the female protagonists; as critics (Sinocentric, Asian American, and feminist) who bring a variety of disciplinary questions, approaches, and contexts to bear on our readings of the text, the multiplicity of impersonation allows for a proliferation of readings that do not necessarily have to be pitted against each other for validation and legitimacy.

Chinese scholars have focused their attention on Mulberry as an exilic figure who represents the wandering Chinese.[6] Such a reading is allegorical, dependent upon a recognition of the ways in which "this story about one woman's personal dissolution . . . allegorize[s] the fate of a divided China" (Yu 144). The Sinocentric frame of reference that interprets Peach's state at the end of the novel as representative of "the Chinese people's inability to replace their lost nation" and her pregnancy as "a sign of hope . . . [regarding]

Chinese exilic/diasporic consciousness" sees the United States as "the back-
drop to the Chinese protagonist's inner morality play, a mere signifier to an
assortment of spiritual ills. It is thus an ahistorical 'place,' or rather non-
place" (Wong 142). Significantly, such a reading depends upon a radical de-
historicizing of the novel's American setting.

Nieh's text has relevance to a number of different cultural contexts and is
amenable to a variety of different reading strategies. Her focus on the shared
body foregrounds, in many respects, the vexing implications of reading *Mulberry and Peach* within the context of Asian American literature. Even as
Peach insists on her difference from Mulberry in the face of the INS agent's
questioning of identity, the text blurs the boundaries between its "Asianness"
and "Asian Americanness."[7] Wong notes that there are multiple reasons to
support the novel's inclusion in the body of Asian American literature. In addition to the "mechanical criterion" of "physical setting" reflecting a textual
interest in applying an Asian American interpretive lens to the novel, the
work's publication by Beacon Press in a series featuring both Asian and
Asian American writers, its inclusion in King-Kok Cheung's and Stan Yogi's
bibliography of Asian American literature, and its winning a Before Colum-
bus Foundation American Book Award in 1990 as a result of a nomination
by Asian American author Shawn Wong all constitute "prima facie 'empirical' support" for considering *Mulberry and Peach* an Asian American text.[8]

By approaching Nieh's novel as an Asian American text, my reading of
Mulberry and Peach does not so much depart from an allegorical interpretation of Mulberry as a figure of the wandering Chinese as identify the ways
in which the body represents a site that allegory both obscures and depends
upon. In writing about allegory, Paul de Man begins his discussion by evaluating the last line of Yeats's poem "Among School Children": "How can we
know the dancer from the dance?" The double meaning that de Man ex-
tracts from this question—rhetorically, the question confirms the insepara-
bility of sign and meaning and literally, the question insists upon differentiating between them—represents the essence of allegory: "the authority of
the meaning engendered by the grammatical structure is fully obscured by
the duplicity of a figure that cries out for the differentiation that it conceals"
(11). An Asian American reading of Nieh's novel that is wary of the allegorical impulse to *decorporealize* the figures of Mulberry and Peach must then
consider the body as a particularly important and generative site.

Clearly, an Asian American approach to the novel privileges different aspects of the text than a Sinocentric one. *Mulberry and Peach* is a unique text through which to explore the politics of performance and bodily negotiation because of its multiple registers of enactment: the text not only "performs" differently in Asian and Asian American contexts, but the friction between the multiple interpretive communities that seek to lay claim to the novel emphasizes the significance of the body as a site of radical performativity. In other words, Mulberry's body both is and is not Peach's body and the paradox that connects and divides them—bodily expression and negotiation—is predicated on an insistence upon the body as nothing more or less than a set of performative possibilities. Such possibilities foreground a process of continual transformation and as Peach gradually supplants Mulberry in the body they both share, the body's betrayal of its own histories manifests itself as a loss of memory. Despite the fact that the body is reshaped as it is alternately—even simultaneously?—inhabited by these two different women in a variety of different geographical locations, the text foregrounds the similarity of pressures exerted on the female body by different "national" interests.

In "What Is a Nation?" (1990), Ernest Renan characterizes national existence as one which is predicated upon a "fusion of component populations" (10). Concerned with unity and the regulation of identity as a documentable condition, the nation is figured as a homogenizing presence. Although the body inhabited by Mulberry and Peach traverses national boundaries, it is continually subjected to the policing forces exerted by national interests. In Taiwan, Mulberry finds herself a fugitive, hiding with her family in the cramped attic of the Ts'ais after her husband is caught embezzling funds from his employer. Ensconced within the attic space where time, represented by Chia-king's irreparable clock that always reads twelve thirteen, has stopped, and hovering on the edge of discovery by the Nationalist police who constantly check to make certain that the bodies inhabiting the nation-state are bolstered by census papers and identification cards, Mulberry's body makes forays into the spaces outside which threaten her existence as a fugitive. Under cover of darkness, the body escapes into the night-time world, simultaneously an outlaw body as well as one which, on the surface, possesses a certain legitimacy within the structure of the state.

As an outlaw body, Mulberry can exist without the cultural authority provided by an identity card. However, in policing the body, the nation-state documents each body as possessing a corresponding identity, one which cannot be challenged after its inscription onto identity cards:

> Papa and Mama both have identity cards. Mama says that an identity card proves that you are a legal person. I'm already ten, but I still don't have one yet. Mama says that people in attics don't need identity cards. Only people on the outside need them. If they don't have identity cards, they will go to jail. I hate it when Mama goes outside every night . . . I want to tear up her identity card. (142)

As her daughter Sang-wa's diary entry details, Sang-wa's lack of an identity card makes her fugitive state different from Mulberry's. While the legitimate status of Mulberry's body—signified by her still possessing an identity card—is threatened by her association with Chia-kang's embezzlement activities, clearly her "freedom" to go outside the attic space problematizes the distinctions between "legal" and "illegal" bodies.

Simultaneously documented and undocumented, Mulberry's body fluctuates between the polarized values assigned the fugitive body and the citizen. The attic, seemingly a refuge from the scrutiny of the Nationalist police, figures as a microcosm of the outside world. When Sang-wa asks about the people moving on the other side of the attic window, Mulberry explains the limitations imposed on bodies that have been regulated: "They can't go wherever they want to, either. There's a wall around the yard. Beyond the wall is the sea. Beyond the sea is the edge of the earth. The earth is a huge attic. The huge attic is divided into millions of little attics, just like ours" (129). The country, figured as a "green eye floating alone on the sea," watches and attempts to control the bodies inhabiting it. Mulberry's notebook from Taiwan records pages of escape fantasies and her attempts to write herself out of her confinement make manifest the difficulties of emerging from the attic. She cannot envision areas outside of the attic that are free of the policing powers of the nation-state: "We can't stop anywhere for long. If we stop, we must report our place of residence to the police station. If we report our residence, we must show our identification cards. Our identification cards will give us away as fugitives" (131).

Despite her vivid imaginings, Mulberry's fantasies of escape are always thwarted or end in capture. The inevitable scripting of failure in Mulberry's escape stories marks the danger and seeming impossibility of moving beyond the control and surveillance of the nation-state. Crossing the threshold of her attic prison, Mulberry's initial attempts to move furtively into the outside are accompanied by sounds and objects that warn her to return. Seeing a cat, hearing a knock, sighting a policeman, Mulberry records a litany of denied entrance and participation in the spaces overtly controlled by the nation-state: "I go back to the attic . . . I go up to the attic again . . . I go back to the attic again . . . I go back to the attic before midnight. It's safer there" (138–40). Torn between the "safety" of the attic space and the imagined freedom of movement outside the attic, Mulberry moves restlessly from one space to another. In her stories, the fugitive body always finds itself searched out and pinned down by the policing agents of the nation.

Unable to resolve the demands of existing as both outlaw body and politically recognized identity, Mulberry finds her body pushed to new articulations of identity. As her previously stable and singular subjectivity fragments itself to accommodate the multiple demands made of her, her diary records the dichotomous nature of her life: "My life splits in half. Daytime in the attic. Night-time at the hospital" (141). As her body moves in and out of various spaces, it develops another identity. In this way, Mulberry and Peach (who remains nameless at this point) begin to deal with the limitations and the possibilities of escape from the female body as it has been constituted in the nation-state. According to Nieh's text, such a process of fragmentation is unavoidable according to the ways in which bodies are forced to choose identities. When Mulberry offers a definition of herself as an "innocent criminal," Uncle Ts'ai asserts the impossibility of the fugitive body as one existing simultaneously with the regulated body: "An innocent person should live outside the attic entirely. A criminal should hide during the day and go out at night" (144).

The focus on documenting the body follows Mulberry/Peach to America. Such interest in documentation of the body speaks to the ways in which the nation-state works to incorporate bodies through a homogenization of their distinguishing features. Such a process results in the formation of the body as a culturally authorized entity, welcome in the larger body politic precisely because of its compatibility with the national ideology of unity and its acquiescence to performing itself as what Foucault terms a "docile body," one "whose forces and energies are habituated to external regulation, subjection, transformation" (Bordo 14). The regulatory practices of the nation-state bent on creating "docile" bodies acceptable for incorporation into the larger communal body are nowhere more pronounced than in the interview between Mulberry and the investigator from the Immigration Service. Focused intently upon ascertaining the acceptability of Mulberry's body for inclusion into the United States, the immigration official poses a series of questions. His initial attempts to determine her position relative to Communism are eventually re-directed toward obtaining information about her relationship with Uncle Ts'ai. His excessively voyeuristic interest in ferreting out the physical details surrounding her affair with Uncle Ts'ai speaks to the only means by which the official can divine Mulberry's fitness for permanent residency in the United States. In response to Mulberry's queries concerning the means by which her application for residency will be decided, the immigration investigator identifies the body as a singular site of inquiry:

'Whom are you interviewing?'
'Some are your friends. Some are people you don't know.'
'Even if they are friends, they don't necessarily know me.'
'That doesn't make any difference. What we want to investigate isn't your state of mind, your emotions, or your motivations. I'll say it again: what we want to investigate is your behaviour. And that can be observed by anybody.' (165)[9]

Unable to verify her true willingness to abide as a member of the nation, the policing agents of the state see the body as the only marker of cultural and political acquiescence. As such, the body must be investigated, regulated and rendered manipulable. Rather than focusing on the identities contained within the figure of the body, the body itself comes under scrutiny. This inquisition of the body seeks to render the infinite postures of subjectivity as quantifiable materiality.

Staged within Nieh's text, the body as it is perceived by the legalizing and policing agents of the body politic represents a loss of individuality: people become bodies which, in their materiality, are rendered indistinguishable from one another. Signified by a number or an identity card, noted and translated into a series of forms and depositions, identities are separated from the body, which then becomes the sole signifier of subjectivity. Defined in this way, identity can only result in fragmentation. Unable to simply *be* the body, Mulberry/Peach can only attempt to move beyond a singular correspondence with it. Far from simply being a struggle for domination, the developing dance for bodily expression between Mulberry and Peach is a process which, by virtue of the limits imposed upon identity through the body, seeks to create a tenuous relation of being and difference which must always escape from the limits of the body. As Peggy Phelan writes in *Unmarked* (1993):

> Identity cannot, then, reside in the name you can say or the body you can see . . . Identity emerges in the failure of the body to express being fully and the failure of a signifier to convey meaning exactly. Identity is perceptible only through a relation to an other—which is to say, it is a form of both resisting and claiming the other, declaring the boundary where the self diverges from and merges with the other. In that declaration of identity and identification, there is always loss, the loss of not-being the other and yet remaining dependent on that other for self-seeing, self-being. (13)

Inherent within the relationship between Mulberry and Peach as they circulate and find momentary expression through the body is the notion of Otherness as a state of being. The notions of the unified body so necessary for the successful construction of the body politic rest on the displacement of difference onto the bodies of certain others, when "[t]he fragmented materiality of bodies helps sustain the illusion of indisputable continuity between biology and culturally constructed identities such as those of gender and race, the illusion of stable categories" (Smith 129). However difference is elided to create the illusion of unity and sameness, the existence of Mulberry and Peach within the same body discloses the burden of maintaining the appearance of a stable identity when the body inhabited has already been marked as "Other": "It is the body, as individual history, memory, and trace, which sets in play the possibility of dialoguing with our being-in-difference" (Chambers 72). Despite the increasing obviousness of the fragmentation and schizophrenia experienced by Mulberry, Peach is always a presence of otherness resting more or less quiescently inside the body inhabited by Mulberry. Conversely, Peach's later surfacing as the dominant identity within the body housing Mulberry/Peach is predicated upon the absent *presence* of Mulberry. Rather than being simply Peach, Peach is also always *not*-Mulberry: as her responses to the questions of the man from the immigration service indicate, the distinctness of Peach's identity stems from her being *other* than Mulberry. In this way, the paradoxical situation described by Phelan of "not being the other and yet remaining dependent on that other for self-seeing [and] self being" writes itself within the spaces offered by a singular body housing alternative identities. And within the body, the performative moves away from the representational, so that the performance of the body by Mulberry/Peach is never taken as the actual body of Mulberry/Peach. Thus difference, always already in place, finds itself continually foregrounded. Such a distinction between the performative and the representational is crucial. As Phelan asserts, "Representation reproduces the Other as the same. Performance, insofar as it can be defined as representation without reproduction, can be seen as a model for another representational economy, one in which the reproduction of the Other *as* the Same is not assured" (3).

Mulberry and Peach dramatize the inadequacies of the body through a series of divergent performances (although Mulberry is never fully cognizant of the other personality which also inhabits her body) in an effort to individuate themselves as part of their processes of self-representation. Mulberry's schizophrenia and the resultant emergence of Peach gesture to the construction of the body as a site of anonymity: behind the mask provided by the body as visual referent, identities become reduced to and conflated with a corporeal figuration, and differences between subjectivities denied. The INS agent, as a representative of the nation-state, is overwhelming in his anonymity. Masked by sunglasses and dressed in a dark suit with "only the anonymous parts . . . visible," he is uniformed as a singularly appropriate member of the larger body politic (3). Swallowed by his vestments, the INS agent symbolizes the erasure of individuality that threatens the body of Mulberry/Peach once it succumbs to the controlling mechanisms working to police what enters the national space. Mulberry's identifying label— "(Alien) number 89–785–462"—prefigures the homologous existence awaiting her once she is deemed acceptable for incorporation into the nation-state. As Peach's struggle to counter the INS agent's insistence on the singular connection between Mulberry and "her" body demonstrates, to live in such a state would be analogous to death. The parenthetical prefix attached to her identification number signals Mulberry/Peach's existence as an alien body and while the investigation by INS officials will decide whether the parenthetical signifier denoting her alien status will remain on her documentation, the number that marks her as simply another body is the identifying label by which the nation-state will always recognize her.

As Peach and Mulberry dramatize throughout Nieh's novel, identities must remain individual and differentiated within the space offered by the body. Thus, when the anonymous INS agent refuses to accept the quiddities that point to the separated existences of Mulberry and Peach, declaring "You two are the same person all right," Peach repudiates his assertion with a listing of performative distinctions illustrating how the two identities in question are not commensurate:

> You're wrong. Mulberry is Mulberry and Peach is Peach. They're not the same at all. Their thoughts, manners, interests, and even the way they look are completely different. Mulberry, for instance, was afraid of blood, animals, flashing lights. I'm not afraid of those things. Mulberry shut herself up at home, sighing and carrying on. I go everywhere, looking for thrills. Snow, rain, thunder, birds, animals, I love them all. Sometimes Mulberry wanted to die, sometimes she wanted to live. In the end she gave up. I'd never do that. Mulberry was full of illusions; I don't have any. (6)

This detailed listing of the different performative choices made by each woman theorizes identity as a construction determined by a series of individual acts that must necessarily be distinguished from the possibilities represented by the body. Judith Butler argues in her article "Performative Acts and Gender Constitution" (1990) that the body "is a set of possibilities [which] signif[y] (a) that its appearance in the world, for perception, is not predetermined by some manner of interior essence, and (b) that its concrete expression in the world must be understood as the taking up and rendering specific of a set of historical possibilities" (272). If the body is nothing more than a set of historical possibilities, some of which must first be "performed" into existence before any given meaning can be assigned to the body, then the notions held by the INS agent and other characters in the novel of an essential identity or an identity which can somehow be essentially represented by the simple figuration of the body are clearly problematic due to their inadequacies in identifying the contradistinctive subjectivities embodied within the figure of Mulberry/Peach. The inability of the people who surround Peach and Mulberry to differentiate them from one another foregrounds the possibilities of the body as a site of performance in the service of self-making and self-representation rather than an iconic symbol for identity.

III.

> It is clear that for a woman to be healthy she must "adjust" to and accept the behavioral norms for her sex even though these kinds of behaviour [sic] are generally regarded as less socially desirable . . . The ethic of mental health is masculine in our culture.
>
> *Women and Madness*, Phyllis Chesler

Nieh's text is largely concerned with an identification and critique of the ways in which the female body has been constructed as a signifier of the difference and powerlessness ascribed to women living under the control of national and cultural authorities who refuse to assign legitimacy to their identities. Female subjectivity becomes trapped by the signifying practices of the body, which are reconstructed by the hermeneutic desire of the authorities of the nation-state into a cipher for identity. Nieh's production of Mulberry's body dramatizes the ways in which female subjectivity finds itself tied to the limiting space of the body as it is perceived by those around her. Through Mulberry/Peach's confrontation with and embrace of "madness," the fragmentation made apparent through constantly existing as a "being-in-difference" reveals itself as schizophrenia, being-in-relation to an/Other that is also oneself.[10]

Similar to the process by which Mulberry's inability to write her family's escape from the attic in Taiwan leads to a spiraling descent into "madness," the identity trapped within the figuration of the female body cannot imagine a release from that site of confinement without suffering a schizophrenic breakdown. In his construction of schizophrenia as a category of mental illness, Sander Gilman has called attention to the evolution of schizophrenia as a term with multiple meanings. Although originally a reference to the fragmentation of mental functions, the popular understanding of it has emphasized the "splitting" of the object (224). Gilman goes on to write that "schizophrenia, which initially had reference to the damaged language of the patient, came to imply a sense of 'truthfulness' in the communication of the schizophrenic" (224). This insistence on verity speaks to a crucial point of tension in the shifting metamorphoses which transform Mulberry into Peach, and back again. Unable to imagine the body as it has already been imagined for the female subject—as a "truthful" expression of her identity—Mulberry gives way to Peach, whose attempts to shape the body and harness its possibilities for herself seem more hopeful. As we watch, Peach's identity fights to mark the surfaces of the body in a manner that will force those who watch her to acknowledge her subjectivity and the validity of her identity. However, such a bid for visibility is problematized as the process of transformation into multiplicity is perceived as duplicity by the INS agent, who cannot separate the solidity of the body from the identities housed within it. The INS agent, David Palumbo-Liu argues, is of critical importance in *Mulberry and Peach* because "it is his interrogation that marks the intervention of the state in the construction of ethnic identity and attests to its need to recuperate that fugitive subject into its political field" (*Asian/ American* 347). I would agree with Palumbo-Liu but suggest, too, that the immigration agent's significance to the text should also be traced to the ways in which his desire to demarcate and sanction a "legitimate" identity for Mulberry denotes an investment in the logic of imposture and an allegiance to the notion of identity as "authentic" that the novel's female protagonists, and the text itself, seek to challenge through participation in a performative repertoire deriving from impersonation's challenge to such ideas as they reveal themselves in embodied form.

As discussed earlier, Nieh's text constructs the female body as a site containing both self as well as other. Complicated by the additional burdens of being determined an alien/exiled body, the "mental illness" experienced by Mulberry seems less a denial or refusal to confront reality than a reflection of the ways in which self and other are always staged in relation to one another. This relationship constantly fluctuates, shifting away from stability because it is marked by inequality: the relationship between self and other "is alluring and violent because it touches the paradoxical nature of psychic desire; the always already unequal encounter nonetheless summons the hope of reciprocity and equality; the failure of this hope then produces violence, aggressivity, dissent" (Phelan 3–4). The encounters between Mulberry and Peach highlight the shifting and unequal nature of being-in-relation. As each identity struggles for dominance, Peach writes to Mulberry, "You and I threaten each other like the world's two superpowers. Sometimes you are stronger; sometimes I am" (183). Because the hope for reciprocity and equality will never be fulfilled in the contest for bodily expression between the two women, violence permeates the edges of consciousness. Mulberry comes back to the body to discover depictions of dismembered penises marking her demise; the INS agent walks into Mulberry's apartment to find Peach celebrating Mulberry's "deathday" with the construction of a "gigantic, swollen penis stand[ing] like a pillar in the middle of the floor" (5). The violence between Mulberry and Peach seeks outlet and release in mobility and sexuality; the images of dismemberment and cannibalism permeating the text contain within them the promise of freedom from the body, figurations of a dark eroticism.

IV.

> Like a prisoner who wants to get out of his cell at any price, the soul keeps torturing its own body in order to be cured. Or perhaps to torment itself.
> *The Memory of the Body*, Jan Kott

As part of the process whereby meaning is both embodied and unbodied, the body inhabited by both Mulberry and Peach moves constantly, mobile in its journey through spaces, times, and alternative modes of semiotic production.[11] The body as constructed by the different women who inhabit it refuses to be pinned down, to stay still and ossify into any one fixed meaning. Rather, the signifying practices of the body are continually invested with meaning, both by the identities inhabiting it as well as by those outside it. Through the avenues provided by mobility and eroticism, Mulberry and Peach attempt to perform the body into freedom from the outside meanings ensnaring it. Choosing at various points to move the body physically or to plunge the body into eroticism, freedom from the body is always momentary and elusive. Thus, the performances of Mulberry and Peach delineate the ways in which mobility never leads to a final destination and identity always returns to its limits as circumscribed by the body. And sexual expression, in the service of releasing the imprisoned identities of the embodied women, acts as a dangerously double-edged mode of escape: a patriarchal understanding of sexuality works to reduce women into nothing more than bodies while the eroticism of female desire provides a way to break free, however briefly, from the boundaries erected by the flesh.

As Mulberry, the body finds itself trapped within a successive series of confining spaces. The confinement of the body is continually dramatized through its staging and production within the enclosed spaces of the Chü-t'ang Gorge, the besieged city of Peking, the attic in Taiwan and the apartment in Lone Tree. While the body itself is capable of movement when inhabited by Mulberry, and finds itself traversing a variety of national, social and cultural spaces, it continually returns to a state of enforced captivity, fettered by its inability to transcend the specular power of those watching it, wanting to control and possess it sexually.

The impotence manifested by Mulberry's body and its powerlessness to resist the sexual demands placed upon it repeatedly return to the stage, each time a re-enactment of the ways in which a woman's body is continually marked and re-marked as an iconic codification of identity by cultural and political authorities. From the beginning of her journey, Mulberry conceives of sexuality as a means of escaping; her flight to Chungking is prompted by her implicitly sexual relationship with her girlfriend Lao-shih. Mulberry's reaction to the presence of the Refugee Student while trapped in Chü-t'ang Gorge further exemplifies the yearning of the body to escape what abuses, confines, and terrorizes it. When the Japanese bombers fly over the gorge, the physicality played out between bodies forced into proximity represents the only way to move beyond the fear of the situation:

> Now our bodies are pressing against each other. He is bare-chested and I can smell the odour of his armpits. Lao-shih's armpits smell the same way, that smell of flesh mixed with sweat, but smelling it on his body makes my heart pound. I can even feel the hair under his arms . . . The thick black hair (it must be black) under his arms tickles me. I'm not even scared of the Japanese bombers anymore. (32)

This basic scenario of sexuality being pursued as a means toward escaping the confinement of the body repeats itself over and over, masked by changes in location, relationship and partner, but essentially a gesture toward flight. Mulberry finds herself engaged in sexual relationships with Chia-kang, Uncle Ts'ai and I-po, each time seduced by the possibilities of breaking free from confinement. This cycle is perpetuated by the construction of iconicity between Mulberry and her body. Chia-kang's dream illustrates how Mulberry has been reduced to a single image, unable to escape from the specular forces that evince a hermeneutic desire to render her equatable with the body:

> Mulberry, I dreamed you were lying in the centre of the altar, naked, looking up at the sky. You were so clean and pure. I had to make love to you.

We rolled over and over on top of the altar, shouting. The space between heaven and earth was filled with our shouting. Between heaven and earth there was only you and me, two naked bodies entwined together. (72)

Defined by the contours of the flesh, there is no way to escape the mesmerizing power of what has already been imagined, and the woman becomes reduced to the body, and the body, in turn, reduced to an instrument for sexual pleasure. Although Chia-kang's dream seems to offer a vision of liberation through the excess of the body, an excess which fills "heaven and earth" with "shouting," its utopic construction of the body elides the different standards of behavior maintained for male and female bodies. His shock, anger and frustration at the fact that Mulberry is not a virgin on their wedding night clearly delineate the limitations of sexuality as a means for female freedom. In using virginity to determine the value and limits of the female self, women are indeed reduced to the body in its most physical definition. As Sidonie Smith argues, "[t]he material and symbolic boundary of the female body becomes the hymen . . . Gender ideologies assign so much meaning to that rupture because they identify that thin skin signed by blood as the irreducible material core of woman's selfhood" (12).

While sexuality does, within patriarchal conceptions of the body, serve to limit and reduce female selfhood and identity, *Mulberry and Peach* also explores the liberating powers embedded within eroticism. Sexuality reduces female identity to the material body; eroticism gestures toward the momentary transcendence of identity from the body. The orgasmic connection between two bodies locked within an erotic embrace opens the "closed bag of impenetrable skin" to reveal an instant of disembodiment which frees the self to be entire in Otherness: "You melt into something that is not you, into that other person, but that other is, at once, 'the other world.' In this entanglement you are both whole and the other who is a part of your own flesh. The boundaries of the flesh are obliterated" (Kott 117). Mulberry and Peach imbue their narratives with images using the obliteration of the flesh as a metaphor for release from the body. The desire to destroy the boundaries posed by the flesh reveals itself in the figurations of cannibalism and dismemberment that permeate the text. Lurking at the edges of textual and bodily consciousness are limbs separated from torsos and heads floating upon turbulent waters, images bespeaking an "erotic imagination [that] never creates a fully developed situation, or a complete person" (Kott 71). According to Jan Kott, "The erotic partner of imagination and desire is created or given only in fragments. Like a broken statue the parts of which we find or examine one by one: torso, arms, legs, head or belly—all separate objects" (71). While Peach and Mulberry each try to lose themselves in sexual acts with other people as a means of escaping the limits of the body, they discover in each other the ultimate erotic partner.[12] Paired but separate, continually exposed as distinct but dependent fragments of a fragmented body, the erotic embrace between them fully discloses the possibilities as well as the limits of the body.

⌐

The body in *Mulberry and Peach* acts as a site of performative possibility, its movements never completely under control but always teetering at the edges of regulation. Nieh's novel stages the theatricality embedded within the strictures of the body as it has been imagined by the state, and also gestures toward the problematics inherent within the construction of the female body as an iconic representation of female identity. The acts of impersonation undertaken by Mulberry and Peach as each woman struggles to challenge the ways in which sexuality, gender, and race are mobilized by the state to overdetermine the identificatory choices available to her invoke the possibility of creating a self that fights against stagnation and disappearance within the body, as if there were nothing more than the body. Nieh explores the depths of divided consciousness and through her focus on the connections, disconnections, and tenuous relationship between the body and consciousness, she problematizes and complicates our understandings of the necessary gaps between the demands of the body and the exigencies of the self.

FIVE

Shamanism and the Subject(s) of History in Nora Okja Keller's *Comfort Woman*

In treating his patient, the shaman also offers his audience a performance. What is this performance? . . . we shall say that it always involves the shaman's enactment of the "call," of the initial crisis which brought him the revelation of his condition. But we must not be deceived by the word *perfor-mance*. The shaman does not limit himself to reproducing or miming certain events. He actually relives them in all their vividness, originality, and violence.

Structural Anthropology, Claude Lévi-Strauss

[Shamans] derive their power from *listening* to the others and *absorbing* daily realities. While they cure, they take into them their patients' possessions and obsessions and let the latter's illnesses become theirs.

Woman, Native, Other, Trinh T. Minh-ha

Shamanism provides the [Korean] people with a profound symbolic language. Most of all, it gives people the "spirit" of resistance. They can "invoke" their own significant spirits and thus transform them into the bearers of their political message. They invoke the spirits of students, factory workers, and nameless masses killed by abnormal causes and translate them into political rhetoric: the resurrection of nation, restoration of history, return of subaltern people, and reconstruction of popular space. All this has been rejected or lost through colonialism, capitalism, foreign domination, and modernization. As spirit possession is a cultural construct for a dialectic play of identity formation . . . shamanistic ritual process attempts to replace a reality imagined by the state with the people's own imagined reality.

"Rituals of Resistance," Kwang-Ok Kim

You are a young woman, still a girl really, and you have been taken from your family. It could be that you were promised a job and, desperate to help those you love, you agreed to work in a factory in order to support your parents and siblings during the war. Or maybe you were walking along a road with your girlfriend one day and the miraculous appearance of a fancy automobile became the occasion for a kidnapping. Perhaps you were forcibly abducted from your home, stolen by soldiers who shot your resisting father as he tried to prevent them from taking you away. And after all this, imagine that you are made a prisoner and repeatedly raped by men who line up, up to fifty at a time, in order to use your body even as they deny that you have a soul.[1] To imagine yourself as one of these women—even as you know that what you imagine is woefully inadequate and can only approximate the shape of these experiences—is to engage in an act of identification so profound, so intense, that it will either illuminate the limitations of imagination or challenge the borders of identity by which you perceive your place in the world. Maybe it will do both.[2]

Such an act of imagination potentially has the power to rupture the seams that suture identity to identification. Such an act of imagination can be, in essence, an act of impersonation through which we can all be held accountable for the recognition or erasure of such witness. Trinh Minh-ha suggests that the power to embody another's experience can be curative; Claude Lévi-Strauss identifies this ability to relive experience "in all [its] vividness, originality, and violence" as the source of the shaman's power. Kwang-Ok Kim asserts that, in the case of Korean shamanism, the power to invoke history through the performance of possession depends upon recognizing the "dialectic play of identity formation" (218); such recognition grants the practitioners of shamanic ritual the power to remember what has otherwise been forgotten. If so, the transformative potential of shamanism to trouble the distinctions between self and other must always begin with a scene of haunting, and, unsurprisingly, Nora Okja Keller's 1997 novel about a shaman who survives her past as a comfort woman is itself the product of an instance of ghostly haunting.

After hearing Keum Ju Hwang bear witness to suffering and surviving her experience as a "comfort woman" in 1993, Keller found her dreams haunted, "filled with images of war and women, of blood and birth" ("Reader's Companion" 6). And in order to wrestle with the ghosts peopling her dreams, Keller had to imagine herself surviving "their daily lives, their physical and emotional anguish, the aftermath" (5). Such a task was not easy but the ghostly presences that demanded her recognition and her imaginative identification to help them testify to forgotten moments of history were both demanding awareness of what they experienced and criticizing the discursive and political ideologies that had kept their stories from being heard.

Avery Gordon asserts that ghosts "pull us affectively into the structure of feeling of a reality we come to experience as recognition[, thereby showing us how h]aunting recognition is a special way of knowing what has happened or is happening" (63). Such "ghostly matters," Gordon suggests, are always inextricably bound up with *"a concern for justice"* (64, emphasis original). Thus it is perhaps to be expected that Keller's novel is not the only literary text about this subject that is haunted by the ghosts of women who have not attained justice. Indeed, in both Therese Park's *A Gift of the Emperor* (1997) and Chang-rae Lee's *A Gesture Life* (1999), comfort women who have suffered unjustly return as ghostly presences to remind others of histories that cannot otherwise be remembered.[3] That the metatextual scene of haunting that Keller describes as the genesis of her novel manifests itself textually in all of the literary works regarding this subject speaks to the ways in which the long-delayed recognition of Korean comfort women as forgotten subjects in our historical records requires that the histories that have thus far been written be revised to include such information. The ghosts in these novels also suggest that in addition to such revision, we embrace the possibility of "a different kind of knowledge, a different kind of acknowledgment" (Gordon 64).[4]

Keller's *Comfort Woman* explores the legacy of trauma and suffering caused by this experience by demonstrating what "a different kind of acknowledgment" might look like. The plight of comfort women—women who were coerced into sexual slavery by the Japanese military during World War II—has gained much international attention in the last decade.[5] In 1991, Kim Hak-soon publicly testified that she had been forced by the Japanese military to be a comfort woman in response to assertions made by the Japanese government that comfort women were prostitutes who voluntarily serviced soldiers during the war. Since then, evidence has surfaced confirming that over 100,000 women from all parts of Asia had been forced into being comfort women by the Japanese military.[6] The trauma suffered by the women subjected to work in comfort stations has been compounded in multiple ways: in addition to surviving their sexual slavery by the Japanese military, these women have had to struggle against a U.S. cold-war hegemony which supported the suppression of their reparation efforts against Japan, the refutation of their testimony concerning the brutalities inflicted upon them, and the Japanese government's refusal to offer an official apology.[7] Much of the public emphasis regarding the comfort women has been on restitution and reparation, with both comfort women organizations and war crimes commissions demanding an official apology as well as monetary remuneration from the Japanese government.[8] Although Keller's novel seemingly avoids issues of reparation, accountability, and ethical responsibility altogether, focusing almost exclusively on the private battle Akiko wages in dealing with the traumatic after-effects of her experience, carefully attending to the ways in which Keller deploys the social, political, and cultural valences of shamanism with relation to the evolution and maintenance of a distinct ethnic Korean identity reveals that the issues at the heart of *Comfort Woman* are indeed about the ethical responsibility we bear as readers and critics of—and also as witnesses to—this story.[9] To cultivate this ethical orientation toward her subject, Keller emphasizes how shamanism emerges as Akiko's response to multiple agents of oppression—the soldiers in the Japanese military; the Christian missionary who marries her and brings her to the United States; and even her daughter, whose ignorance of Korean cultural practices causes her to label Akiko "crazy."

Comfort Woman is actually the story of two women: Akiko, whose horrific experiences in the "recreation camps" of the Japanese army dislocate her from her home and her former identity as Soon Hyo, and her daughter Beccah, who fears her mother is crazy and who will not fully understand her painful relationship with Akiko until she learns of the ways in which the comfort woman experience has affected them both. This chapter focuses on the unique ways in which Keller draws on Korean shamanistic rituals in order to contextualize and respond to the injustices Akiko suffers as a former comfort woman. Akiko's shamanic practices, undeniably important to both her relationship with her daughter and her own understanding of herself, are nonetheless multivalent and open to divergent interpretations. Is she a woman so traumatized by her past that she becomes a victim to a manipulative scheme to exploit the hope of others, a scheme dependent upon her friend and manager's exploitation of her own mental instability? Is she perhaps more of a sham than a shaman, putting on the false face of ecstatic trance in order to support herself and her daughter?[10] Or is she truly able to communicate with spirits, ancestral and otherwise, in an effort to resolve both her personal suffering and the suffering of the community in which she lives?

Although each of these interpretations surfaces as possible in Keller's novel, how we ultimately choose to interpret Akiko's actions and evaluate her relationship to shamanism will illuminate the critical postures and theoretical positions that govern our own modes of reading. In "Under Western Eyes" (1994), Chandra Talpade Mohanty argues that there can be "no apolitical scholarship" (197) and that the assumptions and biases of much Western feminist criticism about third world women results in the uncomfortable re-colonization of the very subjects and practices such scholarship supposedly liberates.[11] Western scholarship's sometimes unintended practical effect of re-marginalizing or "thinking out" as part of the practice of *thinking through* the subjects and objects it studies manifests itself in realms that extend far beyond the scope of the feminist critical practice that Mohanty takes to task.[12] I would argue that Keller is acutely aware of—and actively writes against—the tendency toward this kind of theoretical colonialism in *Comfort Woman*. In cautioning against perpetuating "the authorizing signature of western humanist discourse" (Mohanty 197), Keller deploys an alternative discourse, that of Korean shamanism, in order to provide for readers and critics an interpretive framework for how to think about the experiences of Korean comfort women as represented through the figure of Akiko.[13]

In insisting that her readers think about her character's comfort woman history within the context of Korean shamanism, Keller demands that we acknowledge both the psychic costs of the experience Akiko endured and the regenerative possibilities of reconnecting with ethnic identity, cultural practice, and diasporic community by recognizing the significance of cultural narratives that resist colonial and neo-colonial hegemony.[14] Additionally, Keller grounds her text in a shamanistic framework in an effort to articulate the production of identity as a plural, unbounded process of cultural emergence that nonetheless does not overlook the exigencies of constituting the self as a subject in favor of celebrating the playful pluralities of postmodernity. As part of this endeavor, Keller averts the temptation to theorize comfort women's experiences strictly in terms of their suffering, aware of the ways in which her critical practice can help produce in the ongoing discursive and political struggle comfort women face opportunities not only to testify to their victimization but also to insist upon themselves as agents who actively negotiated, and continue to negotiate, their oppressive circumstances.

Comfort Woman employs the context of Korean shamanism in order to effect a series of messages about the nature of gender-based oppression and resistance, the practice of possession as an act of both imposture and impersonation, the interconnections between legacy and myth, and the importance of theorizing the comfort woman experience within a situated "local" knowledge so as to resist the appropriation of such stories. Keller uses shamanistic rituals and practices to refigure what Beccah and others (mis)-understand as Akiko's "madness." In Korean shamanism, shamans (known as either *mudangs* or *mansin)* are predominantly women who experience tragedy and as a result undergo a psychic transformation that renders them able to call upon the spirits to possess them while they are in trance states.[15] Akiko becomes a *mansin* as a result of her experience as a comfort woman and I propose that by suggesting how the comfort woman-experience transforms Akiko into a shamanic figure, Keller deftly accomplishes three things: she demonstrates the cultural divide separating Beccah and her mother, a divide marked by Beccah's suspicions that Akiko is mad; she illustrates the complicated chain of death and rebirth set into motion by Soon Hyo's metamorphosis into the comfort woman Akiko 41; and she suggests the possibility that through the rituals of propitiation and healing that Akiko performs for others, she is somehow able to transform the injustices done to her into a self-healing ritual of resistance and redemption.

In *Comfort Woman,* Keller offers to us the figure of the female shaman as a particular kind of impersonator: a traumatized individual who must submit to spirit possession in order to constitute her own destined identity; a skilled performer who must embody an/Other by theatricalizing therapy to heal both self and other; a medium whose impostured identity troubles any notion of a Self that exists in isolation from a community made up of those she lives with and those who have come before her; a practitioner of "sympathetic magic"—the embracing of the patient's possessions and obsessions that Trinh Minh-ha articulates so elegantly—whereby the impersonation becomes the real.[16] The shaman's success does not, as Trinh and Lévi-Strauss caution us, depend upon imitative ability. Instead, the shaman figures impersonation as an act of profound identification, an experience of possession that requires the shaman to inhabit a self not her own in order to effect the rituals of healing which she is asked to perform. Only by undergoing the experience of simultaneously enacting *the patient's* obsessions as well as "the initial crisis which brought [the shaman] the revelation of [her] condition" (Lévi-Strauss 180) can the shaman use impersonation to confront the problems she mediates both for herself and her community. In this dualistic performance, the shaman truly displays a double agency—she is both the agent worked upon and the agent working, a figure whose unique positionality ensures her ability to perform the memory-work and rituals of remembrance necessary for incisive social critique.

Divided States

Comfort Woman begins with a ritual performed by mother and daughter, a *chesa* (a ceremonial offering to the ancestors) that the women execute in honor of Akiko's dead husband, Beccah's absent father. Although Beccah and Akiko prepare the food for the remembrance feast together, this opening scene marks the ways in which Beccah and Akiko are separated by a cultural divide that, despite the efforts of both, is difficult to bridge. The rituals that Akiko and her daughter perform together are, for Beccah, more a kind of habit and insurance than reflective of her belief in the spirits that she knows govern her mother's life. Beccah leaves her offerings "as a sacrifice for the spirits or for God, in case either exists" (3). From the very beginning of the novel the division between the pantheism of Korean folklore, characterized by multiple spirits and the possibilities of ghosts that return to haunt the living, and the monotheism of Christianity is established as a boundary not just of religious difference but cultural difference as well. Beccah's undiscerning offerings signal the divide between mother and daughter that disrupts any notion of ritual as a unifying act. Beccah is distanced from the spirits that are manifest in her mother's life, unsure if she is even capable of believing in their existence.

The very different perspectives of mother and daughter are structurally manifested in the format of the novel, which unfolds as a series of first-person narratives. Despite the fact that their stories are inextricably interconnected, a reality emblematized by the choral effect of their alternating narratives, their alienation from one another, both as mother and daughter and as Korean and Korean American, is textually reflected in the discreteness of each re-telling: Akiko and Beccah never tell their stories to each other directly.[17] This lack of mutual understanding even inflects the verbal communication that does take place between the two women. When Akiko confesses during the *chesa* preparation "I killed your father," Beccah does not believe her mother means what she says: "I don't remember what I felt the day my mother told me she had killed my father. Maybe anger, or fear. Not because I believed she had killed him, but because I thought she was slipping into one of her trances. I remember telling her, 'Okay,' in a loud, slow voice, while I listed in my head the things that I needed to do: call Auntie Reno, buy enough oranges and incense sticks to last two weeks, secure the double locks on the doors when I left for school so my mother couldn't get out of the house" (2). As Beccah's response indicates, she is concerned with how Akiko's trances signify a time when she has to become the caretaker, forced into the responsibility of caring for her mother because "when the spirits called to her, my mother would leave me and slip inside herself, to somewhere I could not and did not want to follow" (4).

Beccah fears that Akiko is truly mad. Although she suggests that she doesn't want the responsibility of "explaining [her] mother's insanity" (5), the uncomfortable truth is that Beccah doesn't know how to go about providing such an explanation. Even in Hawai'i, where Beccah's identity as the *hapa-haole* daughter of an Asian mother and a white father doesn't so much set her apart as make her an expected part of the racial spectrum that comprises a creolized society, her mother's bouts with the ghosts and spirits that haunt her make her unintelligible to many and contribute to Beccah's sense of herself as someone who doesn't possess the kinds of cultural competencies that would make her fluent in the two very different worlds of school and home. The very fact that Beccah thinks her mother is insane gestures to a lack of cultural knowledge that would give her the hermeneutic tools to make sense of Akiko's behavior; "insanity" becomes a convenient category to explain the otherwise unexplainable. Her mother's boss, Auntie Reno, takes advantage of the times when Akiko goes into her trances by recruiting customers who desire her talents, telling them that Akiko was a renowned fortune-teller and spirit medium in Japan and Korea. Rather than clarifying the situation, Reno's explanation of Akiko's past strikes Beccah as further confirmation of Akiko's madness: Beccah believes that Auntie Reno is not only greedy enough to abuse Akiko's weaknesses for her own material gain but that the vast divide between her charade of respectful appreciation for Akiko's former status and her actual treatment of Akiko when she is not in trance marks the unlikeliness of Akiko's shamanism being significantly more than a form of madness.

Significantly, Beccah's discomfort with her mother's trance states derives from more than her anxiety about Akiko's distance from her; she is also ashamed of the ways in which Akiko's "craziness" translates into a culturally specific epistemology that proves almost as unintelligible as the demands of the spirits. Warned about spirits like Saja, the Death Messenger, and Induk, the Birth Grandmother; terrorized by the thought that she might fall ill from the *sal* that her mother vigilantly checks for when she reaches adolescence; confused about the idea of *honyaek* ("red disaster") that her mother predicts will befall her when she goes on an unauthorized field trip with her friends: Beccah finds herself lost in the confusing muddle of information that she knows is culturally informed but that she has no real way of comprehending. This confusion is evidenced by an episode in which Beccah mistakes the sounds of the other tenants in the building they live in for the sounds made by Saja, the Death Messenger, one of the spirits whom Akiko simultaneously cajoles and defies. Such an interpretation is a measure of how much Beccah wants to identify with Akiko: "I wanted her to know that I saw him, as clearly as she ever did, and that I knew he was real" (44).

As she grows older, however, this desire to identify with Akiko is transmuted into a disavowal of her mother. During the year that Beccah is particularly prone to what her mother terms "Red Disaster," a pronouncement that accompanies Beccah's burgeoning adolescence, Akiko attempts to purify the campus and visits her daughter at school. Called a "bag lady" and mocked as "crazy" by the students, Akiko seems to Beccah different in a way that proves beyond understanding: "I wanted to help my mother, shield her from the children's sharp-toothed barbs, and take her home. And yet I didn't want to. Because for the first time, as I watched and listened to the children taunting my mother, using their tongues to mangle what she said into what they heard, I saw and heard what they did. And I was ashamed" (87–88).

"The True Voice, the Pure Tongue"

What the schoolyard children and even Beccah initially interpret only as a peculiar form of madness, though, has another explanation. What Beccah doesn't know about Akiko until the end of the novel, although we as readers are made aware of it as the novel unfolds, is that Akiko has suffered through the experience of being a comfort woman in the recreation camps of the Japanese military. Sold by her sister in order to procure a dowry, Akiko (who is at this point still known by her original name Soon Hyo) is considered too young to be pressed into service when she first arrives at the camps. Instead, she runs errands and performs necessary acts for the other comfort women. However, when the comfort woman Akiko 40 goes "mad" and refuses to comply any longer with the brutalizing conditions she faces, proclaiming her true identity—"Induk"—and challenging her tormenters to try and dehumanize her in the face of her insistence on her fundamental humanity, she is killed and Soon Hyo is christened "Akiko 41" and made to take her place.

Although Beccah knows that her mother calls out to Induk as one of the spirits who haunt her, Beccah has no idea of the complicated and interdependent relationship between the two women. For Akiko, Induk is an ambivalent figure: she is both friend and tormenter, savior and seducer. The soldiers ultimately kill Induk because she refuses to give up her Korean identity, refuses to acknowledge the Japanese name she has been given, refuses to be quiet or to give up her right to express her outrage. Significantly, Akiko sees Induk's last moments not as a sign of her insanity, but as a ritual by which Induk resists the madness of the camp:[18]

> To this day, I do not think Induk—the woman who was the Akiko before me—cracked. Most of the other women thought she did because she would not shut up. One night she talked loud and nonstop. In Korean and in Japanese, she denounced the soldiers, yelling at them to stop their invasion of her country and her body. Even as they mounted her, she shouted: I am Korea. I am a woman, I am alive. I am seventeen, I had a family just like you do, I am a daughter, I am a sister. (20)

Induk's murder sets into motion a complicated cycle of death and rebirth: Akiko 40 dies so that Induk might reclaim life, Soon Hyo is symbolically murdered so that the new Akiko 41 might live, and eventually, Akiko will call upon Induk's spirit to possess her and in the process, a new life—as shaman, rather than only as victim—will be made possible. Although Akiko will never, as Induk does so spectacularly, reclaim her name and former identity as Soon Hyo in the life she lives subsequent to her comfort woman experience, Keller suggests through Akiko's eventual development of shamanic identity that she is able, as I will demonstrate, to connect with and claim a fundamental aspect of her Korean-ness. By emphasizing the multiple misreadings Beccah has of her mother—as a crazy woman, as someone who is not in control of her own behavior, as someone weak and as a mother who doesn't teach her own child to understand her—Keller reveals how Beccah's lack of cultural and historical context necessarily results in her inability to interpret properly the role and function Akiko occupies in her life and in the life of the community. In this way, *Comfort Woman* reveals the paradox that Beccah has to work through if she is ever to understand her mother, herself, and their relationship: the Korean identity that both Japanese soldiers and U.S. Christian missionaries see as justification for their brutalization of and condescension toward Akiko is also what enables Akiko to resist those who would oppress her.

The scene that Beccah remembers so vividly—of her classmates taunting her mother and, even more significantly, of her own sense of shame in her first recognition of the "truth" of their insults—emblematizes one of the central concerns of the novel.[19] *Comfort Woman* wrestles with the ways in which naming and acts of language constitute a kind of psychic violence that is as traumatic as the physical assaults upon the bodies of the women forced to serve the soldiers in the camps. Indeed, language enacts a kind of physical violence for naming becomes the avenue by which women like Akiko are reconstituted into sexual objects that can be used and discarded.[20] Again and again, Keller emphasizes how the act of naming someone demarcates relative states of power and powerlessness, an issue that undergirds the entire text. Beccah learns that the children in the playground have the ability to use "their tongues to mangle" Akiko's words and her very self into a derogatory portrait that Beccah also then sees and hears as well. This is a lesson that Akiko has already been taught, a lesson encapsulated in the name that she chooses to use throughout the novel.

Although originally named "Soon Hyo, the true voice, the pure tongue" (195), Akiko discovers in the camps that in addition to being silenced, all of the women are renamed and given Japanese names with numbers at the end that signify what number they are in the line of women who have been thus re-named and abused. The re-naming constitutes an act of power, signaling for the Japanese not only the power they wield over the fates of the women in the camp, but also the nature of the very women themselves. Despite the saying that "Koreans have an inherent gift for languages, proving that [they] are a natural colony, meant to be dominated," the women "were not expected to understand and were forbidden to speak, any language at all" (16). Thus, language—as a mark of power, as an expression of domination, as a way of erasing identity and constituting a different reality—enforces even as it demarcates a particular kind of power relationship between the soldiers and the comfort women. As the very names of the "recreation camps" and "comfort women" make clear, naming is no ideologically neutral act but instead "a coercive system of norms and rules, a primary means of correction and appraisal" (Min 313). Through the names imposed on both women and camp, the Japanese seek to control the ways in which both should be interpreted and understood.

This way in which language marks both power and powerlessness, conformity and a site of possible resistance, is noted by Akiko, who sees that the distinctions the Japanese seek to impose on the comfort women with their injunctions against speaking are ones that necessitate such strictures precisely because they can and are constantly undermined. Even as Akiko and her fellow prisoners are commanded not to speak, they devise alternative ways of communicating with each other: "to communicate through eye movements, body posture, tilts of the head, or—when we could not see each other—through rhythmic rustlings between our stalls; in this way we could speak, in this way we kept our sanity" (16).[21] The questions of sanity and of the nature of resistance that arise from this period in the comfort camps return at critical moments throughout Akiko's later life and punctuate the nature of the connection Akiko seeks to have with her daughter. For Akiko, keeping sane concerns the ability not to speak but to communicate through the body and to form a community with the women whose fate she shares. Keeping sane depends upon recognizing a coercive linguistic system that normalizes the horrific, seeing through the euphemisms that turn rape into "comfort" and oppression into "recreation." Keeping sane is to acknowledge the rightness of resistance and although Akiko considers herself too much of a coward to follow in Induk's path, keeping sane is ultimately about re-asserting her Korean identity not through violence but through the rituals of shamanism.

The desire for community, and to resist the oppression that attends language, is something Akiko learns from her mother and strives to pass on to Beccah. The many moments of closeness, of connection, that Akiko narrates between her and her mother are striking in that they all center on the ability to communicate the deepest feeling without the hindrance of language. Thus, what Akiko remembers to pass on in her story are the "secret signals[, . . .] the rocks singing out messages" she and her mother pass to each other while washing clothes in the river together; the song her mother hums under her breath after her miscarriage in the rice fields; the first death ritual Akiko performs for her mother, waiting silently on the roof with her wedding dress to ensure that her *Omoni's* spirit flies to heaven. Her choice to pass these lessons on to Beccah—lessons whose difficulty is emblematized by the fact that Beccah bears a name that her mother cannot pronounce properly—translates into a vocabulary of bodily touch that she hopes will counter the effects of a language that "dissects her into pieces that can be swallowed and digested by others not herself" (22).

Although Akiko's suspicion about the dismembering and cannibalistic possibilities of language reflects her own experience of the ways in which language separates her from one identity and renders her partial, incomplete, and fragmented into another, the emphasis on the bodily connection between mother and child is also particularly characteristic of shamanistic belief and practice.[22] Despite the fact that Akiko believes herself cut off from her Korean identity by virtue of the transformations she has undergone, the basis of her actions for and regarding Beccah clearly reveals this to be inaccurate. Specifically, Akiko's insistence on communicating with Beccah via touch isn't meant simply to overcome the language barrier between the two of them. The attempt to construct an alternative vocabulary—like the one shared by the women of the camps or between Akiko and her own mother—stems from a desire to resist the "forked tongue" of colonialism, the duplicitous messages articulated by both soldier and missionary.[23]

As Akiko has learned, language can lull and deceive, confuse and subjugate. Thus, her suspicion of its capacity to effect these things is directed, too, toward her husband and his facility with languages. To the world, he is a learned man, one who speaks four languages and is learning a fifth (21).

With Akiko, Rick seeks to use his linguistic ability to charm her, suggesting—despite bodily evidence to the contrary—that he is not much older than she and that their "names somehow match" (93). However, Akiko sees beyond his words and realizes that he desires her in much the same way the soldiers desired her, that his desire is not to save her for God but for himself.

With her husband as with the soldiers, Akiko develops an ability to impersonate the people they wish her to be. For the soldiers, Akiko and the other comfort women learn to imitate the silent stance required as part of their sexual subjugation. Thus, despite the evolution of their secret language and their hidden ways of communicating with one another, the women of the camps understand that their survival is contingent upon learning "to walk the same, tie our hair the same, keep the same blank looks" because "[t]o be special there meant only that we would be used more, that we would die faster" (143). After the comfort camps, Akiko learns that in order to be sheltered by the Christian missionaries, she must acquiesce to being the saved convert they wish her to become. Similarly, when Akiko becomes Rick's wife, she realizes that she must act the part of minister's wife by wearing the uniforms various occasions require: either the sober, conservative clothes signaling her conversion to Christian decorum or the Korean dress somehow necessary as illustration during her husband's lectures on "Spreading the Light: My Experiences in the Obscure Orient" (107).

Akiko becomes adept at assuming a shape not her own in order to survive the various oppressive conditions she undergoes. This ability to perform convincingly the roles she is given to play is a skill necessary to survival, as Akiko learns from her own mother's story about the importance of change and adaptability that Koreans had to embrace as colonial subjects under Japanese rule. Indeed, Akiko credits her mother's lesson about how to hide her "true self" by impersonating the colonized subject who learns to "answer to a new name [and] to think of herself and her world in a new way" (153) as the very reason she is able to survive her experience as a comfort woman and an immigrant. The impersonations she performs as wife, as convert, and as comfort woman lay the groundwork for the spiritual impersonations she enacts as shaman, performances that ultimately confirm what her many experiences have taught her: that her many selves can only emerge when identity becomes that which is constituted as a performance that both questions and establishes the reality within which she lives.

Akiko's impersonations thus constitute a strategy of both accommodation and subversion. On multiple levels, Akiko's evolving performance of identities—as daughter, as sister, as comfort woman, as minister's wife, as mother, as shaman—can be read as registering both the scripted desires of others as well as her own understanding of how there can never exist a seamless fitting between self and body. Significantly, her acts of impersonation produce their own imitations and the resulting multiple performances leave traces such that impersonation becomes for Akiko not so much a practiced routine whereby she can fool others into believing in the authenticity of the self she performs as a lived strategy through which she must learn to enact her multiple selves.[24] This experience of impersonation as the performance not of a false identity but as the process by which identities are constituted as neither entirely true nor entirely false is enacted most compellingly in the experience of possession that proves so critical to the establishment of shamanic identity and practice.

The Possibilities of Possession

The idea of possession—what Beccah sees only as an uncontrollable lack of agency—must be contextualized by Akiko's earlier invocations of Induk. Indeed, possession becomes an important trope in *Comfort Woman,* signifying the multiple transformations and power struggles that permeate the novel. At its most basic level, the issue of possession is linked to the colonial struggle between Japan and Korea. The majority of comfort women were Korean, used by the Japanese in large part because they were Japanese subjects and their government was under Japanese control. Ironically, although rape as an act of attempted possession relegates women to being objects to be owned—literally possessions themselves—Hyunah Yang has noted that because colonial Korea was part of Imperial Japan, the issue of possession as enacted by rape is rendered an even more complicated notion. Specifically, although Koreans as colonial subjects of the Japanese empire were rhetorically part of the Japanese nation, Yang asserts that "the invention of the Korean comfort woman project would not have been possible if there had not been a discrete Korean identity" (63). Possession thus requires the notion of distinct entities whereby one can control or dominate, by incorporating into itself, the other.

Akiko experiences the ways in which rape, operating as an act of both physical and symbolic import, depends upon gendered power dynamics as well as colonial definitions of sovereignty and ideological superiority. What Akiko resists is not only the physical violation of her body, then, but also the threatened erasure of the self: "the Japanese, like all that was evil, would wait in the shadows, shape-shifting and patient, hoping for a chance to swallow you whole" (67). Because the Japanese soldiers figure the nature of their possession as the obliteration of Korean identity, a reading supported by the genocidal nature of the entire comfort woman project, Akiko and Induk both realize that it is their ethnic identity that they must insist upon and reassert.

As Akiko discovers, though, it is not only the Japanese who seek to possess her. Their attempts to control her body by denying her soul—the doctor who examines her when she is pregnant feels no compunction in wondering aloud about the lascivious propensities of lower-order Korean women—are later reversed when Akiko runs away and is left with a group of missionaries. Akiko learns that in order for the Christian missionaries to save her, she must give herself to God so that "His body will become your body; your flesh, His" (94). Tellingly, the minister who urges her to give herself up thus also desires her for himself. In order, then, to save her soul, the minister would possess her body as his wife. The notion of possession, of body and soul, is thus marked in negative ways through Akiko's many encounters with men. She perceives that despite differences in language, practice, and exhortation, the Japanese soldiers she serves in the camps and the Christian minister she eventually marries all wish to eradicate her identity in favor of one that they themselves have created.[25]

These dynamics serve as the foundation for Akiko's life. Since she considers herself a dead person, her original self killed by the brutality of her experiences, her very continuation as Akiko, the woman who becomes both a mother and a shaman, can be viewed itself as a form of possession. Even more significantly, Akiko's relationship with Induk also depends upon a kind of mutual possession that transforms her by complicating her previous notions of who she was and who she is destined to become. Ironically, Induk's possession of Akiko operates, in many ways, exactly as the minister tells Akiko possession should if she is ever to give herself to God and to him. Keller draws clear parallels between religious and sexual ecstasy by revealing Rick's obsession with Akiko's conversion to Christianity as one predicated upon his sexual interest in her combination of "innocence and experience." Keller suggests explicitly the conflation of sexual and religious ecstasy in her depiction of the ongoing relationship between Akiko and Induk: "I open myself to her and move in rhythm to the tug of her lips and fingers and the heat of her between my thighs. The steady buzzing that began at my finger-tips shoots through my body, concentrates at the pulse point between my legs, then without warning explodes through the top of my head. I see only the blackness of my pleasure. My body sings in silence until emptied, and there is only her left, Induk"(145). The spiritual and sexual inter-relationship between Akiko and Induk echoes eerily the rhetoric of salvation that Akiko's husband delivers as gospel: rather than submitting to Christ and her husband, Akiko gives herself over to Induk so completely that "there is only her left, Induk" (145). Importantly, the kind of giving-over of the self Akiko practices with Induk results in a paradox: only by opening herself to Induk can Akiko ever remember the self she was before the comfort camps; only Induk's possession of her body—the exchange that gives Akiko her shaman-ic powers—can result in Akiko's partial self-possession of her own soul.

While Akiko's relinquishment of self to Induk echoes the threatening obliteration of self dictated by both the rhetoric of Japanese ethnic superior-ity and the dynamics of Christian salvation, the unfolding of the nature of Akiko's relationship with Induk suggests very different priorities and condi-tions, differences that are perhaps only apparent when we are sensitive to the impact of shamanic worldviews on their relationship. According to Kwang-Ok Kim, "unlike Christianity, which teaches total submission of man to God, shamanic practices provide people with the notion that one interacts with superhuman beings in the same way that one interacts with mortal hu-mans; through negotiation, compromise, bribery, and fights" (209). Kim's assessment of the relationship between human and spirit holds true for the relationship between Akiko and Induk. While Akiko sees Induk as the one who saves her by possessing her and Beccah only understands Induk as a spirit with the power to steal her mother away from herself, the text clearly demonstrates that the connection between Induk and Akiko is not a uni-directional one but one of give-and-take. Akiko in trance becomes Induk but remains, ultimately, herself, a shaman with the ability to admonish In-duk and compel her to do her bidding even as she enacts what the spirits would have her perform.

True, Induk's spirit descends upon Akiko and possesses her so that there is "only her, Induk"; however, Akiko also possesses Induk, bringing her again to life and voice. This type of mutuality is not always considered when thinking about the nature of possession in relation to individual subjectivity. However, possession as a way of negotiating the fluid boundaries between individuals, as a way of articulating the *intersubjective* nature of identity itself, is characteristic of shamanic belief. Thus, Akiko tries to teach Beccah that despite their discreteness, they are one in each other and even "as [Beccah] grows into the person she will become . . . we share one body, one flesh" (97). The intersubjective relationship that produces identity through a form of mutual possession becomes the gift that Akiko hopes to give Beccah. Such a gift is one Beccah will not appreciate until she learns that her mother's spirit won't so much murder her, a fear emblematized by her repeated dreams of Akiko pulling her into a pool of water and drowning her, as become the spirit she must inhabit in order to come into a sense of herself.

The emphasis on multiple aspects of possession in *Comfort Woman*, both positive and negative, makes it imperative to consider the special status of the shaman in Korean society and to ponder the implications of Keller's decision to render Akiko as a woman whose past as a comfort woman becomes the impetus for her later transformation into a spiritual medium. As we shall see, possession, particularly the trance state experienced during shamanic ecstasy, emblematizes the uniquely ambivalent position of the shaman in Korean society and marks the shaman as a unique impersonator whose negotiation between identities challenges the limits of knowledge and the boundaries between body and spirit. Seen as a key component in the shaman's calling, possession signifies both power and powerlessness, the ability to intercede with the spirits on behalf of those in need but an inability to resist the supernatural ordination that demands great suffering and the relinquishment of the self.

In Korean culture, shamans occupy a vexed social position: they are both called upon to intercede for others in the spirit world and as such, possess an authority that grants them a certain privilege and respect from those who need their help, and denigrated for their calling, which many, including some shamans themselves, look upon with suspicion and distrust. The denigration of shamans, and their suspect social status, stem from a number of different reasons: the belief that some shamans are charlatans who "fake" their contact with the spirits in order to take advantage of those who are in need of special assistance and, even more importantly, a general understanding of the psychic and spiritual preconditions that are integral for those who are truly destined to be *mansin*.

According to Korean shamanistic lore, shamanism is indeed a calling: true *mansin* all experience great hardship in their lives, suffer from bouts of *sinbyong* ("possession sickness"), feel alienated from their husbands and families due to the jealousy of the spirits that call to them, and have the ability to give themselves over to spirit possession whereby they can prophesy and perform rituals of propitiation and healing for others in the community. Although many *mansin* try to resist the blandishments of the spirits, they must eventually succumb or indeed become mad. Thus, the distinctions between a shaman's powers to see the spirit world and the insane person's inability to distinguish between reality and the non-real are sometimes tenuous—another reason for viewing practicing shamans with suspicion and distaste. Even those *mansin* who are truly in communion with the spirits are looked down upon, primarily because popular beliefs dictate that those predisposed to be shamans are those whose psyches have been fractured so as to allow the spirits to enter.

Korean Shamanism—The Culture and Contexts of Resistance

Although Beccah doesn't realize for most of the novel the reasons for her mother's psychic trauma, she accepts that such trauma exists and manifests itself in the form of a peculiar kind of insanity. As I have argued, Beccah's diagnosis of Akiko as mentally ill is a misreading insofar as it doesn't account for the Korean cultural contexts that render inadequate what might otherwise in a Western cultural framework be considered as madness. However, the connections between shamanism and mental illness have long been considered by anthropologists who study shamanic behavior. While the role and practices of shamans differ from culture to culture, certain shared ideas about the shaman's ability to communicate with the spirit world and to intercede on behalf of the community with immaterial forces—abilities that are clearly suspect in Western cultures—have contributed to a varied critical discussion concerning the nature of shamanic identity and its relation to madness.

Mircea Eliade in his foundational study of the "archaic techniques of ecstasy" views the shaman as "not only a sick [person, but] above all, a sick [person] who has been cured, who has succeeded in curing himself" (27).[26] According to Young-sook Kim Harvey, research on the relationship between a shaman's mental health and her or his ability to enter the states of trance and possession necessary to communicate with the spirit world can be distilled into four general theories: "(1) the shaman is a pathological personality; (2) the shaman is a 'healed madman'; (3) the shaman may be either a pathological or normal personality; and (4) the shaman is a normal or even a super-normal personality capable of reformulating and thus of providing clients with a new synthesis of world views" (241). Clearly, while the role of shamans in mediating between their communities and the spirit world has been documented and studied in a number of different cultures, there are many interpretations of what grants the shaman his or her powers and how these abilities relate to the psychopathology of the practicing individual.

In a Korean context, shamans indeed walk the line between madness and spiritual ecstasy and the difference between the two is not always clear. I. M. Lewis suggests that while the mentally ill and the future shaman begin at the same starting point in that they both undergo "involuntary, uncontrolled unsolicited possession (or other seizure, e.g., illness or other trauma)" (89), what differentiates the two is that the shaman must at some point accept the spirits haunting her. The notion regarding the importance of accepting one's state of possession is a key characteristic of Korean *mansin*.[27] One of the prevailing preconditions necessary for someone to be called as a shaman involves experiencing *sinbyong*, or "possession sickness." Literally meaning "sickness brought on by spirits" and believed to be an integral precursor to shamanic identity, *sinbyong* is usually characterized by a range of somatic, mental, and behavioral symptoms that are quite similar to the symptoms of schizophrenia. These symptoms can include auditory hallucinations, restlessness, the inability to eat, heightened dreaming, and the eventual inability to distinguish dreams from reality (Kim Tae-gon 122). Documented cases of people suffering from *sinbyong* for up to thirty years coincide with folk beliefs in the nature of the shaman as one who can only attain such status by accepting the inevitability of shamanic destiny. For those who continue to refuse the invocations of the spirits as represented by *sinbyong*, there is no cure: "*sinbyong* will last as long as necessary . . . to convince the victim of the need to accept the shaman role, or it is terminated when the resisting victim dies" (Harvey 237).

While the symptoms of *sinbyong* can be confused with the symptoms of mental illness, Korean folk beliefs dictate that there indeed exists an important distinction between the two behaviors. Once the person suffering from *sinbyong* accepts her identity as shaman and undergoes an initiation *kut*, the problems of *sinbyong* cease. Such termination of *sinbyong* would seem compelling evidence that the "sickness" suffered by Korean shamans cannot be understood merely as a culturally specific equivalent to the Western medical diagnosis of schizophrenia but must instead be theorized as a unique expression of Korean spirituality. Additionally, the issue of gender must also factor into an analysis of *sinbyong*. As Harvey in *Six Korean Women* has argued convincingly, *sinbyong* might be most productively understood as both a reflection of the limited opportunities available to Korean women who continue to exist under a rigid Confucian social system *and* a stratagem by which women are able to subvert the restrictive gender codes imposed upon them: "*sinbyong* provides a mechanism whereby the oppressed turn the table on the oppressors with the latter's cooperation and support while the shaman role provides a mechanism for maintaining it or, failing that, of permitting the shaman a viable means of escaping from the family situation" (239).

Sinbyong thus becomes a socially sanctioned, although continually marginalized, experience through which shamans are able to negotiate their positions both within and without the family unit.[28] The distinction between mental illness and shamanic possession, then, to return to and extend Lewis's definition, rests not simply upon the individual's acceptance of her own destiny by accepting the spirits that haunt her, but also depends upon the agreement of her family and society in legitimizing her experience by recognizing her possession as spiritual authority rather than madness. This particular context of cooperation in the production of possession as a meaningful spiritual experience undergirds what *Wangsimni-mansin*, a practicing shaman, reveals as the importance of possession to the shaman's ability to commune with the spirits . . . and the fine line between shamanic ecstasy and madness: "When I heard the *changgu*, I seemed to forget everything instantly and lose all sense of inhibition. I wanted to dance and chant to it. It is this helpless sense of being swept up and away in a weightless sort of a way that makes you dance and be a *mudang* in spite of anything else . . . You can see how people who are possessed by spirits can go insane if they are improperly initiated" (31).

Whether or not Akiko was ever properly initiated as a shaman is an important issue to consider, particularly given the significance attached to the issue of the shaman's psychopathology. It can be argued that Beccah's confusion about her mother's abilities results not so much from her misunderstanding of Korean cultural and religious beliefs but derives from Akiko's status as an improperly initiated shaman. Folkloric beliefs indicate that without recognizing *sinbyong* for what it is and taking the proper steps to address it, sufferers will either become mad or be considered *as if* they were. This distinction between madness and its appearance, while critical, becomes negligible to those who are trying to decipher and diagnose mental illness. For example, in the documentary *An Initiation Kut for a Korean Shaman* (1991), one shaman recalls the experience of a woman whose possession sickness was treated not as shamanic calling but as mental illness. She suggests that while the woman in question clearly suffered from *sinbyong,* the refusal of her family to recognize her symptoms as evidence of *sinbyong* and their decision to treat the woman as insane by placing her in a mental hospital in effect transformed the woman from potential shaman into an actual crazy person.[29] The power of the audience to enforce imposture—the subsumption of any notion of the real into the purely performative—constitutes a very genuine threat and highlights the ways in which meaning is produced relationally. Clearly, impersonation thus depends to a great degree upon the cooperation between both performer and audience. The stakes of this drama are high: even as the shaman has power to impersonate spirits in order to challenge and maintain social order, the audience has power to turn the possibility of impersonation into a debilitating act of imposture that produces its own imprisoning experience of the "real" through the category of "craziness."

While Akiko has clearly suffered in ways suggesting that she should be initiated, the shaman to whom Induk sends her to consult, Mansin Ahjuma, is a woman who has converted to Christianity and thus refuses to perform a *naerim kut* (initiation ritual ceremony) for Akiko.[30] Although it would seem that Akiko hasn't been properly brought into the profession, I would argue that Beccah's unwitting record of her mother's ability contains information that would make the opposite case a compelling argument. Beccah represents Akiko as someone who cannot control the spirits who haunt her, who loses herself so completely in the process of entering into trance that she becomes the unwitting pawn of both whatever spirits possess her and Auntie Reno. And yet, a careful examination of the details of Akiko's shamanic activity as recorded in Beccah's memories about her mother clearly reveals that Akiko possesses the skill that shamans must acquire: the ability of mastering the spirits even as she gives herself up to spiritual possession.

Thus, although Beccah believes her mother has no control over her own trance states, a close reading of the scenes of Akiko's shamanic accomplishments reveals that Akiko is clearly capable of practicing shamanism responsibly and indeed maintains a level of awareness while possessed by the spirits without which performing the requested acts of fortunetelling and rituals of propitiation would be impossible. At the request of the many who come to see her, not only is Akiko able to address the issues of "death and unfulfilled desire" that trouble them but also to "pray and advise" her clients by "fold[ing] purified rock salt, ashes from the shrine, and the whispers of their deepest wish into a square of silk" (11). On another occasion, Akiko's attempts to call down the Birth Grandmother spirit to disclose Beccah's yearly fortune results in signs of unluckiness, at which point Akiko "chanted and swayed until she fell into a trance" (74), after which she is able to identify a way to combat what divination had earlier revealed. These actions are clearly rituals of healing and propitiation Akiko performs on behalf of her clients and herself; the degree of consciousness and will required for these efforts, while unregistered in Beccah's direct assessments of her mother's behavior, is nonetheless recorded in the memories Beccah must revisit once Akiko dies and she must figure out how her interpretations of her mother's stories, actions, and ultimately life must evolve.[31]

Keller's use of shamanistic lore in *Comfort Woman* rearticulates the central concerns of the comfort woman experience in ways that signify on multiple levels. The systematic, gender-based oppression of Korean comfort women occupies an inverted relationship to the fact that *mansin* are predominantly women. Due to the possibility of understanding the shaman role for women as a potentially empowering role, one that allows women access to both public and private domains and to resist patriarchal codes of female behavior in Korean society, Keller's resituation of the comfort woman experience within the context of Korean shamanism foregrounds the importance of seeing female oppression as a social condition that can be resisted, even if at great cost to the self. This lesson is repeated throughout *Comfort Woman,* as Akiko discovers her fate in the contexts of family, comfort camp, and Christian mission house to be directly linked to her identity as a woman.

Although Akiko's stories about her family include moments of tenderness and great love, she identifies the death she dies in stages as a process that begins "with [her] birth as the fourth girl and last child in the Kim family" (17). In the comfort camp, she is valued only in terms of the service she fulfills for the soldiers; denied language, name, and identity, Akiko is counted "still good" by the doctor in the camp on the basis of his evaluation of her genitalia as still capable of providing sexual service. Even after she escapes her tormentors and finds refuge with a group of Christian missionaries in Pyongyang, she discovers that the minister sees her salvation as one that must be mediated through him as her husband. By emphasizing how Pastor Bradley's efforts to "save" Akiko are predicated on his own sexual desires for her, Keller plainly figures the hypocrisy of U.S. imperialism in Korea and highlights its continuity with what Akiko experiences as a marginalized subject once she enters the United States as Mrs. Bradley. Thus Akiko repeatedly confronts the ways in which to be a woman is to be discarded, abused, and exploited.

So, although Keller's novel emphasizes the multiple obstacles Akiko must confront as a woman, *Comfort Woman* also illuminates the shaman role as one uniquely suited to redressing gender inequity. While Beccah sees her mother's trances as signs of powerlessness, episodes wherein Akiko loses her identity and is unable to figure her place in the real world, the novel also stresses that Akiko's shamanistic relationship with the spirits that haunt her provides her with a singular opportunity to address and redress the tragedy that she has experienced. On a prosaic level, enacting the role of "famed fortuneteller and spirit medium" that Auntie Reno advertises brings Akiko a series of patrons whose financial donations enable her to take care of Beccah after her husband dies and she is left to support her daughter in an unfamiliar country. The separation from family that signals the advent of her time in the camps, a separation dictated not only by the fact that she was the youngest daughter but also because her older sister needed to provide herself with a dowry in order to safeguard her own future, is also resolved via her shamanic role. At the end of the novel, Beccah finds a tape of a ritual that Akiko performs for her own mother. Faithful in her role as a daughter,

Akiko is also a shaman who is able to perform the ceremonies of remembrance and invocation that will eventually reconnect her not only with her lost mother but also with her distant daughter. Even in her marriage to the minister who brings her to a country where she is "faceless" and again nameless, Akiko manages to shift the power balance more in her favor by opening herself to her shamanic destiny. While her husband never sees her as a shaman and doesn't countenance shamanism's claim to her identity, Akiko's acquiescence to Induk's possession of her makes it impossible for him to claim her for himself: "After the night Induk came to me, opening my body to her song, I saw the soldiers' fear of death and disease in my husband's eyes. His fear that instead of saving me, he had damned himself. . . . And I knew then that he would not use me again like that. I knew then that he could not" (148).

These moments are staged not in order to repudiate the significant trauma Akiko survives but to highlight an equally important aspect of her experience: her ultimate refusal to relinquish her right to resist the harm imposed on her. Beccah sees her mother as weak and helpless, a victim to circumstance and the spirits that haunt her; Akiko's own rhetoric of self seems to support such an assessment. She admits that she didn't have the courage to choose her own death; she thinks of herself as a ghost who floats among the living; she attributes her own survival to Induk. Yet, despite these assertions of her own weakness, Akiko's past is characterized by a sustained pattern of resistance. In every situation she encounters, Akiko is able to negotiate the strictures imposed upon her: she conveys secret messages to the other women of the comfort camp before she is herself made a comfort woman; as a comfort woman, she insists on maintaining a connection with the other women that the Japanese soldiers would deny her; as Rick's wife, she counters his linguistic lessons to Beccah with her own instruction in the bodily language of touch; as a shaman, she turns out not to be, as Beccah imagines, an unwitting pawn in Auntie Reno's fortune-telling enterprise but a shrewd businesswoman who was "so sharp . . . [s]he knew exactly what she made, down to dah last cent in dah Wishing Bowl" (204).

In such ways, Akiko insists on her own agency: more than a victim, she is a resourceful woman who is able to challenge many of the restrictions that have been imposed upon her as a woman, a Korean, a wife, a "convert," and an Asian American immigrant. Keller's representation of Akiko as a woman who is, in Reno's words, "one survivah," redresses the potential hermeneutic danger of "freez[ing] the identity of the former comfort women as international victims, 'existential comfort women' " (Yang 66). By emphasizing the ways in which Akiko inhabits multiple identities—she is both victim and agent, shaman and comfort woman, mother and daughter, sharp and neglectful—Keller writes against the kind of pre-existing narrative structures that would "permit no space for the depiction of the women as agents who suffered and yet who actively negotiated with their harsh situation" (59).[32]

Clearly, Keller's deployment of shamanism in *Comfort Woman* constitutes an attempt to re-figure the victimization of the comfort woman by capitalizing on the ways in which the shaman, herself an outcast and perceived as a victim of fate, might pursue strategizing victimization. According to anthropologist Laurel Kendall, "women use possession as a strategy; in trance, they speak the unspeakable. Possession, institutionalized in healing rites, becomes a 'means by which women, and sometimes other subject categories, are enabled to protect their interests and proffer their claims and ambitions through . . . affliction' " (24). Induk's possession of Akiko enables her to confront her husband's accusations of "self-fornication" by insisting upon the difference between "what happen[s] spiritually" and "what [goes] on between men's and women's bodies" (146). She is also able to resist the patriarchal oppression of Christianity and the demands of a conversion that would expect her to acquiesce to a new identity in much the same way that the Japanese expected the comfort women to submit. This emerges most clearly in a half-forgotten memory that Beccah is only able to recall near the end of the novel, a memory of her mother "dancing in the alley of our yard and my father on his knees before her, begging her to come inside before someone saw them" (195). Akiko's husband's plea—to "[r]emember the woman of Luke . . . [who] had been inflicted by evil spirits"—is accompanied by his command for Akiko to "bow down . . . just as that woman did" in order to "be free" (195). With the help of her spirits, Akiko is able to assert her independence, an independence that is, ironically, dependent upon creating bonds with the women who came before her and the daughter she leaves behind. While Akiko's shamanism offers her perhaps the most visible way of strategizing against the victimization of her past, Keller presents it as a logical extension of a history of resistance that takes place even before Akiko accepts her possession by Induk and her shamanic destiny.

Shamanism as a particularly *gendered* and a particularly *Korean* practice offers a paradigm for interrogating the conflation of the comfort woman's body with the Korean nation that Induk articulates just before she is killed. Significantly, Induk's resistance manifests itself not only as a refusal to be silent; she insists that the Japanese soldiers' abuse of her body parallels the Japanese invasion of Korea. The identity of comfort woman bestowed upon both Induk and Akiko, an identity signified by the name they share, masks the other similarities that mark the spiritual unity of Induk and Akiko throughout the novel. In many ways, Akiko sees Induk's murder as a definitive point of distinction between them: unlike Induk, Akiko doesn't use words as a weapon against the Japanese, doesn't take back her Korean name, and claims not to insist upon her Korean identity in the face of efforts to eradicate it.

And yet, Akiko, through her understanding of herself and her experience within a shamanic context, *also* refuses to be severed from her Korean-ness, refuses to submit to the eradication of her humanity. After escaping from the recreation camp, Akiko, bewildered and wandering, experiences a vision:

> I walked and slept, walked and slept, and throughout the journey kept my eyes fixed on Induk beckoning before me. At times, her form would blur until it doubled, then quadrupled, and she would become Induk and my mother, and in turn my mother's mother and an old woman dressed in the formal *top'o* of the olden days. I realized I was walking with my ancestors. (53)

As this passage makes clear, Induk becomes for Akiko an ancestral presence; it is through her spiritual intervention that Akiko sees the path of shamanism as one that she might pursue. The key to Akiko's survival is a recognition of her ties to community and family, a reaffirmation of a previous identity that cannot be re-assumed, but can act as the foundation for her new occupation and new identities. In this vision, ancestral guidance offers a way for Akiko to bear with her by containing within herself the very existence of female community and Korean identity that enabled her to survive the camps. What a shamanic world-view provides for Akiko is a double reinscription of her place in the world: the shaman's role as spiritual intermediary grants her the opportunity to move beyond her victimization by allowing her to choose her future; the "dynamic process" (Kendall, *Life* 8) of familial interaction that is so crucial to shamanic practice also reminds

Akiko that the comfort woman experience is not the only context through which she might understand herself—and Beccah should know her.

Akiko's own "death in stages" is a ghostly echo of Soon Hyo's remembrance that her "mother [also] died more than once in her life" (175). And like her mother, Akiko comes to understand that her story isn't one that can be summed up easily, that it is possible to not know a single name by which someone can be identified. Thus when she tries to convey to Beccah a legacy by which to live, she decides upon a story of her own mother that illuminates the expansive capacity to be more than a single personality: "She was a princess. She was a student. She was a revolutionary. She was a wife who knew her duty. And a mother who loved her daughters, but not enough to stay or to take them with her" (182). As princess, student, revolutionary, wife, and mother, Akiko's *Omoni* plays a lead role in the narratives of both an individual's life and a nation's past that Akiko would have Beccah remember. Thus, the story that Akiko generates for her daughter becomes itself a generative act of resistance in its invocation of memory, a gift she passes from her mother's and Induk's examples to her daughter.

The fundamental spirit of Induk's death as a generative act of resistance lies in her assertion of her Korean identity as something distinct and unacknowledged by the Japanese soldiers lining up to use her body. This is precisely what Akiko seeks to assert through her shamanic practice. Scholars like Kim Tae-gon consider shamanism "the source of the Korean people's spiritual energy" (qtd. Kendall, *Shamans* 35) while others argue that it is the "primitive ethos of the Korean people" (S. Palmer 5). Interestingly, Korean *kut* ("shaman rituals") are now avidly recorded because they are viewed as cultural practices infused by "abstract issues of national identity and the preservation of a Korean cultural heritage" (Kendall 35). As one practicing *mansin* puts it, "Not only do the *mudang* patch up broken hearts and shore up sagging hopes of the many who need succor, today's *mudang* are probably the only and the best source of knowledge if anyone wants to study old Korean tradition now becoming obsolete . . . People my age who studied under the Japanese don't know any better than today's children how ancient Korean was spoken; *mudang* are a valuable repository of traditional Korean culture" (Harvey 126).

In addition to representing Korean national identity through cultural practice, shamanism invokes a history of resistance to colonial and neo-colonial efforts to eradicate it. Keller's novel presents a serious critique of Japanese colonialism in Korea; her representation of Akiko's comfort woman experiences during the war highlights the ways in which the Japanese government sought to suppress on *institutional* levels the free expression of a vibrant and energetic Korean identity. To this end, Keller's emphasis on the role of Korean shamanism in the rescue and redemption of Akiko constitutes a way of foregrounding and reinforcing the history and significance of Korean resistance to colonial rule.

Shamanism is an indigenous religion in Korea that has survived contact with Confucianism, Buddhism, and Christianity—all imports that were introduced to Korea as part of its long history as a colonized nation.[33] During Japanese occupation, the Japanese response to Buddhism and Christianity was quite starkly opposed to its position with relation to shamanism. According to Wi Jo Kang's study of Korean religion and politics, while Japanese attitudes toward Christianity and Buddhism in Korea fluctuated and were characterized by various levels of both accommodation and resistance between Japanese administrators and the practitioners and leaders of these two organized religions, the Japanese policy of "benevolent assimilation" was not welcomed by many of Korea's indigenous religious groups whose nationalistic feelings were, generally speaking, very pronounced. Kang asserts that the "Japanese government saw these religions as disturbers of the peace, misguiders of the people, strong adherers to Korean tradition, and opposers of the new orders established by Japanese administration" (70). The Japanese response to the potential problems posed by the nationalistic bent of Korea's indigenous religious groups was two-pronged: on the one hand, the government considered shamanism to be "superstition" rather than a legitimate religion. On the other hand, recognizing the ubiquity of shamanistic beliefs in Korean life, Japan also periodically attempted to co-opt shamanism's influence on the Korean people—to little effect.[34]

Shamanism's unique position in the formation of resistant Korean national identity has resulted in contemporary efforts to deploy "shamanistic performance in the ritualization of violent protest" (Kwang-Ok Kim 197). Interestingly, the shamanistic elements adopted by protestors seeking to revive traditional culture in a search for national identity—including open-air folk dramas (*madang kuk*) and the more traditional ritual performances of *kut*—have now transcended the religious beliefs of individual protestors to become a national "idiom of protest" (199). Thus, even Christians embrace the props and performance of shamanism to testify against certain ellipses in national memory and historical consciousness; shamanism, celebrated as a symbol of a "pure Korean cultural tradition," has itself become ritualized as a representation of the strength of Korean identity to resist the oppressive structures of the state—in large part because of shamanism's past as a set of beliefs occupying the "alienated space that is negated by the official discourse of the state" (209).[35] Akiko's reliance on shamanism thus carries with it attendant significances concerning the establishment of a Korean identity that is distinct from colonial definitions of it, particularly as defined by the Japanese during the period of occupation.

Shamanic Interventions: Filiality, Rituals, Healing, History

By insisting on shamanism as the interpretive framework for her novel, Keller essentially writes against the potentially colonizing effects of our theoretical practices and urges us to commit to a kind of analysis that will force us to undertake the imaginative acts of impersonation with which this chapter began. *Comfort Woman* suggests that while Western discourses of mental health, psychoanalytic theories of trauma and postmodern strategies of reading offer possible hermeneutic frameworks for evaluating the form and content of Akiko's story, they are, ultimately, singularly inadequate to the task of analyzing fully the significance of Akiko's experience surviving her comfort woman past. In cautioning against both a too-easy diagnosis of Akiko's schizophrenia and a psychoanalytic emphasis on the racialized subject as pathologized by virtue of the twin traumas of race and sexuality, Keller demands that we focus on the possibilities of resisting the oppressive circumstances that women like Akiko survived and recognize the importance of the communal in the formation of the self's vigorous insistence on its own possibilities. In essence, Keller engages shamanism in order to demonstrate the importance of foregrounding agency even as we apprehend the divided allegiances of subjectivity.

Although we might consider the acknowledgment of Akiko's position as a "multiply interpellated" subject one that shares with other postmodern subjects the space for identity that is always in play, *Comfort Woman* also demands a committed critical investment in the serious consequences of its subject matter; for many of the elderly comfort women who now live in impoverished circumstances, denied home, family, and financial stability as a result of their pasts, how we choose to consider the stakes of our investment, and theirs, can literally be a matter of life and death. The nature of this commitment is one that postmodern strategies of reading and thinking have sometimes been slow to respond to.[36] Shamanism as both a lived strategy and a framework for interpretation, on the other hand, demonstrates a history of commitment to the kind of serious investment that is necessary in order to do justice to this subject.

In offering shamanism as a way of reading and responding to the historical weight of what we do and do not choose to remember from this episode of the enforced sexual slavery of Korean women during World War II, Keller proposes a hermeneutics that capitalizes on what we can learn from historically and culturally grounded theoretical frameworks. As such, the figure of the shaman stands as a cultural critic, exhorting us to remember the histories that have made us what we are and parrying attempts to co-opt these events into a generic narrative of trauma that would possibly minimize its particular genealogy and thus its specific effects. What emerges from Keller's critical use of shamanism to contextualize the aftereffects of Akiko's comfort woman experiences is a set of interpretive paradigms that illuminate the nature of our own critical investments in the practice and politics of remembering what history threatens to forget. In *Comfort Woman,* the shaman acts as a figure of critical interrogation whose cultural performance of memory structures political and social critique in deeply personalized terms. The shaman's invocation of, and ritual interaction with, ancestral spirits articulate the problem of family dynamics as rooted in the larger social and political contexts of both Asia and the United States.

Significantly, Keller's deployment of shamanism as an interpretive frame for the novel not only critiques Japanese imperialism but also illuminates the ways in which the U.S. neo-colonial presence in Korea impacts Korean American subject formation. As such, Beccah proves an important figure of consideration. Her nostalgic attachment to her dead father, deified as "an angel" who possessed "the face and voice of Mr. Rogers" (2), and her desire to identify *against* Akiko's seeming madness with the normalcy represented by her romantic fantasies of a father who "would spirit me away, to a home on the Mainland complete with plush carpet and a cocker spaniel pup" (2), are revised not so much as a result of understanding "cultural differences" in ways that ultimately reify the United States as liberatory space. Instead, Beccah's interpellation as a "normal" U.S. citizen is interrogated from the perspective of Korean shamanism to reveal the consequences of not acknowledging the oppressive conditions that produce Akiko as unwilling missionary wife and unwelcome immigrant and Beccah as an Asian American subject who has trouble identifying who and what she is and wants to be. In delineating the problems and possibilities Beccah experiences in relation to Korean shamanism, Keller engages what Kandice Chuh has identified as an "ongoing interest in Asian American studies[: . . . the utilization of] transnational paradigms of knowledge for understanding such matters as national identity and subject formation" ("Introduction" 2). Ironically, Chuh reads Keller's novel as one that "privilege[s] the mode of 'breaking silence' without critical reflection on that process" (17), in large part because "despite its invocation of histories and stories that are arguably unfamiliar to many U.S. readers, the novel may be seen to operate on [the] well-trodden, even clichéd grounds" of generational reconciliation and an over-emphasis on "happiness for the next (U.S.) generation" (19). Understanding the significance of shamanism as a hermeneutic paradigm for *Comfort Woman* challenges the conclusions Chuh makes about the pedagogical functions of Keller's text. Despite the novel's reiteration of mother-daughter conflict and cultural opposition, *Comfort Woman*'s emphasis on the implications of Akiko's shamanistic performance as transnational critique and Keller's insistence on shamanistic practice as Beccah's legacy from her mother works against the romanticism of narrative closure that Chuh suggests as the text's most obvious conclusion.

As Beccah discovers, the gaps and distortions of her own family dynamic not only result from a problem between individuals who come from different backgrounds but reflect the uneven historical, social, cultural, and political conditions of oppression and resistance that mark the evolution of Korean and Korean American ethnic identity. Keller's figuration of the shaman as cultural critic derives, in part, from Harvey's characterizations of female shamans as people who "were critical of cultural norms others accepted as givens in their lives, were hypersensitive to cultural inconsistencies, and suffered from a deep and abiding sense of having been morally injured as human beings" (237). By delineating Akiko as a shaman, Keller is thus able to bring these particular dimensions of the shaman's role to bear upon the as-yet unresolved questions and problems surrounding the issues of culpability and ethical behavior with regard to the current comfort woman controversy. *Comfort Woman's* metatextual commentary on issues centered on the status of Korean comfort women in the construction of a national identity in postwar Korea arises as a result of its emphasis on shamanism's significance as a discourse that emphasizes the role of women in community and the nature of affliction as the defining moment of shamanic identity. Additionally, Keller's emphasis on shamanism's discursive significance addresses the historical amnesia evidenced by both the Japanese government's response to the comfort women issue and U.S. discourses about sexual slavery in Asia that disavow the United States's complicity in perpetuating such atrocities.

As we have seen, the concerns Keller demonstrates about proper registers of response to the history and lessons imparted by what happened to women like Akiko are aptly addressed by her invocation of the shaman as figure of gendered resistance. The shaman's ability to remember through performance a shared past and a communal spirit of resistance in order to address the social and political problems of the contemporary situation asserts both the importance of witness as well as the significance of claiming agency. By occupying herself the paradoxical position of cultural agent and spiritual pawn, the shaman embodies through possession the precarious positionality that impersonation makes manifest. As impersonator, Akiko's ability to enact the spirits is to make them both more and less "real," to challenge the ellipses of history, to suggest that the boundaries between self and other must be negotiated even as their very palpability is acknowledged. Keller suggests that the theatricality of shamanic ritual proffers a grounded framework for theorizing the evolution of ethnic identity and the means by which subjects survive and even triumph over traumas such as those experienced by the Korean comfort women of World War II.

Finally, shamanism exists as a kind of performed memory—its chants and rituals comprise a legacy of stories that need to be told, memories that must be remembered. The paradoxical, synchronic act of providing a corrective to memory as well as performing rituals that perpetuate the traditions of the past emblematizes the dual nature of impersonation as a performance that celebrates the past by problematizing its claim to truth. Although

Keller's emphasis on shamanism in the novel constitutes an attempt to ensure that the stories of Korean comfort women are not co-opted in the name of Western feminism, her insistence on the significance of Korean shamanism in the text also attempts to counter what Hyunah Yang has identified as "the discursive hegemony of Japan" in the revelation of the "facts" and "truths" critical to these women's stories. Yang urges those interested in the recovery of the "truth" of comfort women's experiences to shift their focus away "from institutional history to personal memories, thereby rescuing the comfort women from becoming informants and restoring their status as subjective agents" (Choi viii).

In this shift away from institutional history to personal memory, the space for contested meaning opens to include provisionality and indeterminacy as markers of that which should be considered true. Beccah grasps the implications of such contested meaning when she considers the ways in which some of Akiko's stories—stories that "sounded good" and included the phrase "It was a hard time but a happy time"—were "just stories told to people who didn't really matter" (32). She comes into her own awareness of the possibilities of such contestation when she realizes after years of hearing only her own stories that "not only could I not trust my mother's stories; I could not trust my own" (34). Beccah discovers she cannot trust the stories she grows up with to reflect an unchanging past; instead, she must rely on them to show her, truly, the contemporary effects of what has happened in the past.[37] She learns, through the painful process of becoming sensitive to the forms and structures favored by Akiko in teaching her daughter how to communicate with her, that the narrative forms preferred by her shaman mother are myths whose meanings continue to evolve to reflect her own changing understanding of "truth," filiality, and the legacies of the past.

The myths and fables that Akiko tells Beccah become a testing ground for determining Beccah's interpretive ability and the cultural contexts that she brings to bear in learning the lessons Akiko needs to teach her before she can remember the histories that belong to them both. As with so much else in this novel, the stories that bind the women together also expose the disjunction in worldviews that makes the mother-daughter relationship so difficult to negotiate. Akiko often exhorts her daughter to remember the story of the Heavenly Toad whose loving adoptive parents and obedient wife reveal him to be not a toad but "a young man as handsome as an angel and truly one of heaven's messengers" (159). As a child, Beccah considers the story with trepidation, paralyzed by the possibility of being married, killed, or taken to heaven by the toad. Only later does she realize that the character she regarded with such apprehension as a child was likely intended as a benevolent figure. Given Beccah's anxieties about her mother's possession, the Heavenly Toad—"in his ability to transform himself, to hide in the skin of others—seemed more frightening" (159) than anything else. Thus, even as Akiko attempts to convey to Beccah the roles and rituals of family devotion through her storytelling, Beccah's own anxieties about the nature of possession and Akiko's shamanism result in her utter confusion about how to interpret the significance of these tales.

While it seems that Akiko doesn't do a very good job of passing on the contexts and lessons that would prepare Beccah to witness to her mother's life, Akiko's method of telling, like her shamanic practices, can only be understood when Beccah learns the proper way to listen. "Like the river in my blood, my mother waited for me to fly to her, waited for me to tell her I was ready to hear what she had to say. I never asked, but maybe she was telling me all the time and I wasn't listening" (191). Although Akiko never tells Beccah explicitly the story of her past, the messages she transmits about the nature of her suffering, the importance of filiality, the significance of remembering the histories of those important to us, and the need to perform rituals by which we can both free and remember the ones we love are encapsulated in the myths that confuse Beccah because their meanings keep changing as her understanding grows. Not until Akiko has passed on does Beccah realize that the stories themselves provide a way for Akiko to bring Beccah into a shamanic relationship with her. The myths themselves comprise "a cure and a protection [that] is at once musical, historical, poetical, ethical, educational, magical, and religious" (Trinh 140).

The most important of these stories is the story of Princess Pari, the filial daughter who risks death in order to save her parents. In Akiko's version of the story, Princess Pari is an unwanted daughter who cleverly outwits Saja the Death Messenger by going to hell and distracting him with a feast. With Saja distracted, Princess Pari is able to identify the souls of her parents from the other human souls in hell and bring them to the Lotus Paradise, where they are reborn as angels. Beccah understands this story as a story about filiality: Princess Pari is a daughter who is willing to risk her own life in order to rescue her parents while Beccah herself fails to save her mother from her demons or from death. However, Beccah's interpretation of what filiality *means* and how she might come to perform such a quality in her own relationship with Akiko evolves as she learns more about her mother and the demands that, until the end, have always seemed unbearably burdensome and even suffocating. "Implicit in the tale of Princess Pari is the message that unwanted daughters have unacknowledged powers and a stubborn will to survive and be vindicated" (Kendall, *Life* 33). Such a message has resonance for Beccah for multiple reasons: in addition to understanding how *Pari Kongju's* tale illuminates Akiko's comfort woman experience, Beccah eventually learns that Princess Pari is significant because she is not only celebrated as a model daughter; she is also considered Korea's first shamaness and revered as a model for *mansin*. Princess Pari's ability to rescue others from death, her talent for communicating with the spirits of the dead, her willingness to descend into the depths of Hell—all of these are shamanistic abilities that *mansin* also take upon themselves. For Beccah to understand Akiko, for her to demonstrate true filiality, she needs to undertake herself the rituals of death and comfort that Akiko so fears she will not be able to perform.

At novel's end, Beccah listens to a tape that her mother made for her before she died. The tape is meant for Beccah, but not in the ways that Beccah initially thinks. Her mother's voice, her mother's story—these are invoked on tape as part of a death anniversary *chesa* that Akiko performs for her own mother, Beccah's grandmother. What the tape offers Beccah is a model for the ritual she must perform for Akiko so that her soul may depart in peace. In it, she hears a word she doesn't know: *Chongshindae*.[38] She looks up the word, makes a possible translation—"battalion slave"—and discovers a story she has never heard before: "Even though I heard her call out 'Akiko,' the name she had answered to all my life, I could not imagine her surviving what she described, for I cannot imagine myself surviving" (194).

At this moment, Beccah is confronted with an opportunity, a demand even, to imagine herself in Akiko's place. Not until this moment does she realize that her awareness of the limitations of her imagination constitutes the necessary first step she must take in order to inhabit the experiences that Akiko remembers and passes on. Only by realizing that she needs to learn to listen truly and be open to the mutual possession she has feared all her life—to know, in Akiko's words, that *"we will carry each other always. Your blood in mine"* (197, emphasis original)—will she be able, finally, to perform the act of impersonation that would allow her to imagine herself as Akiko and to re-member, through shamanic rituals of remembrance, the importance of the past. Because Beccah is able to discern the importance of shamanic ritual, fi-nally, in her mother's life, she is able, at novel's end, to perform her own ver-sion of a *chesa* for Akiko. Even though she "doesn't know if [she's] doing it right," she does it anyway. In the process, she takes on the role she once thought impossible: she chants the song daughters use to rescue their par-ents, singing "And if you fall, if he lures you into hell, wrap the vines around you, and I will be your Princess Pari, pulling you through" (208). By re-in-voking Princess Pari while performing a shamanic ritual to ease another soul into death and beyond, Beccah finally understands the filial obligations that bind her to Akiko, and the healing acts through which Akiko has tried to heal both herself and others.

There's no simple resolution for Akiko—we see that she is indeed able to bring comfort to others as a result of her shamanic abilities, but the peace she craves for her own life is only ever partially attained and the under-standing that she wishes to achieve with Beccah is denied her until after death. While Akiko's shamanism proffers a way through which she is able to process the traumas of her comfort woman past, only after Beccah moves away from the ways in which she records the lives of the dead as an obituary writer for the newspaper and enters into a more communal, fluid shamanic ritual of remembrance can Akiko be truly cured. Beccah proves critical to such an endeavor because, according to Trinh Minh-ha, "Curing means re-generating, for understanding is creating. The principle of healing rests on *reconciliation,* hence the necessity for the family and/or the community to cooperate with, partake in, and witness the recovery, de-possession, regener-ation of the sick. The act of healing is therefore a socio-cultural act, a collec-tive, motherly undertaking" (140). By accepting the shamanic legacy of her mother, Beccah does perform the motherly functions of nurturance and pro-tection that she so resisted as a child. Indeed, the novel's final image—wherein Beccah's repeated dream ends not with a drowning but with her sleeping, "coiled tight around a small seed planted by [her] mother, waiting to be born" (213)—supports Trinh's assessment of the structural similarities between shamanic healing and mothering.

Comfort Woman insists that the contexts that help us fathom the unfathomable are, nonetheless, inadequate for addressing the problems of colonialism, neocolonialism, and the eradication of culture. Any solutions found are partial and temporary; they must be enacted again and again if they are to perform the cultural work of resisting history's oppressive forgetfulness. To that end, shamanism's capacity to remember through ritual comprises one possible way of ensuring that the ghosts of history will not be left alone to fade away into oblivion.

As I noted at the beginning of this chapter, ghosts figure prominently in contemporary literary representations of Korean comfort women. As an emergent trope in Korean American literary production about this topic, such ghosts perform multiple functions. They embody, as in the brief sighting Soon-ah has of her friend Kyung Hwa's ghost in *A Gift of the Emperor,* the fear of death . . . and the guilt of surviving the unsurvivable. In *A Gesture Life,* the ghost of K., the comfort woman who suffered a brutal, horrifying death because the man who loved her did not have the courage to kill her quickly as she requested, reminds us of the material effects that phantoms can exert. As Chang-rae Lee shows us, the ghostly can render the living "not really here" (286), in effect turning the living into ghosts themselves. Lee reveals that the singularly solid world of Bedley Falls that his protagonist Franklin Hata inhabits is, in fact, a shadow realm whose very existence is made possible only if Hata's "latent history, if [he] could so will it, would be left always unspoken, unsung" (289). As a sign of history "unspoken, unsung," the ghosts of Korean comfort women haunt these novels, occupying what Frantz Fanon has identified as the "zone of occult instability" (227) in order to force us to acknowledge their spectral presence as fundamental to returning to the past in order to learn from the mistakes we have made, the episodes we have forgotten.

Clearly, *Comfort Woman* offers to us the most elaborate articulation of the ghostly as a form of knowing the world and remembering the injustices of the past so as to sketch a politics of resistance to current oppression. Keller's use of shamanism does more than provide a particular cultural framework through which to understand why Akiko is haunted. In proffering to us the lessons to be learned from Korean shamanism, Keller teaches us that we must, at all costs, *resist exorcism.* To exorcise the ghost would be to forget the reasons it comes to haunt us in the first place. To exorcise the ghost would be to convince ourselves of the illusion that justice can be served by anything less than continued vigilance and wholehearted commitment. As Akiko knows, the only way to co-exist with Induk's ghost is to invite her in, to offer her Akiko's "own hands, [her] eyes, [her] skin" (96). Thus, the scene of mother-daughter reconciliation at the end of *Comfort Woman,* a scene that would seem to indicate that Beccah has successfully exorcised the demons of her past in order to resolve harmoniously her differences with Akiko, gestures to what lies beyond the scene itself. Even as Akiko reconciles with Induk's ghost in order to find a kind of salvation, Beccah reconciles with Akiko's ghost in order to embrace her own legacy. And even as we know that Akiko's life with Induk is filled with moments when the ghostly demands of the spirits refuse to be denied, we know that the peaceful image of Beccah wrapped around the seed planted by her mother will mean that she *will* continue to be haunted by Akiko, and not always in benign ways. As shamanism understands, to recognize ghosts means not to banish them from life but to live with the demands they have made, and will continue to make, on the worlds we call our own.

SIX

Impersonation and Other Disappearing Acts: The Double(d) Agent of Chang-rae Lee's *Native Speaker*

And yet you may know me. I am an amiable man. I can be most personable, if not charming, and whatever I possess in this life is more or less the result of a talent I have for making you feel good about yourself when you are with me. In this sense I am not a seducer. I am hardly seen. I won't speak untruths to you, I won't pass easy compliments or odious offerings of flattery. I make do with on-hand materials, what I can chip out of you, your natural ore. Then I fuel the fire of your most secret vanity.

Native Speaker, Chang-rae Lee

I am an invisible man. No, I am not a spook like those who haunted Edgar Allan Poe; nor am I one of your Hollywood-movie ectoplasms. I am a man of substance, of flesh and bone, fiber and liquids—and I might even be said to possess a mind. I am invisible, understand, simply because people refuse to see me.

Invisible Man, Ralph Ellison

Henry Park is an invisible man. Like the nameless protagonist of Ralph Ellison's *Invisible Man,* he suffers from the refusal of others to see him. However, unlike Ellison's character, his invisibility is both a matter of the refusal of others to see him and the logical effect of his occupation. In Chang-rae Lee's *Native Speaker* (1995), Henry Park *is* a spook, haunting those against whom he is paid to spy. That Lee's protagonist is a spy is no coincidence: Henry's vanishing acts, a professional opportunity to enact the spy's "multiple roles," are a logical extension of his personal history as a Korean American struggling to negotiate the divide that separates how others perceive him and how he sees himself. *Native Speaker* weaves an intricate web of intrigue in order to examine the multiple forces that create Henry as a spy who gets caught up in the messy tangle of his many deceptions. Lee writes about a spy yet the novel is not a typical spy novel. Henry's stories—lyrical, cryptic, introspective—do not conform to the conventions of the spy story. The disjunction between the teller and his tale marks Lee's deliberate reworking of the genre of the spy story, altering it to accommodate the exigencies of a spy whose racially determined invisibility signals not license but a debilitating erasure of self and power. Although Henry's spying is a metaphor about his uneasy position as a Korean American struggling to figure out his place in American society, spying in *Native Speaker* moves beyond metaphor and provides Lee an opportunity to criticize formally the generic conventions that make the telling of Henry's story such a difficult thing. By rewriting the generic conventions of the spy story, Lee designates Henry as a postmodern operative whose troubles with language and performance lead him to question the roles he has been given to play and the ways in which he has been encouraged to speak.

Native Speaker explores its preoccupations—with the conventions of genre and of narrative, with racial invisibility and disappearing acts, with linguistic fluency and rhetorical style—on levels both formal and thematic. Henry's exploration of what it means to be a spy and a storyteller represents not only the self-examination of a man who is afraid he has lost his identity; it is also the chronicle of immigrant success and failure, and the price exacted by the immigrant practice of "gently and not so gently exploit[ing] one's] own" (50). The tensions that structure Henry's story make the telling of it a difficult thing. His lyricism and eloquence falter into strange silences, broken narratives, cryptic phrases. Such problems with how to fashion narrative symbolize the multiple anxieties that Henry experiences: as a Korean American whose American birth does not preclude his grappling with linguistic fluency and a cultural legacy of silence; as a man who woos his speech therapist wife without truly fathoming the mysteries of how to make himself heard and understood; and as a spy whose professional success is predicated upon his ability to impersonate someone else, to speak a story not his own.

Henry is a problematic storyteller. There are questions that others—his boss, his wife, his colleagues and his friends—have about his reliability. Even more importantly, Henry himself cannot always distinguish his facts from his own narrative impulses: his confusion about which stories to tell and how to tell them is the result of his multiple betrayals, each one contributing to the unraveling of both narrative and identity. A good father, a dutiful son, a loving husband, a trustworthy friend, and an accomplished spy: he is, at times, all of these things as well as none of them. Lost behind the masks and impostures he effects as part of his job, he discovers that his consummate ability to cast for others "the perfect picture of a face" (12) carries with it a heavy price: the dissolution of self-coherence. Working as an undercover "ethnic operative" for Glimmer and Co., an intelligence firm specializing in the accumulation and exchange of information, Henry eventually confronts "the magnificent and horrifying level of [his own] virtuosity" (150) in all areas of his life. That confrontation, provoked by the death of his son, his wife's subsequent decision to leave him, and his interactions with councilman John Kwang, forces Henry to deal with the extent to which his identity is the result of his own performative choices as well as the role his American education has taught him to play.

Ultimately, Henry discovers that he is both victim and perpetrator of the crimes he commits. Before he can own up to the ways in which his many betrayals lead to a self-betrayal, Henry must wrestle with the histories that shape him: the conditioning that teaches him his "truest place in the culture" is as a spy; the practice of imposture that problematizes the "authenticity" he craves; and the difficult mastery of linguistic fluency. His engagement with these dilemmas implicates him in a romantic notion of identity as the final mask that will not fall away even as they mark him as a cultural informant whose acts of "serial identity" foreground the impossibility of ever fully removing the masks he wears. As Henry discerns the paradoxical truth, that the masks he wears prevent him from speaking even as they are the very things that enable him to articulate a semblance of self, readers of *Native Speaker* discover that Lee's novel itself operates behind the mask of the spy story in order to expose the limitations of form in narrating Henry's story . . . but also to acknowledge the important role conventions play in dictating the stories by which we know ourselves and others.

Rewriting the Story, Recasting the Spy

Henry is a spy but his story is not a "spy story" in the conventional sense. Although Eric Ambler claims that the only ingredient one needs to create a spy story is a protagonist who happens to be a spy, critical discussions of the genre detail the importance of a number of conventions in the construction and consumption of the spy story. As is the case with all formula fiction, the spy story relies on a set of well-defined narrative formulas for its shape and meaning. Marty Roth argues that, unlike the conventions of "literature," which "are regarded as scaffolding," conventions in spy and detective fiction are "the crucial relays of meaning and pleasure" (10). These generic conventions extend beyond subject matter to include the style and structure of the narrative, the social positioning of the protagonist, the ways in which the plot unfolds, and the functions of conspiracy, suspense, and resolution. With "its own methods of plot construction, characteristic techniques of presentation, and a code of ethical values peculiar to itself" (Murch 11), spy fiction exists as a form whose meaning and pleasure derive from a relatively strict adherence to the formulas with which it is associated and which its readers both expect and demand.[1]

In writing the story of Henry Park, Lee rearticulates the standard concerns of the spy story—a fascination with the trope of undetectability; an exploration of the license and voyeuristic thrills that characterize the "fantasy of invisibility"; the double plot of detection; and the presentation of the spy as a storyteller, the story a paradigm for the processes of reading and writing—to accommodate the inflections of race on the spy's invisibility as well as to expose the failure of the conventions to narrate the story of such a spy. *Native Speaker* begins its rewriting of genre by examining the spy's authorial agency and revealing the ways in which recasting the spy necessitates rewriting the spy story. Henry's Korean background proves valuable to his boss, Dennis Hoagland, who

> constantly bemoaned the fact that Americans generally made the worst spies. Mostly he meant whites. Even with methodical training they were inclined to run off at the mouth, make unnecessary displays of themselves, unconsciously slip in the tiniest flourish that could scare off a nervous contact. . . . They felt this subcutaneous aching to let everyone know they were a spook. (160)

Henry's lack of flamboyance, the quality that makes him an excellent mole, is also ironically what makes him an unconventional spy hero. However unrealistic, one of the genre's primary conventions involves the nature of the protagonist as hero and the representation of his mission as dangerous and exciting. Ian Fleming's James Bond, whose espionage practice is characterized almost entirely by the "unnecessary displays" that Hoagland despises, is perhaps the best-known example of such an agent. While it would seem that 007's excessive displays make him a bad spy because they are so at odds with the secret agent's injunction to be unnoticed, what makes James Bond a bad spy in reality is precisely what makes him a popular fictional character. Citing the "non-mimetic" nature of the spy thriller as its most distinguishing characteristic, Bruce Merry argues that the literary representation of espionage activity almost never "corresponds to the known and ascertainable facts about real-life spy networks and intelligence operations" (1). As Somerset Maugham notes, "The work of an agent in the Intelligence department is on the whole monotonous. A lot of it is uncommonly useless. The material it offers for stories is scrappy and pointless; the author has himself to make it coherent, dramatic, and probable" (qtd. in Merry 47).

Glimmer and Co. specializes in the accumulation of information, and the methods Henry uses to obtain his intelligence are decidedly unromantic. The set-pieces of the popular spy story are curiously absent: there are no flagrant disguises, no hairsbreadth escapes, no specialized technologies at use.[2] Henry employs only a computer, which he uses to record indiscriminate literary snapshots of his subjects. He represents himself as detached from his literary production, fulfilling his charge "to be a clean writer, of the most reasonable eye, and present the subject in question like some sentient machine of transcription" (189). In essence, he is commissioned to provide *nothing but* the "scrappy" and "pointless" material of which Maugham speaks, cautioned not to give his reports too much shape or "drama." Henry's efforts to remove himself from his narratives emblematize as well as perpetuate his lack of agency as an Asian American spy. In order to find voice and expression, Henry must move away from his position as "a clean writer" and acknowledge his own investments in the stories he writes.

Jack Kalantzakos, Henry's sole friend at Glimmer and Co., signifies both the conventions that Lee wishes to rewrite as well as the lack of authorial agency Henry experiences as one of Hoagland's ethnic operatives. Jack's story is a textbook example of the representational conventions of the spy story. His history, which Henry concedes could very well be fabricated, reads as if straight out of a spy thriller:

> Hoagland told me how Jack had been abducted in Cyprus by a red insurgent faction in sixty-four. At the time he was working piecemeal for the CIA. In Cyprus, Hoagland said, Jack's captors decided they were going to

break every bone in his body with a small hammer, from the toes up. Then they would put a bullet in his brain. They started the job but stopped when someone crashed a donkey cart into the bottom of the house. The way Hoagland tells it, when they went down to deal with the ruckus, Jack struggled with his guard, shot and killed him, then dragged himself onto the roof and flagged down a policeman from a prone position. (25)

This brief biography depicts Jack as a hero who refuses to compromise or sacrifice his mission. It presents spy work as dangerous and operates according to the basic conventions of the genre, including a prolonged torture scene which, despite its grisly threat, allows the hero just enough time to kill his captors and avoid death. Notably, Jack's story is narrated by Henry's boss. By punctuating the narrative with a number of reminders that the story is the product of Hoagland's telling, Henry foregrounds the narrative's fictionality, thus emphasizing the distinctions between spy and storyteller, tale and representation. In addition to providing the reader with a trenchant example of the conventional spy story and the representational process by which it comes to assume an expected form, this biographical vignette foregrounds Jack's lack of agency in the writing of his own story.

Henry himself demonstrates an extended knowledge of his reader's generic expectations from the very beginning of his own story. In fact, he begins the narrative with a warning that our expectations, expectations that have been shaped by the nature of the genre and the conventions inherent to it, will not be met.[3] Cautioning us that he and his fellow operatives "weren't the kind of figures you naturally thought of or maybe even hoped existed" (15), Henry goes on to refute, quickly and concisely, all of the popular conventions structuring the spy story:

We pledged allegiance to no government. We weren't ourselves political creatures. We weren't patriots. Even less, heroes. We systematically overassessed risk, made it a bad word. Guns spooked us. Jack kept a pistol in his desk but it didn't work. We knew nothing of weaponry, torture, psychological warfare, extortion, electronics, supercomputers, explosives. Never anything like that. (15)

By thus casting himself as an anti-heroic protagonist, Henry rewrites one of the basic rules of the spy story. Such a rewriting is rendered necessary by virtue of his compromised social positioning as a "virtual" American. Although the spy is always marked by his status as an outsider, the transformation of what Jerry Palmer identifies as the spy hero's "insider-outsider" status into a condition that more closely resembles the "total outsider" positioning usually associated with the villain of the genre allows Lee to figure Henry as a highly ironic and self-conscious narrator.[4]

Since irony involves a "signaling of difference at the very heart of similarity" (Hutcheon, *Irony's Edge* 26), the reader's familiarity with a genre's forms and conventions leads to "conventions [being] paradoxically functional in the disintegration of . . . genre" (Tani 43).[5] Henry ironizes the conventions of the genre throughout *Native Speaker* by highlighting the readerly expectations created by the spy story. He parodies the improvisational adventure associated with spy work, noting that the while a "camera . . . installed behind the mirror[ed door]" at Glimmer and Co. was monitored by the office secretary via video screen, "no one had ever shown up unexpectedly" (26). He mocks Hoagland's office rituals, critiquing the "thespian formality" that governs their meetings even though the meetings to drop off information between agents are "always routine and uneventful" (295). Hoagland's operational strategies, which include a distrust of the mails, a penchant for sending unknown couriers who "display an edge, some suspicion" (295), and a special fondness for using his own name as a code phrase during transactions, are parodic reenactments of popular ideas regarding the practice of the secret agent. Given the lack of danger characterizing the work performed by Glimmer and Co., the scenarios mimic, in an excessive and theatrical fashion, the conventions of the genre.

However, even as Henry pushes his readers to acknowledge the expectations they bring to his story by parodying the established representational practices governing the genre, he also admits to the allure of conventional representation. Linda Hutcheon, elaborating on the observations of Hayden White, states that irony's "transideological nature" means that "irony can and does function tactically in the service of a wide range of political positions, legitimating or undercutting a wide variety of interests" (*Irony's Edge* 10). The ambivalence of positionality made possible by the ironic mode informs Henry's wry notice of his own attraction to the very conventions he ironizes. While watching a "new technothriller" replete with "laser-guided weapons, gunboats" and "[m]uscular agents," he thinks of Jack and embellishes upon Hoagland's narrative by "imagin[ing] Jack in Cyprus, both knees broken, blood gluing his teeth, taking aim and shooting his young captor in the eye while lying on the ground" (227, 228). Although Henry professes a distaste for the movie, his fantasies about Jack's past exploits triggered by watching the film mark his own susceptibility to the romance of conventional representation. His mocking awareness of the invincibility of the film's hero is, in turn, parodied by the gymnastics of his own imagination forcing him to concede that "[i]n our fictions, a lucky shot saves your life" (228).

Disappearing Acts

Henry is at pains to distance himself from the spy hero. The unheroic nature of his daily work and his inability to divorce his personal problems from his professional obligations make him an unlikely candidate for such a role. Nonetheless, his own participation in the construction of "*our* fictions" reveals a fascination with the exploits and abilities of such a figure. According to John G. Cawelti and Bruce A. Rosenberg, the secret agent protagonist is an immensely popular mythical hero (2). Such popularity stems not only from the spy's role as facilitator of the reader's secret desires and fears, but also from the power afforded by a "fantasy of invisibility":

> The spy is invisible in a number of senses: he is the secret observer who, himself unseen, watches through a peephole or, in our modern technological age, through a telescope or some electronic device; he is invisible in the sense that his commission as a spy frees him from responsibility and gives him license to do things he could not ordinarily do without serious consequences . . . These aspects of invisibility—voyeurism, self-concealment, and license—clearly have a powerful attraction quite apart from the purpose that they are intended to serve. (13)

The invisibility of the spy hero delineated by Cawelti and Rosenberg results in a license that may allow him to kill and otherwise transgress the boundaries of social policy that constrain the rest of society. Henry feels destined to engage in spying because he considers his marginal position in American culture as one that easily translates into the spy's marginalized status as "the secret observer." The qualities that make Henry a good spy are the result of his successful racialization; his history as "the obedient, soft-spoken son" within his family and the invisible Asian Other in American society prepare him to move unseen when he wishes.

Despite his ability to perform the disappearing acts required of a spy, Henry discovers that the spy's empowering positionality is confounded when the invisibility of the spy coincides with the in/visibilities of race. Cawelti's and Rosenberg's characterization of the "fantasy of invisibility" as liberating figures invisibility as a mode of awareness and control, a position of power from which the spy is able to manipulate and observe others. This emphasis on the powerful aspects of invisibility is further developed by Peggy Phelan in *Unmarked: The Politics of Performance* (1993), her study of the ideology of the invisible. Phelan argues for a reconsideration of the political emphasis on visibility and the corresponding implication that invisibility is characterized by impotency.[6] Contending that visibility is, as often as not, a trap that "summons surveillance and the law . . . [and] provokes voyeurism, fetishism, the colonialist/imperial appetite for possession" (6), Phelan emphasizes the liberating possibilities of invisibility by encouraging an exploration of being "unmarked, unspoken, and unseen" (7).

Although Phelan identifies a number of critically important insights regarding the imbrications between the "given to be seen" and the careful blindnesses that demarcate it, her discussion of the unmarked fails to take into account the fissures that problematize any easy correspondence between that which we cannot see and that which is unmarked. Despite the potential of "the unmarked [to] summon the other eye to see what the mark is blind to—what the given to be seen fails to show, what the other cannot offer" (32), being invisible is not necessarily the same as being unmarked. As Lee's novel makes clear, it is indeed possible to be invisible and yet still bear the marks of that erasure. Such a condition is one of in/visibility, where the hypervisibility of race is the precondition for the ways in which one is misseen or unseen. For all of Henry's performative forays into the realm of invisibility, his enactment of the "active disappearance" that constitutes Phelan's unmarking leaves an imprint that cannot simply be shrugged off: "My years with [Hoagland] and the rest of them, even good Jack, had somehow colored me funny, marked me" (19).

The marks that Henry cannot shrug off are the direct result of the complicated in/visibility he bears. He discovers that his in/visibility is not privileged in the ways that Cawelti, Rosenberg, and Phelan argue. Unlike the performers of which Phelan writes, Henry cannot simply "give up the mark." His marks, contoured on his face and lodged in his over-careful speech, are ones that cannot be voluntarily relinquished. Henry, burdened by his "difficult face," operates within a visual economy wherein being visible is the precondition for his in/visibility. While the power of the spy is predicated upon an aptitude for exploiting his invisibility, the license granted the spy occupying the position of "the secret observer who [is] himself unseen" eludes Henry, whose position is more akin to that of the voyeur at the keyhole who is himself confronted by *"le regard"* or "an awareness of himself-as-spectacle" (Silverman 164). According to Kaja Silverman, "[t]he voyeur's apprehension of his own specularity . . . leads to the discovery . . . that he 'exists for the Other' " (165). Henry's position as a minority subject compels his awareness of the ways in which his professional voyeurism shadows how he himself is observed and defined. The power of the gaze has been understood as coextensive with the power to limit and define. David Palumbo-Liu argues that the gaze grants "the dominant Other . . . one power inaccessible to the minority Self—it can withhold . . . possibilities [of self-definition] and foist upon the minority Self a set of predetermined and necessarily limited sites of representation" (76).

Henry's entry into espionage is certainly the result of the limitations he feels imposed upon him, a matter of exploiting one of the "predetermined sites of representation" to which he feels constrained:

> I had always thought that I could be anyone, perhaps several anyones at once. But Dennis Hoagland and his private firm had conveniently appeared at the right time, offering the perfect vocation for the person I was, someone who could reside in his one place and take half-steps out whenever he wished. For that I felt indebted to him for my life . . . for I thought I had finally found my truest place in the culture. (118)

His talents as a spy depend upon the cultural negotiations he learns as a Korean American. Marked as a foreigner although he is American by birth, Henry is familiar with "that secret living" demanded from those who are not seen as "native." And significantly, he sees his entry into Glimmer and Co. as one granting that experience "a bizarre sanction" (163). Working as a spy, Henry feels the useful conjoining of his life experience with his professional interests. His outsider status and the alienation that delimit his cultural position as an "American" are precisely the qualities that his spymaster values.

Unlike the white Americans characterized by Hoagland, Henry feels no compunction about staying in the background. He grows up experiencing a feeling of doubleness, his self-observation a manifestation of the ways in which he senses his in/visibility.[7] Looking in the mirror and practicing his elocution, Henry remembers the double consciousness that prevents him from believing in his own ability to speak easily and without accent: "When I was young I'd look in the mirror and address it, as if facing the boy there; I would say something dead and normal, like, 'Pleased to make your acquaintance,' and I could barely convince myself that it was I who was talking" (167). In his father's grocery store, the lesson of his in/visibility—the impossibility that he could break out of the preconceived ideas about who he was and might be—is meted out in non-confrontations with the customers who "didn't seem to see [him]" and "didn't look at [him]" because he "was a comely shadow who didn't threaten them" (49).

Henry's anger over the in/visibility that encourages a customer to call his family "Oriental Jews" while standing right behind him finds no release in physical or verbal confrontation. Unlike the narrator of Ellison's *Invisible Man*, whose anger about his invisibility as a Black man is vented, however momentarily or unsuccessfully, in a physical attack on the man he bumps into on the street, Henry is schooled in restraint. Witness to his father's nightly frustration, vented only after he comes home, with men who cheat him and degrade him, Henry is taught to endure and persevere. His mother's patient example; his father's stoicism in the face of provocation; the cipheric blankness of Ahjuhma, the Korean housekeeper who enters the Park household after the death of Henry's mother—all encourage him to accept the definitions that others have of him. As an adult, Henry begins to understand how his upbringing has taught him to accept the social determinations of his identity. He comes to believe that by "misapply[ing] what our parents taught us" (180), Asians exist "silent in our guises" and play the roles that others cast for them, no matter how uncomfortable the performance or how inaccurate the perception.

A history of self-effacement prepares Henry for his performances as a spy. Hoagland requires the impossible: self-effacement so complete that the spy becomes nothing but a camera eye, recording without the subjectivity of interpretation. In his work for Glimmer and Co., Henry must dissect his subjects and present them for analysis, neat packages of information from which strategic decisions might be made. He specializes in sterile deconstructions—a fact that is reflected in his reports, which are "exemplary."

Henry seeks to pinpoint the essence of a man's identity by stripping his own prose of interpretive nuances:

> In the commentary, I won't employ anything that even smacks of theme or moral. I will know nothing of the crafts of argument or narrative or drama. Nothing of beauty or art. And I am to stay on the uncomplicated task of rendering a man's life and ambition and leave to the unseen experts the arcana of human interpretation. The palmistry, the scriptology, the rest of their esoterica. The deep science. (189)

Although Henry represents his task as "uncomplicated" and purports to be good at it, he must eventually acknowledge that it is not so easy—in fact, impossible—to transcribe without narrative or interpretation. To help him maintain, as much as possible, his pose as "a clean writer" and prevent the possibility of his own biases and judgments getting in the way of performing the role of "the most reasonable eye," his superiors never divulge to him the reasons behind his missions. Rather than looking for particular details, Henry's undercover assignments involve recording all and leaving "the arcana of human interpretation" to others. Significantly, those to whom such a task falls, the "unseen experts," are those whom even Henry cannot perceive, elusive by virtue of the fact that their invisibility renders them immune to the scrutinizing gaze they train on their subjects as well as those they employ.

The distinctions between the spy's invisibility and Henry's in/visibility are confirmed by the multiple betrayals that lead to John Kwang's downfall. Henry's identification with and admiration for Kwang begin to compromise his effectiveness. After Kwang's campaign headquarters are bombed, Henry writes a report that identifies Glimmer and Co. as a probable suspect. In effect, he sends a warning to Hoagland, informing him that "whatever I was giving him should be considered, for his purposes, to be suspect, mistold prose. Perhaps you can't trust Henry Park, I wanted him to think, you can't abide anymore what he now sees and says" (268). In the end, Henry discovers that he has been in Hoagland's sights all along. When he discovers that Kwang himself is responsible for the firebombing, an act of revenge targeted against another spy who has infiltrated the campaign, Henry realizes that Hoagland must have had "many minions and pawns surrounding a case, a swarm invisible even to the spy" (292). While he operates blindly, unaware of who else might be involved in Hoagland's operations, Hoagland has occupied a vantage point from which he might engineer the ways in which Henry "might effect [his] own undoing, all along contriving to witness and test [his] discipline and loyalty" (292).

Acknowledging the psychological damages of in/visibility, *Native Speaker* is a meditation about fractured identity, the loss of internal coherence, and the longing for a wholeness that is ever deferred, ever impossible to attain. Ultimately, Henry recognizes that his impostures and false acts as a spy have come to mark him personally: he is a man whose very identity is in question. The list that Lelia leaves Henry at the beginning of the novel, "visions of [him] in the whitest raw light" (1), is meant as a compass by which he might realize how far away he has drifted from her and from the person she wishes him to be.[8] However, Lelia's careful compilation reveals nothing concrete, mapping only the shadowy outline of a man whose (pre)occupation with serial identity renders him no longer able to distinguish between "real" and "fake" performances—even when those performances are ones of his own staging. Without the ability to figure out what makes each act of impersonation a false act founded upon a "true ontological bearing," Henry feels cut off from the identities he would claim as his own.

Spying the Native Speaker

Henry's paradoxical distance and proximity to the identities, both personal and professional, he would claim are signaled by Lee's focus on the figure of the native speaker. As its title suggests, *Native Speaker* is deeply invested in the examination of linguistic fluency. Stylistically, the novel evinces an absorption with the texture of language and its evocative potential. Lee writes elegantly, his carefully measured phrases displaying a rhetorical polish that belies Henry's professional injunction to fashion his own prose using "nothing of the crafts of argument or narrative or drama. Nothing of beauty or art" (189). While the lyricism of the prose is unquestioned, Verlyn Klinkenborg's review for *The New Yorker* notes that it is at cross-purposes with the narrative pacing usually characteristic of a spy novel: ". . . the pleasure of *Native Speaker* [is] also its problem. Henry Park will declaim to himself on any occasion, and the result is usually wonderful, instructive. . . . But every sentence is a climax and an understatement, a *koan* of his own. It's the right language for insight, for revelation, even for threats, but it's the wrong language for telling a spy story" (77).[9] While *Native Speaker*'s language may be wrong for the telling of a conventional spy story, its flourishes and digressions are exactly right for representing the contradictions and coincidences that characterize Henry's position as both a spy and a non-native speaker.

Native Speaker is very much interested in how stories are told. Just as Lee rewrites and redeploys the conventions of the spy story in order to relate Henry's story, Henry must himself learn to write against the narrative formulas he has inherited. In spite of his claim that he is "the secret writer of all moments imminent" (185), Henry tends to relinquish authorial agency to those around him. His long practice of serial identity renders him curiously willing to play the roles that others would have him play; his talent for mimicry makes him the student who strives to compose his subjects (and himself) according to the definitions he has been given.

In trying to master language and its potential for articulating a self and an identity, Henry must first learn to negotiate a cultural legacy of silence learned from his parents. His domestic schooling in relationships contributes to the "intricate and open-ended emotional conspiracies" (16) that he eventually contrives as a spy. While those professional conspiracies are perpetrated in order to allow Henry a vantage point from which to "write out" the identities of his subjects, Henry ironically allows those close to him to write out his identity. Before Henry can deal with the effects of his personal and professional betrayals, he must determine how to narrate outside the boundaries and conventions that others have set for him, to acknowledge the complexity of a "larger narrative" that encompasses contradiction and irresolution.

Although Henry's story spills outside the boundaries of his relationship with his wife, his marriage to Lelia symbolizes his general willingness to let someone else determine who he is. When they first meet as strangers at a party, Lelia is excited by the novelty of Henry's knack for being simultaneously inscrutable to her gaze and reflective of her desires. She immediately deciphers him as "not a native speaker" (11).[10] While she feels confident in making this pronouncement on the basis of the fact that Henry "looks like someone listening to himself" (11), she is later unable to discern how he is responding to their first kiss.[11] His inscrutability arouses her, and significantly, her arousal provides Henry with the information he needs in order to perform into existence a man she would desire:

> I did something then that I didn't know I could do. It was strangely automatic. Instantly I was thinking of the lover she might want, the man whom she'd searched out but hadn't yet found in her life. . . . I put myself in her place and imagined her father and mother. Boyfriends, recent loves. I made those phantom calculations, did all that blind math so that I might cast for her the perfect picture of a face. (12)

His blankness turns him into a screen for her desire and the face he casts for her is not so much a false one as it is only partially his. His eagerness to become "an impeccable mate" by performing into existence the man she initially wishes him to be is precisely what turns Lelia against him. Eventually, she sees this early moment in their relationship as emblematic of her inability to know him and of his underlying refusal to speak truly. His acceptance of her evaluations about his identity, their marriage, and his response to their son's tragic death causes her to leave.

Although Henry purports to be able to create multiple identities for himself, he actually depends upon others to sketch the shape of his identity, which he then fills in according to his training. This tendency to rely on others to determine who he might and should be at any given time proves problematic when Lelia demands that he "be himself" after Mitt suffocates to death at the bottom of an impromptu dogpile at his own birthday party. The practice of continually being someone else renders him somehow "inauthentic" and when Henry does not voice his grief over his son's tragedy, Lelia cannot accept that his pain might be real, that he might express truthfully his anguish over the death of their son. The list that Lelia gives Henry when she leaves emblematizes Henry's lack of agency. Although she claims the list to be neither "exhaustive" nor "complete," its very compilation marks the ways in which her perceptions—of Henry and their marriage—dominate their relationship. The list describes him unflatteringly as, among other things, "stranger, follower, traitor, [and] spy" (5), but the charge Henry feels most deeply is one found written on a scrap of paper underneath the bed: *"False speaker of language"* (5). Yet rather than contest Lelia's characterizations of him, Henry accepts her assessment as his due, the necessary price exacted by professional secrecy bleeding into personal relationship.

Henry's sensitivity to that final accusation—"False speaker of language"—denotes the importance of his struggles with language, belonging, and the attempt to write and speak an identity that will somehow prove "true" in the face of his deceits and betrayals. In *Native Speaker*, the writing of a self is intertwined with the ways in which both language and silence constitute subjectivity. Just as his ability to do the "blind math" that would make him into Lelia's ideal partner when they first meet is the logical result of a childhood spent practicing the roles that others would have him perform, his silence after Mitt's death is the result of an apprenticeship in restraint. Raised as "the obedient son," Henry's parents inculcate him into a narrative characterized by a "fine and terrible ordering . . . [which] casts you as the golden child, the slave-son or daughter, the venerable father, the long-dead god" (6). Such a family drama brooks no wayward gestures or rebellious refusals to play one's given part, even as it also provides a "basic comfort . . . where the relation abides no argument, no questions or quarrels" (6).

Whatever comfort Henry derives from his familial role(s) is accompanied by an anxious negotiation of the silence he grows up with and the language he struggles to master. While he professes that "[o]ur mode at the firm was always to resist history, at least our own" (25), Henry discovers that such resistance is indeed difficult. Henry sees his upbringing as one which encourages him to "depend too often on the faulty honor of silence, use it too liberally and for gaining advantage" (88). His mother's "exquisite control" over her facial muscles, her "subtle power of inflection over them, the way a tongue can move air" (28), teaches Henry to speak through gesture, nuance, and bodily articulation. "She believed that displays of emotion signaled a certain failure between people" (28), and this lesson is impressed most forcefully upon Henry by her death. After her demise, his father "seemed instantly recovered" (54); there is no discussion of their mutual suffering. Instead, ten-year-old Henry is left to wonder whether he cries alone. He attempts to glean some insight into his father's feelings through those moments they share in restaurants, "both of us eating without savor, unjoyous, and my wanting to show him that I could be as steely as he, my chin as rigid and unquivering as any of his displays, that I would tolerate no mysteries either, no shadowy wounds or scars of the heart" (54). Despite the pain and incomprehension he remembers experiencing as a result of such behavior, Henry continues to practice an outward stoicism with Lelia: after Mitt dies, he follows his father's example by "show[ing] Lelia how this was done, sometimes brutally, my face a peerless mask, the bluntest instrument" (88).

The stoic displays of his father at the dinner table produce in Henry a sense of constant emotional confusion burdened by the "shadowy wounds" that are no less painful for being unseen. In a home where "[e]ven the most minor speech seemed trying" (119), Henry necessarily acquires a performative repertoire in order to communicate with his father:[12]

> To tell [my father] I loved him, I studied far into the night. I read my entire children's encyclopedia, drilling from aardvark to zymurgy. I never made an error at shortstop. I spit-shined and brushed his shoes every Sunday morning. Later, to tell him something else, I'd place a larger bouquet than his on my mother's grave. I drove only used, beat-up cars. I never asked him for his money. I spoke volumes to him this way, speak to him still, those same volumes he spoke with me. (119)

The "volumes" spoken in the Park household disturb Henry, partly because they force him into a mode of performance that he finds uncomfortable, and partly because he grows up without fully understanding the nuances of the "troubling, expert power" (159) that silence bestows. As King-Kok Cheung has maintained, the "equat[ion of] speech with (self-) expression and silence with passivity" (169) represents a faulty binarism that chooses to ignore the communicative potential of silence, its resources as well as its hazards. Despite an appreciation of the ways in which silence has shaped his own identity, Henry finds himself too often wishing for an opportunity to express the "burning language" that he feels trapped inside him.

Although Henry claims to "celebrate every order of silence borne of the tongue and the heart and the mind" (159), he too perceives silence as hazardous. He grows up not understanding the silences of his parents. As a child, he mistakes his mother not asking his father about the stores as a sign of her disinterest in the particulars of their business. Only later does he learn that his mother's silence is calculated, a tacit acknowledgment of the "true courage and sacrifice" represented by his father's decision to "discard his excellent Korean education and training, which were once his greatest pride, the markings by which he had known himself" (309), and work as a grocer. The silences that govern the Park household are instructive, heralding not only a cultural practice of reticence but also denoting the social and economic restrictions that delimit the possibilities available to immigrants like Henry's parents and native-born sons like Henry himself. Mr. Park shares many of the burdens borne by the "tight-lipped husbands" of Hisaye Yamamoto's stories, men who "are themselves caught in loveless marriages, marooned within the larger society, and, above all, constrained by the patriarchal code of masculinity" (Cheung 46).

Henry fears the ways in which silence can be misinterpreted, misunderstood, and mistaken for blankness. Although he is afraid of how his own silence marks him, Henry himself is guilty of not always being able to interpret the ways in which silence can be "articulate" (Cheung). Ahjuhma, the woman who enters the Park household after the death of Henry's mother, is characterized by a seemingly impenetrable silence. Unlike the unspoken requests and admonitions of his parents, Ahjuhma's quiet is "unnerving" and renders her more alien than Henry can accept. Henry's childhood memories remember her as "some kind of zombie" who "[w]hen she wasn't cleaning or cooking or folding clothes . . . was barely present" (60). Despite Henry's inability to "read" Ahjuhma, he recognizes that her noiseless isolation probably masks a history no less tragic or compelling for remaining unspoken. Just as the protagonist of Maxine Hong Kingston's *The Woman Warrior* (1975) takes her mother's injunction to remain silent as an opportunity to write and rewrite her No-Name Aunt's story into multiple narratives, so Henry excavates the possible histories behind Ahjuhma's silent presence in his home: "I imagined that something deeply horrible had happened to her when she was young, some nameless pain, something brutal, that a malicious man had taught her fear and sadness and she had had to leave her life and family because of it" (60).

In a novel where "language spoken, written, stumbled over, learnt, misunderstood, [and] found wanting" is identified as "the heroine" (Pavey 32), the anxieties Henry experiences as a spy are intimately connected with his relationship to linguistic fluency and his existence as a non-native speaker who tries desperately to overcome that handicap. Henry's attraction to Lelia is fated: her skill in "executing the language, . . . her wide full mouth sweep[ing] through her sentences like a figure touring a dark house, flipping on spots and banks of perfectly drawn light" (9), makes her the ideal to which he aspires when trying to learn the "scabrous mouthful" that is English.[13] For someone whose earliest memories of learning English are of his tongue "struggl[ing] like an animal booby-trapped and dying inside [his] head" (217), Lelia's linguistic mastery is as close as Henry will ever come to achieving the "lowing rhythm of ennui and supremacy" (218) that he both desires and despises. Even more, her work as a speech therapist with immigrant children represents an opportunity to revisit his past encounters with both the promise and difficulty of learning to speak English.

Henry's struggles with silence, language, and authenticity stem from his existence as a non-native speaker of English. Remembering his difficulty in learning English, aware of his susceptibility to "mak[ing] bad errors of speech" because of "mental pathways of speaking that can never be un-learned" (218), Henry longs for "a life univocal" (249). This desire for fluency is undergirded by the power that "purely spoken" English represents to the Park family. In an effort to improve business, Mr. Park urges Henry to show customers "how well I spoke English, to make a display of it, to casually recite 'some Shakespeare words'" (49). Although he eventually attains the "dead and normal" voice of a native speaker, he is forever reminded of the disjunction between Korean and English that lurks beneath his surface mastery: ". . . I always hear myself displacing the two languages, conflating them—maybe conflagrating them—for there's so much rubbing and friction, a fire always threatens to blow up between the tongues" (218). Henry's hope for Mitt—that he would grow up with "a singular sense of his world . . . which might have offered him the authority and confidence that his broad, half-yellow face would not" (249)—is one he has already relinquished for himself. As such, language represents an unattainable self-coherence for Henry, whose ambivalence concerning such "assimilist sentiment" is a result of the ways in which he is formed by his "own ugly and half-blind romance with the land" (249).

The "authority" and "confidence" that Henry sees in linguistic mastery is embodied by the figure of the native speaker. Understood as "a common reference point for all branches of linguistics" and generally regarded as "the gate keeper of authenticity" regarding spoken language, the native speaker is simultaneously the subject and object of formal linguistic inquiry (Coulmas 1; 5). Claire Kramsch suggests that "within the humanities[,] native speakers . . . enjoy a *de facto* authority and prestige that the nonnative lacks" (359). Following Thomas Paikeday's *The Native Speaker is Dead!* (1985), linguists have begun to direct critical scrutiny not only at the idealization of the native speaker as "expert" arbiter of what is grammatically correct and acceptable in a given language, but also at the very construct of the native speaker itself.

Jacob Mey's tongue-in-cheek theorization of the spurious status assigned to the native speaker identifies "King Native Speaker" as a sort of royal figurehead. Mey contends that "King Native Speaker's power is exercised in strict accordance with the directives of his ministers, the wily, seemingly subservient linguists, who in reality wield almost Machiavellian powers" (70). Mey asserts that the foundation for the native speaker's lofty position is shaky. More perceptually convincing than representationally accurate, the concept of native speaker raises the issue of false identity even as it posits the existence of linguistic authority and accuracy. If the distinctions between the *perception* of native speaker's authority and the actual authority that a native speaker who ventriloquizes the linguist's desire wields are indeed operating in any given construction of the native speaker, then does the native speaker not possess an identity which is not his own? Given the constructed nature of the native speaker, the falseness of his identity is based upon more than his illusory determinative capabilities regarding linguistic competence: since "nobody is born a speaker[,] . . . the native speaker is a figment of our imagination" (Mey 70).

The native speaker shares more than the ontological condition of "false" identity with the spy. Exposed as an artificial construction, a helpless figurehead, or even the linguist herself, the native speaker is also an informant. Werner Kummer identifies colonial expansion as the original historical context for the relationship between the linguist and the native speaker. Taking as his example La Malinche, the native woman who proved useful to Cortez not only as a translator but as a spy and a leader of negotiations with high Aztec officials, Kummer argues that "the representative role of informants functioned in the relationship [between linguist and native speakers], not only as deliverers of speech data, but also as 'collaborators' of the colonizers, be it as missionaries, agents furthering the cultural assimilation, translators, representatives of the colonial power in lower governmental positions or colonial intelligentsia" (175). Charged with the gathering and reporting of information, native speakers, like spies, are involved in practices of cultural negotiation and information transfer.

The spy and the native speaker are valued for the information they are able to deliver regarding the communities that spymaster and linguist wish to examine. These similarities between spies and native speakers have been noted by Florian Coulmas, who sees a "perfect command of the language" as a quality shared by those who would be successful spies as well as reliable native speakers. By focusing on the non-native speaker as spy, Coulmas foregrounds the ways in which performance, linguistic and behavioral, affects the spy's success. For such a figure, the issue of pretense is doubly important:

> The spy cannot concentrate on linguistically manifesting his faked identity while disregarding the context of what he says. Neither can he confine his efforts to the unequivocal expression of whatever he has to say. It is not enough that he takes care *what* he says, he must also be on his guard with his accent and, more generally, *how* he says what to whom. His nefarious profession requires him to do all this at the same time, and if he is not able to perform this feat, he surely isn't an ideal spy and hence of little interest for our present discussion. (356)

The two levels of performance of which the spy must be aware—contextual and ontological—are heightened when the linguistic dimension of the non-native speaker's performance is factored into the spy's enactments. Henry himself occupies a linguistic no-man's-land. Caught between being a native speaker and a non-native speaker, Henry finds himself interpreted and used as both. Despite his English fluency, he is forever marked as a non-native speaker by his tendency to "say *riddle* for *little,* or *bent* for *vent*" (218). For Hoagland and those who hire Henry to infiltrate the Asian American community, Henry is considered a "native," someone who can exploit the "minor power we can have over each other, that exercise of influence and duty which we know from our families, our fathers" (238). Lee refashions the native speaker's domain. In addition to mastering language, Henry must acquire a bodily syntax and grammar in order to gain access to those he seeks to betray.

As Coulmas makes clear, the linguistic dimension of a spy's enactments is predicated upon a heightened notion of realistic performance. Ironically, such realism is itself based upon a foundation of duplicity. While the spy's deceit stems from his impersonations and the native speaker deceptively represents linguistic authority and accuracy, the linguist's complicity in sustaining the fiction of the native speaker makes him analogous to the secret agent: "It is not only that every scientist is something of an investigator. His cunning and capacity to attain knowledge should not be inferior to that of a spy. Clearly, knowing how to perform properly is what the spy is after . . . Both linguist and spy aim to detect the secrets of the native; the spy in order to copy his skills, the linguist in order to explain them" (Coulmas 365). *Native Speaker* speaks to the multiple performances that constitute Henry as spy, (non)native speaker, and "linguist of the field" (159). In so doing, the novel exposes the complications that problematize the practice of ventriloquization and insists on Henry's complicity in voicing himself in the ways that others would have him speak.

Performing Impersonation

The distinctions between real and fake with which Henry struggles on a daily basis are clearly problematic, especially regarding issues of identity and performance. Henry's confusion about the authenticity of performance, whether the act is one that he performs or one he is paid to "see through," also manifests itself in a professional crisis. While attempting to extract information from Dr. Emile Luzan, a suspected Marcos sympathizer, Henry's pose as Luzan's psychiatric patient comes dangerously close to violating the unseen boundaries that separate his "real" identity from the one that is, ostensibly, "only an act." Before making contact with Luzan, Henry prepares a "legend," an "extraordinarily extensive . . . autobiography [whose . . .] minutiae of life experience . . . required a truthful ontological bearing, a certain presence of character" (20). Although the legend capitalizes on the intimate relationships between "truth" and fiction by marshaling "a truthful ontological bearing" to sustain the force of his fictionalizations, Henry's enactments on Luzan's couch acquire a depth of persuasiveness only achievable when the once self-conscious performer succumbs to his own fictions.

Significantly, Henry's lack of performative self-consciousness is framed as a loss of self. Becoming "dangerously frank, inconsistently schizophrenic" (20), Henry metamorphosizes from impersonating Luzan's patient to actually *becoming* Luzan's patient.[14] The psychiatric sessions take on an air of cathartic confession as the initial irony of Luzan's promise to his "patient"— "You'll be yourself again"—is supplanted by the literalization of such an occurrence. When Henry finds himself "running short of my story, my chosen narrative," he forgoes retreating and revising in favor of "stringing the legend back upon myself . . . looping it through the core [and] freely talking about my life, suddenly breaching the confidences of my father and my mother and my wife. I even spoke to him about a lost dead son" (20).

This failure to maintain the distinction between his "false" identity and his "real" self results in Hoagland pulling him from the case. After ordering Jack to retrieve Henry from his compromised mission with Luzan, Hoagland deems it necessary to recalibrate Henry's performative technique before sending him out to report on John Kwang:

> I need you to work carefully through your legend with Jack before you come back to me with it. . . . You're coming off a tough loss with that shrink and we're all pulling for you. . . . What happened to you has happened to all of us once. That shrink only got to you because he believed in you so fully. You were giving a fantastic performance. You were never better than in those sessions. . . . Christ, *I* even wanted to help you with your problems. *I kept forgetting why you were there.* You were brilliant. (38; emphasis mine)

Hoagland's admonishment contains equal measures of praise and caution about the "brilliance" of Henry's performance, his disappointment at Henry's inability to execute successfully his directive concerning Luzan tempered by an appreciation of the overwhelming believability inspired by Henry's enactment. Hoagland's assessment of the situation pinpoints both the pleasures as well as the dangers of theatrical realism. Not only does Luzan, the uninformed audience for Henry's act, believe fully in what Henry tells him, Henry himself and even Hoagland are drawn into the authenticity of what is being presented. By "forgetting why you were there," spy and spymaster lose the frame of reference that makes the impersonation less "real" than the narrative injunction sustaining any life story. Clearly, the category of what Phelan identifies as "the Real-real" is predicated upon the unseen assumptions of authority that "contain within [them] a meta-text of exclusionary power" (3). Therein lies the danger of forgetting which reality is *the* authentic one.

The desire for authenticity can overwhelm. The temptation of the "Real-real" exists both as form and function. In theatrical performance, realism has been decried as a dangerous practice, primarily because of its potential to interpellate an audience into a passive subject position. The potential of realism to imprison a spectator's imagination stems not only from the vision of authenticity and authority that it presents to an audience but also from the methods of representation it employs. Thus, critics have identified the dramatic conventions associated with realism as ones that subtly compel the spectator to occupy a viewing position that implicitly accepts the "truth" of that which is presented. And while realism itself is not necessarily a politically suspect mode of theatrical performance, critics maintain that it can be alarmingly persuasive because of its tendency to naturalize its subject and perspective. According to Josephine Lee, the

> argument [against theatrical realism] is not so much with its formal or representational qualities as with the more subtle coercion of perception that informs it. Although realism purports to be a faithful representation of ordinary life, it is in fact a more complex ideological practice, a manufacturing rather than a mirroring of some construct of "real life." . . . Recent reassessments of realism have been most critical of the ways in which realism calls . . . for a particular relationship between the spectator and the stage event. (34)

The nature of the "relationship between the spectator and the stage event" that has undergone critical reassessment, particularly by feminist theater critics, is predicated upon the assumption of a specific kind of spectator and characterized by a certain level of intimacy and trust.[15] The alchemy of belief created by theatrical performance involves a spectator who enters a theatrical space prepared to witness an illusion but, nonetheless, is seduced into belief. Although feminist critiques of theatrical realism emphasize the vulnerability of the spectator, the realism of Henry's performances is doubly threatening: in addition to commanding the belief of his witnesses, witting and unwitting, he also manages to lose himself in his roles. While the illusions of performance are usually thought to be directed at the spectators who witness it, they can prove seductive to the unvigilant actor as well. Time and again, Henry succumbs to the illusions of his own performances, his confused role-playing with both Emile Luzan and John Kwang a mark of his inability to separate the fictions of his enactments from those acts that he deems reflective of his "real" identity.

Henry's difficulty in distinguishing the performance of identity from that which is ostensibly "real" problematizes his initial belief that masks can be taken off, facades stripped away to reveal the concrete foundations that structure who we are. When Henry begins reworking his legend during his psychiatric sessions with Luzan, he considers his personal confessions a sign of his "real" identity breaking through his act. However, the legend itself, which is based on the "ontological truth" of who he "really" is, is a performative framework that capitalizes on the theatrical practice of "utiliz[ing] everyday objects, situations and people as raw material . . . to construct fictions that by employing these materials have an unusual claim upon actuality" (Carlson 53). Rather than simply substituting a fiction for reality, Henry's impersonations "are neither totally 'real' nor totally 'illusion' but share aspects of each" (Carlson 53).

This commingling of reality and illusion speaks to the complicated issues of authenticity that undergird Henry's performances of self.[16] Although Henry yearns for a "singular sense of the world" (249), he embodies what Jean-Louis Barrault identifies as "the problem of the double": "In man there is a double position: the first one is real, visible, palpable; the second is impalpable, only apprehended, present, yes, but invisible—that is the double. . . . The human being that [theater] brings to life on the stage is, in fact, *as double as he can be*" (121–22). According to Hillel Schwartz in *The Culture of the Copy* (1996), impostures such as Henry's are "never far from theater" (69). Characterized by a drama of "seamlessness[,] . . . . imposture is the incessant Siamesing of one's life. It is compulsive, it feeds upon itself, it is unrepentant" (69–70). Henry discovers that impostures can take on a life of their own and the impostor can become a victim of his own double agency.

Henry's impostures effect an intimacy that undermines the spy's mimicry even as they exploit the spectator's guilelessness. Without the explicit framing of performance provided by theatrical presentation, Henry's enactments collapse the psychological and physical distance between spectator and performer. In the process, Henry becomes enmeshed in the complexities of his own performance; he is a performer who leaves behind the self-consciousness of impersonation to embrace the seamless transformation of imposture. As Bertolt Brecht suggests in his concept of Alienation *(Verfremdungseffekt),* the distance between spectacle and spectator that foregrounds an audience's awareness of the ideology behind any performance is also what keeps the actor "safe" from his own enactments.[17] This is doubly true in the case of the spy. By insisting on the artificiality of his acts, Henry assures himself of a discrete and yet-unviolated ontological core, an identity that remains somehow "real." However, each act of imposture heralds a paradox: only by first losing himself in his performances with Luzan and Kwang can Henry "find" himself. Imposture teaches Henry "to look at [his] life not just from a singular mode but through the crucible of a larger narrative" and in so doing, he learns to appreciate the nuances that trouble his original notions of truth and authenticity: "Is this what I have left . . . ? That I no longer can simply flash a light inside a character, paint a figure like Kwang with a momentary language, but that I know the greater truths [that] reside in our necessary fictions spanning human event and time?" (192).

Detecting the Asian American Agent

Like Henry, Lee acknowledges in his work with genre the ways in which "greater truths" are concealed in his "necessary fictions." The necessary fictions with which Lee engages in *Native Speaker* are manifold. As a careful reading reveals, Lee's novel writes both with and against a variety of disparate textual and representational legacies: the thematization of racial invisibility offered by the African American literary tradition; the ongoing literary revisions of the generic conventions of spy and detective fiction by minority and women writers; and the development and re-assessment of the figure of the Asian/American as one of stealth and subterfuge.

As Catherine Hong noted in her review for *Vogue*, "[w]ith echoes of Ralph Ellison, Chang-rae Lee's extraordinary debut speaks for another kind of invisible man: the Asian immigrant in America" (236). While Ellison's protagonist is clearly not a spy in the vocational sense, he shares with Henry a thematic preoccupation with the problems and possibilities of racial invisibility. Even so, the figure of the racial minority as spy emerges (or should I say lurks?) in Ellison's text as surely, if not in the same ways structurally, as it does in *Native Speaker*. In a conversation with his grandfather, an ex-slave who was "the meekest of men" and "never made any trouble," the narrator of *Invisible Man* (1952) discovers that underlying the acquiescent exterior his grandfather presents to the world is a keen understanding that "our life is a war and I have been a traitor all my born days, a spy in the enemy's county" (17). Clearly, despite—or rather, *because of*—the "tranquillized mask of subordination" (Accardo and Portelli 78) that the protagonist's grandfather dons, he is able to perform the dangerous role of "a spy in the enemy's country," an operation dependent upon one's ability "to overcome 'em with yesses, undermin 'em with grins, agree 'em to death and destruction, let 'em swoller you till they vomit or bust wide open" (Ellison 17).

In many ways, the kind of double performance proposed in *Invisible*

Man is precisely what Henry is asked to perform on behalf of Glimmer and Co. . . . and what he struggles to learn to enact for himself. Significantly, Lee's metafictional double performance with regard to genre echoes the practice of his protagonist and offers a textual contribution to the work of a number of Ethnic American, women, and gay and lesbian writers who are also seeking to revise the spoken and unspoken conventions dictating the form and meaning of contemporary spy and detective fiction. John G. Cawelti suggests that popular fiction acts as a kind of "social or cultural ritual" ("Concept" 734) that proffers different groups an opportunity to participate in synthesizing divergent values, (re)affirming shared understandings, and exploring new social values or relations; thus, the "creation of representative detective [and spy] heroes has become an important social ritual for minority groups who would claim a meaningful place in the larger social context" (Cawelti, "Canonization" 8).[18] Linda Hutcheon echoes the efficacy of such an engagement with popular form on the part of minority writers who seek to subvert the very forms they utilize when she theorizes that "[p]erhaps the most potent mode of subversion is that which can speak directly to a 'conventional' reader" (*Theory* 202).[19] Although the particularities of how individual minority and women writers have chosen to revise the genre vary, it would be relatively safe to state that the incorporation of "new" content within the "old" form of the spy story or detective fiction by such writers oftentimes results not only in the questioning of form but also in the innovation of the conventions by which formula fiction derives its meaning. As Ellison affirms in *Shadow and Act* (1964), "protest [in art]. . . does not necessarily take the form of speaking for a political or social program. It might appear in a novel as a *technical assault against the styles* which have gone before" (137; emphasis mine).

Although Lee, like many other minority writers, revises many of the conventions of the spy novel to accommodate his Korean American protagonist, the figure of the Asian spy is itself a cultural convention. Stereotyped as sneaky and inscrutable, Asians and clandestinity have proven a particularly compelling combination. The internment of Japanese Americans during World War II was justified by the suspicion that Japanese Americans were secretly working as "spies, saboteurs, and fifth columnists" for the Japanese government (qtd. in Daniels 200).[20] Although no Japanese Americans were ever proven to be enemy spies, the condemnation of the entire Japanese

American community on the basis of such fears represents the material effects of a Yellow Peril mentality that had influenced American responses to Asian immigration since the nineteenth century.[21]

In casting Henry as a professional spy who succeeds by exploiting his own community, Lee presents a provocative thematization of racial in/visibility. The use of espionage as a formal and thematic trope not only highlights the myriad ways in which Asian American bodies have been represented as in/visible but also provides an opportunity for Lee to redress the popular stereotypes of Asian secret agents created by Anglo-American writers. (In)famous sleuths like Charlie Chan, created by Earl Derr Biggers in 1925, and Mr. Moto, the Japanese secret agent invented by John P. Marquand, captured the public imagination with their powers of detection. These two characters are generally considered a response to the figure of Dr. Fu Manchu, whose very name became synonymous with Asian secrecy, cunning, and threat.[22] Marty Roth traces one of the spy thriller's defining characteristics, "a conspiracy of deception or evil" (226), to Sax Rohmer's Yellow Peril romances about the Devil Doctor. The "racist ambivalence" that writers like Lee are addressing when they rework the figure of the Asian spy is identified by Cawelti and Rosenberg as the primary ingredient of the heroic spy story, where "a fascination with alien cultures coexists with an overt fear and condemnation of these cultures" (44).

While a number of contemporary Asian American artists have participated in the project of revising and redeploying the stereotypes of Asian secrecy and cunning through their use of the figure of the Asian American spy or detective, Lee's particular contributions in this area can be demonstrated through a brief comparison with David Henry Hwang's award-winning 1989 Broadway play *M. Butterfly* and Leonard Chang's recent crime novel, *Over the Shoulder: A Novel of Intrigue* (2001).[23] As a discussion of these texts will demonstrate, Lee participates in an on-going conversation with other Asian American writers that explores the nature of Asian/American hypervisibility and challenges the representational forms of popular culture through the secret agent protagonist. As I discussed in chapter 3, *M. Butterfly* joins *Native Speaker* in examining images of Asian invisibility, inscrutability, and stealth by recasting Song Liling as an agent whose spying activities are problematized by as well as contingent upon his racial identity. Like Lee, Hwang suggests that the stereotype about and practice of Asian subterfuge is emblematized by the figure of the Asian/American spy. While Song Liling's flamboyance as a secret agent—his gender masquerade in many ways an "open secret" in the play, his ability to impersonate a female Chinese opera singer contingent on not only his skill in deception but also his partner, Rene Gallimard's, willingness to believe in the fantasy of the submissive Asian woman that he exploits—runs counter to Henry's "silent guise," both Lee and Hwang insist upon the dangerous possibilities of the impersonation of espionage work turning into a debilitating imposture of self. Because Hwang's play attempts to deconstruct the stereotype of the submissive Asian woman, particularly as it was represented in Puccini's opera *Madama Butterfly*, Song's spying does predominantly act as a metaphor through which issues of desire, secrecy, and racial in/visibility can be explored.

In *Over the Shoulder*, many of the same concerns illuminated by *Native Speaker* are taken up and given a different twist. On the surface, the two texts seem remarkably similar: both feature Korean American male protagonists who are trained to capitalize upon their Asian backgrounds to do their jobs as secret and not-so-secret agent; both men face difficult family issues; both authors have been praised for the ways in which they have explored issues of racial assimilation by developing the uncanny conflation of their protagonists' occupations and preoccupations; and both novels have been characterized as "literary" revisions of popular forms. *Native Speaker*, which preceded *Over the Shoulder* by six years, differs from Chang's novel in both the nature and effect of its revision of genre. Chang makes much more visible than Lee his revision of genre: applauded for the ways in which he has produced "an absorbing blend of literary novel and crime thriller" (Zaleski 57), Chang ensures that despite the distinctive characteristics of his protagonist whose "dis-ease" with life (50) manifests itself in a philosophy of *"removement,* the state of being removed from everything" (89), he also includes all of the generic expectations—of plot, of pacing, of technical execution—that conventional readers of thrillers would expect. In contrast, Lee is both more reluctant than Chang to gratify his reader's conventional expectations even as he is more subtle about the ways in which he actively (re)writes the generic conventions whose "absence" is still acknowledged as of critical importance to his novel's meaning.

The genre's inherent fascination with the effects and functions of invisibility paradoxically reinforces as well as opposes the perspectives that minority detectives and secret agents bring to the story. One reviewer of *Native Speaker* applauds the ways in which "the spy's sense of doubleness is doubled by the immigrant's sense of doubleness" (Klinkenborg 77). This redoubling exposes unspoken assumptions about the ways in which race, power, and privilege structure the spy story, often to the point where the story is transformed into a new form whose ironic connection to the old signifies less a reworking of genre than a radical departure from it.[24] This departure may confuse and frustrate readers who misrecognize the new form or simply regard it as a bad attempt to write according to the conventions of the genre. In her review of Lee's novel for *New Statesman & Society,* Ruth Pavey's sole criticism of the text stems from just such a misrecognition: "But was it necessary to add in the spy story as well, fun though it is? Henry is so much more like a writer than a spy; perhaps he could just have been one" (32).

Suggesting that maybe Henry "could just have been" a writer is to miss the implications of Lee's work with genre. As I've argued, Henry's spying is not just a metaphor for his cultural dividedness as a Korean American but also provides an opportunity to examine the complicated negotiation with genre and the conventions of narrative in which both Henry Park and Chang-rae Lee engage. Clearly, the adaptation of the form of the spy story to take into account the exigencies of racial in/visibility is fueled by a skepticism with the genre that finds expression in a number of ways. Henry's wry acknowledgement of the narrative expectations of genre exists alongside a recognition of his own investments in some of the very conventions he decries. Similarly, Lee manifests a complex relationship to the genre: he is drawn to the ways it illuminates the in/visibility of his protagonist even as he writes against the genre to reflect Henry's ontological dilemmas. As such, *Native Speaker*'s ironic treatment of the conventions of the spy story, its subversion of the rules of the genre, render it a kind of postmodern spy story and Henry himself, a man constantly deconstructing the rules by which he plays the game, a kind of postmodern operative. Significantly, while Henry might be seen as a postmodern operative and *Native Speaker* may be read as one version of the postmodern spy story, Lee refuses to abide by the conventions of either genre. The text refuses the clarity of division and categorical distinction, demonstrating a keen awareness of the conventions of both the traditional and postmodern spy story even as it experiments with the assumptions by which conventions work to delimit the genre. In essence, both

Henry as a subject and *Native Speaker* as a text share an ambivalent relationship with the conventions of narrative that embodies the not-so-secret nature of impersonation as a performance of divided allegiance to both authenticity and mimicry.

The spy story shares with the detective novel a divided nature. The protagonist is both a hero and a criminal, the narrative a cover story for the process of uncovering and recovering the secret(s) at the core of the text.[25] On a metatextual level, genre may be bound by convention and also a way of challenging the conventions by which we read. Lee might be drawn to the genre of the spy story because of both its subversive potential and its symbolic status as an important social ritual. His commandeering of the genre for exploring the double-consciousness comprising one aspect of Asian American subject formation in the United States produces exciting new innovations in form and structure.

Henry's awareness of his own double nature highlights the vexed nature of certain distinctions—of self from impersonation, of performance from reality, of spy from spied upon. As part of its deconstructive project, Lee's text emphasizes repeatedly the impossible distinctions between criminal and victim, spy and subject. While Henry may be victimized by his minority status and driven to his debilitating performances as a spy by virtue of his in/visibility, he is also a criminal who betrays those who trust him. He cannot simply refute his acts of disloyalty toward others as performances that have been forced upon him. Despite Jack's comforting assurance that "People like you and me can only do what is necessary. We are not the ones who have the choices" (272), it is his own complicity in such acts that Henry must eventually accept: "I have always known that moment of disappearance, and the even uglier truth is that I have long treasured it. That always honorable-seeming absence. . . . Is this my assimilation, so many years in the making? Is this the long-sought sweetness?" (188). Similarly, John Kwang is both a victim of Henry's betrayals, his political and personal downfall a direct result of Henry giving Hoagland the list of immigrants who participate in the *ggeh*, and a villain who is responsible for his protege Eduardo's death once he discovers that Eduardo, too, spies against him. By representing each man as both agent and victim, Lee targets the complicated issues of identity and authenticity that are at the heart of Henry's ontological quest.

For Henry there is no "solution" to the dilemma of his identity. At the end of the novel, he gives up espionage to be Lelia's assistant as she teaches ESL to summer students on a temporary basis. Despite the closure seemingly offered by the ending—Henry's retirement from the deceptions of espionage signaling the end of his role-playing and the possibility of, finally, being himself—Henry's desire for solidity, belonging, and a "true" identity remains, at the end of the novel, unfulfilled. He attends Lelia's classes as a "part of her materials" and contributes by "wear[ing] a green rubber hood and act[ing] in my role as the Speech Monster" (323). Although Henry can be more honest about the roles that he plays, the novel resists the temptation of celebrating Henry's liberation from the masks and impostures that he found so debilitating in his spy work. Even the "happy ending" represented by his reconciliation with Lelia is unsettled by a game of perpetual pretense: "Now, I am always coming back inside. We play this game in which I am her long-term guest. Permanently visiting. That she likes me okay and bears my presence, but who can know for how long?" (322).

Stefano Tani suggests that the reworking of genre often renders conventions "deceitful clues planted by the writer to rouse the attention of the reader before disappointing his expectations" (42–43). *Native Speaker* does not attempt to deceive the reader about the ways in which it reworks genre. Rather, the novel emphasizes the limitations of the spy story's narrative conventions in order to expose Henry as an agent who struggles to write himself into the picture. Through his use and deployment of narrative conventions, Lee demonstrates an interest in authorial agency and the difficulties that attend the kinds of stories Henry wishes to tell about himself, his father, and John Kwang.[26] By not just using Henry's spying as a metaphor for his cultural dilemmas as a Korean American but by engaging with the ways in which the genre of the spy story affects the ways in which Henry's acts of (self)-impersonation can be narrated and understood, Lee illuminates the complex entanglements of voice, desire, and performance that motivate any attempt to articulate minority subject-formation. In this way, Lee suggests that Henry's discovery must also be our own: the constraints of convention that limit our ways of reading are also integral to understanding the powerful fictions by which we live.

Coda

"What is an Asian American?" As I often tell my students at the beginning of my classes on Asian American literature and culture, they will not, at the end of the semester, leave with a concrete answer to that question. Indeed, I assure them that such an entity does not exist in any culturally or racially authentic way: that the term, descriptive and invented as it is, is useful to us primarily as a way of conceptualizing a "politico-cultural collectivity" (Espiritu 2) that symbolically reinterprets its histories of both inclusion and exclusion in order to effect social, political, and artistic articulation. To borrow words from Tam Lum, a character in Frank Chin's *Chickencoop Chinaman*, Asian Americans "are made, not born." Although Lum refers to "Chinamen" in his statement, the sentiment is equally applicable to if not even more appropriate for describing the figure of the Asian American, that figure birthed and given name in the identity movements of the 1970s who has come to stand in for so many different populations whose differences, we are reminded, might be more significant than their similarities.[1] In thinking about how Asian Americanness operates, then, this book has argued that Asian American identity *must* be impersonated in order for it to function as the category of personhood that we understand it to be. And, even more significantly, impersonation highlights for us the ways in which we must keep in mind disparities in performance if we are to remember the double project—of both undermining and yet not annulling identity—that this study pursues.

Central to the critical enterprise of this book has been an emphasis on how impersonation's double structure of performative embodiment might provide Asian American artists and critics a paradigm through which to enact this twinned project. As I have tried to demonstrate in my readings throughout the book, acts of impersonation depend upon a notion of performance that recognizes, even insists upon, alterity. This emphasis on difference, embodied by the structural dimension of Asian American acts of impersonation that foreground the possibility of being "not-me/not-not-me," manifests itself as a being-in-difference that necessarily challenges the assumed coherency if not the ultimate efficacy of Asian Americanness as a viable subject category. My efforts to implement impersonation as both a metacritical reading practice for Asian Americanists and a paradigm of performance through which Asian American subjects can claim for themselves a "complex personhood" (Gordon 5) should be understood as part of a larger, on-going critical project in Asian American literary studies. By re-evaluating the subject(s) around which the field itself has developed in order to challenge—but not necessarily dismantle—the constructions of identity that have given the discipline a practical coherency, Asian Americanists themselves have, like many of the characters studied here, acted as double agents with multiple allegiances.

Although it might be controversial to suggest that there is something essentially impersonative about Asian American identity formation, the space opened up by de-coupling imposture from impersonation and considering the multiple allegiances that characterize Asian American subject formation is critical if we are to continue re-thinking how Asian America is (in)congruent with the subjects it claims for itself. To that end, charting the representational contexts for how impersonation operates within the contested site of Asian America as a strategy for the performance of self is a necessary project and one that I have undertaken here. By focusing on the heightened self-awareness of the acts of (literary) impersonation performed by contemporary Asian American writers and by acknowledging the ways in which literary criticism can emerge from the quotidian practices of what it means to be Asian American, I mean to make *Double Agency*'s critical endeavor self-reflexive. Thus, the emphasis throughout these readings on the dangers and the pleasures of impersonation—along with an insistence on seeing simultaneously the demarcations that trouble any easy dis-affiliation of imposture from impersonation, impersonation from identity—demonstrates the ways in which I have been engaged throughout this study in my own act of doubled agency: aware of a critical need to produce a seamless theoretical product yet suspicious about the possibilities such a project demands be repressed.

Let me conclude by returning to the site of the university and suggesting something this project has helped me to understand about my teaching practices and what it means to be a member of an academic community. All too often, teachers and academics feel themselves to be impostors. The anxieties such a feeling produces are compounded when what one teaches and studies revolves around the issues of race, gender, and the inequities of power. Enacting on a daily basis my roles as a teacher and a critic, roles bound by a U.S. educational system that does not always recognize the contradictions in what it asks its subjects to perform, has taught me how crucial it is to maintain distinctions between what it means to imposture and what it means to impersonate. Although the multiple affiliations and injunctions I experience are not always contradictory or oppositional, sometimes they are; indeed, sometimes they have to be. I have learned from the examples of the texts and characters examined in this book about the need to distinguish for myself, and for those I perform with and for, the differences between betrayal and double agency. This is a realization that many of the Asian Americanists before me have experienced firsthand but it bears repeating so that we might understand the continued relevance of the politics of impersonation for contemporary Asian American intellectual work, both in theory and in practice.

Notes

Chapter 1: Impersonation and Double Agency

1. One of the distinctions embedded in the different responses offered by Yamada's speaker and Gotanda's character derives from the gendered expectations each character confronts. As this chapter goes on to demonstrate, impersonation as a strategy evolves from specific encounters in the Asian American historical past and such contexts—which included restrictive immigration laws and highly unbalanced gender ratios in immigrant "bachelor societies"—necessarily foreground gender as a critical site through which to consider the ways in which Asian American performances are both constructed and contested. For a study of how gender affects both immigration conditions and immigrant responses, see Yen Le Espiritu's *Asian American Women and Men: Labor, Laws, and Love* (1997). In Patricia Chu's *Assimilating Asians: Gendered Strategies of Authorship in Asian America* (2000), gender figures as a critical lens of literary inquiry; Chu argues convincingly in her study for the necessity of different rhetorical strategies for representing the sometimes antagonistic, sometimes complementary efforts of Asian American male and female writers in articulating identity formation.

2. The pronoun shifts here and as the chapter progresses are deliberate, a reflection of the ways in which I undertake in the act of literary criticism an act of impersonation, too. Impersonation is a performance that responds to a history of always already constructed roles, acknowledges the framework of response such enactments offer, and makes manifest through the performer's partial habitation of his or her performance the deconstruction of the roles in question. By shifting

pronouns and making my own investment in the project apparent, I write against criticism's desire to present a seamless argument—what I term the unremarkable virtuosity of imposture—and instead adopt a rhetorical stance that favors the partiality and self-reflexive accountability that characterizes impersonation as a trope in Asian American literature.

3. In order to focus on the "quotidian dimensions" of Filipino diasporic life, Manalansan advocates using a concept of "positioned performance" whereby "performance is structurally located within various hierarchical relationships and implies divergent engagements of actors with so-called scattered hegemonies. . . . [This] concept of positioned performance is grounded not only from the vantage of theory, but more importantly, from the actors' point of view and cultural knowledge" (158).

4. Performance has been mobilized as an important theoretical lens and conceptual paradigm to investigate not just the roles we perform as part of the identities we claim, but also the constructed nature of the real. The questions that concern performance within the context of theatrical (re)presentation—"questions of subjectivity (who is speaking/acting?), location (in what sites/spaces?), audience (who is watching?), commodification (who is in control?), conventionality (how are meanings produced?), politics (what ideological or social positions are being reinforced or contested?)"(4)—are, as Elin Diamond suggests, still operative in the critical discussions that use performance as a theoretical mode of inquiry into nontheatrical sites and events. As Judith Butler demonstrated in her foundational work on performativity, a term she derives from J. L. Austin's concept of the utterance that produces the very reality it claims to speak, issues of agency and enactment are critical areas of consideration in the field of performance studies. To wit, Butler's work has claimed gender to be performative in that "it is real only to the extent that it is performed" ("Performative Acts" 278). Criticism of this argument—which Diamond characterizes as "anti-essentialism pushe[d] past constructionism" (4)—resulted in a different conceptualization of performativity in *Bodies That Matter* (1993), where Butler avoids the appearance of claiming a subject who possesses an agency outside of the cultural and social apparatuses that determine gender identity and instead theorizes performativity as, above all, dependent upon the repetition of always already existing acts whose reiteration instantiates sex, gender, and even the body itself. In her words, "There is no power that acts, but only a reiterated acting that is power in its persistence and instability" (*Bodies* 9).

5. The condition of in/visibility and the relationship it articulates between hypervisible Asian American bodies and unseen or mis-seen Asian American subjects is, not coincidentally, inverted in the case of whiteness: "the structural visibility of white subjects relies on the ideological invisibility of their race . . . In order to se-

cure itself, whiteness is visible only by the default resulting from the specularity of the other" (Traise Yamamoto 67).

6. The most well-debated instance of this charge in Asian American literary studies is still the Maxine Hong Kingston-Frank Chin conflict.

7. In his recent study *Race and Resistance: Literature and Politics in Asian America* (2002), Viet Thanh Nguyen provocatively pinpoints the ways in which Asian American intellectuals have, quite singularly, "been most interested in representing themselves and the object of their study—Asian America—as sites of political and cultural contestation against forms of racial and class hierarchy integral to American society" (11). While this is clearly one model of response to U.S. American constructions of Asian Americans as somehow dangerous to incorporate into the national body politic, Nguyen argues that it is imperative that Asian American criticism become more self-reflexive about the limits of Asian America and the "disavowed roles" that Asian American academics play as "panethnic entrepeneurs" (12). In contrast, Gary Okihiro characterizes resistance as an "underdeveloped and hence 'emerging' . . . interpretive paradigm" that has "implications for Asian American history as a whole" (*Columbia Guide to Asian American History* 164). Impersonation's "resistant" dimensions are about acknowledging the very "disavowals" that Nguyen encourages us to consider as well as attending to the "emergent paradigms" that thinking about the nature of Asian American accommodation and resistance can produce.

8. As Garrett Hongo makes clear in his introduction to *Under Western Eyes: Personal Essays from Asian America* (1995), the issues of betrayal and authenticity are intimately linked and, moreover, operative in policing how Asian American identity and subject-formation are regulated by both those within and without Asian America. Significantly, Hongo notes that artists, in addition to resisting the pressures placed on them by "mainstream" critics and academics to conform to certain liberal ideas of difference and sameness, also need to challenge—despite accusations of "inauthenticity"—"the further notion that a given group could claim exclusive proprietary rights to all representations of itself created in the culture [. . . for fear that] this would establish that ethnic topics, ethnic identities, and the literary portrayal of ethnic voices were the *exclusive cultural properties* of a group that would somehow be deemed 'authentic,' licensed with the cultural 'right' to represent itself as the ethnic *Other*" (31; emphasis original).

9. In her study of Asian American drama, Josephine Lee argues for the importance of differentiating the viewing positions occupied by "mainstream" and Asian American audiences while also acknowledging that such different positions do not necessarily subvert the notion of how pleasure operates in producing theatrical identification and disidentification. Lee suggests that, particularly with regard to

the re-deployment of stereotype, the Asian American spectator might feel "a perverse pleasure" that is not simply about "the subversion of stereotype" but also about the complicated issues of mastery and desire that stereotype generates even in those subject to its exaggerations (118).

10. Browder argues that ethnic impersonator autobiographies are significant because of the ways in which they mark and revise national mythologies about the nature of success, the performance of racial and ethnic stereotypes, and the marketing of the self and the possibilities of (ethnic) self-fashioning.

11. A kind of anti-imposture has figured prominently during those periods of yellow peril anxiety when specific Asian American ethnic communities have been the target of discriminatory social and legal practices—particularly during World War II when Japanese Americans were interned. Yen Le Espiritu discusses the practice of ethnic disidentification—"the act of distancing one's group from another group so as not to be mistaken and suffer the blame for the presumed misdeed of that group" (20)—in *Asian American Panethnicity* (1992). In Hisaye Yamamoto's story "Wilshire Bus" (1988), the Japanese American protagonist encounters another Asian American wearing an "I'm Korean" button; in Julie Otsuka's novel *When the Emperor Was Divine* (2002), a boy remembers seeing "real Chinese—Mr. Lee of Lee's Grocers and Don Wong who owned the laundry on Shattuck—on the street wearing buttons that said, I AM CHINESE, and CHINESE, PLEASE" (76).

12. The relationship between poststructuralism and identity politics has been a subject of considerable critical debate. As critics have argued, poststructuralist conceptions of identity (and their accompanying emphases on the impossibility of coherency, the suspicion of realism, and the naïve idealism and essentialism of identity politics) have been embraced in the academy at precisely a moment when minorities are claiming for themselves the right to speak as subjects and agents. Similarly, Coco Fusco asserts that "[s]cores of feminists and postcolonial theorists have rejected formulations of poststructuralism that declare the death of the subject, the end of meaning, the decline of the social, and the failure of political resistance; these proclamations, they argue, speak only to the realities of those few who once could claim absolute rights, absolute truth, and absolute authority" (*English Is Broken Here* 32). Paula Moya identifies the critical problem postmodernism and its poststructurally informed notions of identity pose to minority scholars who are still interested and invested in the epistemic significance of identity as one where "the prevalence of postmodernist thought has created an intellectual atmosphere in which invocations of identity, appeals to experience, and claims to truth have been judged to be both theoretically naïve and ideologically suspect" (6). According to Moya, it is imperative that ethnic studies scholars develop theoretical models for demonstrating how identity is still an indispensable category of inquiry, a

site of investigation upon which an effective political agency is dependent. To that end, Moya argues in *Learning from Experience: Minority Identities, Multicultural Struggles* (2002) for a "postpositivist realist theory of identity" which conceives of objectivity "as an ideal of inquiry necessarily involving theoretical bias and interest, rather than as a condition of absolute and achieved certainty that is context transcendent, subject independent, and free of theoretical bias" (14). The result of such a reconceptualization of objectivity is "an interpretive approach that resolves the dilemmas that attend absolutist conceptions of identity, objectivity, and knowledge, going beyond both dogmatic certainty and unyielding skepticism" while also accounting for "the causal influence that categories of identity like race, sex, and socioeconomic status have on the formation of identity even as it accounts for how identities can adapt to changing historical circumstances" (16, 17).

13. The suspicion about this incorporation is revealed in the polarized dynamics underlying yellowface performance as a kind of dis-incorporating maneuver. Robert Lee argues in *Orientals: Asian Americans in Popular Culture* (1999) that yellowface is a performance that capitalizes on as well as constructs Asian/Americans as aliens in this way: "Yellowface marks the Asian body as unmistakably Oriental; it sharply defines the Oriental in a racial opposition to whiteness. Yellowface exaggerates 'racial' features that have been designated 'Oriental,' such as 'slanted' eyes, overbite, and mustard-yellow skin color. Only the racialized Oriental is yellow; Asians are not. . . . Yellowface marks the Oriental as indelibly alien" (2). Lee uses the March 1997 *National Review* cover depicting President Clinton as a Chinese houseboy, Hillary Clinton as a Maoist Red Guard, and Vice President Gore as a Buddhist priest as a prime example of this type of impostured performance. A recent example, which masks the motivating impulse of whiteness in the performance of yellowface, can be found on the Internet in the Mr. Wong cartoons. Critical to keep in mind here are the ways in which race is stylized into a particular set of enactments—and rooted in the body. This stylization is at the heart of stereotype and is discussed further in chapters 2 and 3.

14. As Gary Okihiro argues in *Common Ground: Reimagining American History* (2001), the experiences of Asian Americans should be used not to demarcate the binaries that structure how many interpret the U.S. American past but rather to demonstrate the disruption of binarism itself. By identifying four prominent schematics through which we understand U.S. American history and character—"West and East," "White and Black," "Man and Woman" and "Heterosexual and Homosexual"—and demonstrating how the experiences of Asian Americans continually challenge the coherency of social orders produced by such binaries, Okihiro encourages us to rethink the usefulness of thinking about the polarities marked by "American" and "Asian."

15. Chapters 2 and 6 of *Double Agency* take up the ways in which the issue of

foreign allegiance as emblematized in the figure of the spy/secret agent stereotype is addressed both as impostured Asian American performance (yellowface) and through various acts of impersonation in Asian American literature. Sax Rohmer's archetypal Asian villain, Dr. Fu Manchu, yokes Asianness to atrocity; according to Jenny Clegg, "In him the qualities of being exotic and evil are bound together, connecting the characteristic of the Chinese with crime, vice and cruelty" (4). The legacy of Fu Manchu has generated a number of different responses by Asian American writers seeking to reconfigure the stealth and secrecy associated with Asianness and to use that figure in order to make domestic critiques (as opposed to identifying foreign threats). Thus, as chapter 6 delineates, Chang-rae Lee's *Native Speaker* takes up the trope of the Asian American spy to challenge the charges of imposture and betrayal that inevitably accompany the figure of the Asian American secret agent. Recent research conducted by Marilyn Alquizola and Lane Hirabayashi reveals that noted writer Carlos Bulosan was under FBI surveillance from 1950–1956; his file, only recently declassified and released under the Freedom of Information Act, indicates that Bulosan was considered "a very serious threat" and perhaps part of an "international communist conspiracy" (Guillermo). Ironically, Bulosan articulated in *America Is in the Heart* (1946) the perception of Asianness which made such government scrutiny not only possible but probable: "I came to know that in many ways, it was a crime to be Filipino in California. I feel like a criminal running away from a crime I did not commit. And this crime is that I am a Filipino in America" (121).

16. According to Ling-chi Wang, the term "honorary whites" first "began during World War II when American attitudes toward Chinese slowly and generally turned more favorable because Chinese in China were deemed allies of the U.S. in the fight to defeat Japanese imperialism. The honorary white status was extended to the Chinese in Mississippi as James Loewen suggested in Chapters 3 and 4 in his book, *The Mississippi Chinese* (1971). After the war, America's public perceptions of the Chinese ran on two separate and conflicting tracks: demonization and assimilation. The Cold War drastically reversed the wartime favorable images to vicious, aggressive, untrustworthy, and menacing images. At the same time, the favorable images, during the 1950s, were supplemented by reports of low juvenile delinquency rates among Chinese Americans and of incredible Chinese American accomplishments in science and engineering. At the height of the civil rights movement in the 1960s, the media and academics introduced the 'model minority' image to contrast Chinese and Japanese American successful assimilation with other racial minorities fighting for rights and welfare" (posting to AAAS listserve). Mia Tuan offers a good example of the way in which achievement and model minority status can co-exist with the perception of illegitimacy in her reading of the

MSNBC headline—"American Beats Kwan"—reporting the results of the 1998 Olympic Games' women's figure skating competition. As Tuan's analysis and the headline itself make clear, Kwan's achievement was undergirded by the perception that Tara Lipinski was somehow more "naturally" representative of what an "American" looks like.

17.   Such logic obviously supported the internment of Japanese Americans during World War II. Although Japanese American internment has variously been explained as the result of wartime hysteria, military necessity, and a government effort to protect Japanese Americans from acts of racial violence, the Munson Report—which asserts that "There is no Japanese problem on the Coast. There will be no armed uprising of Japanese" (90)—reveals one of the primary forces behind internment as the perception of Asians as aliens and somehow, despite appearances of being law-abiding, subject to suspicion. Ronald Takaki in *Strangers from a Different Shore* (1989) writes that while there were indeed Japanese American agents involved in the spy trade during the war, they were actually working for the United States rather than for Japan. For more on the internment, see Michi Weglyn's *Years of Infamy: The Untold Story of America's Concentration Camps* (1996).

18.   The use of "Asian American" in this chapter is anachronistic at points since the identity category itself was not mobilized until 1968, when activists at the University of California, Berkeley founded one of the first pan-Asian political organizations: the Asian American Political Alliance (AAPA). However, the disjunctions registered by the anachronism of the use foreground the sense of slippage and the contestation of identities that would otherwise be rendered oblique through use of the term "Orientals."

19.   Yamamoto's *Masking Selves, Making Subjects: Japanese American Women, Identity, and the Body* (1999) is a brilliant study about the trope of masking as it operates in post–World War II writing by Japanese American women. Yamamoto identifies the "highly problematic" relationship that such authors have had to negotiate and carefully analyzes masking—"which, at its most literal level, is directly connected to the construction of the Japanese face as the mask of difference" (5) but which also, despite being "[i]naugurated by the trauma of the racially marked, gendered, and still sexualized body's positioning in the social economy of the United States, . . . [still constitutes] a resistant strategy by which the body and, through the body, subjectivity may be claimed" (100–101).

20.   For more on the Chinese Exclusion Act and responses to its strictures on the part of the Chinese American community, see Elmer C. Sandemeyer's *The Anti-Chinese Movement in California* (1939, 1991), Alexander Saxton's *The Indispensable Enemy: Labor and the Anti-Chinese Movement in California* (1971), Stuart C. Miller's *The Unwelcome Immigrant: The American Image of the Chinese* (1969),

Claiming America: Constructing Chinese American Identities During the Exclusion Era (1998, eds. K. Scott Wong and Sucheng Chan), and *Entry Denied: Exclusion and the Chinese Community in America, 1882–1943* (1991, ed. Sucheng Chan).

21. The practice of Japanese and Korean men sending for picture brides became more prevalent after the Gentlemen's Agreement of 1907, which limited migrant labor to the United States until 1921, when the Japanese government ended the practice under pressure from the U.S. (Okihiro, *Columbia* 20). For more information on picture brides, see *The Passage of a Picture Bride* (1989) by Won Kil Yoon and *Japanese Women in Hawai'i: The First 100 Years* (1985) by Patsy Sumie Saiki. The official website for Kayo Hatta's film (http://www.naatanet.org/picture-bride/index.html) contains links to information about the picture bride experience as well as a useful bibliography.

22. As this example and the earlier examples taken from the paper son/daughter contexts make clear, the material and state-enforced reasons that made/make Asian American impersonation necessary can be traced, in part, through the history of exclusion, restriction, regulation and resistance documented via the legal battles waged by and on the part of Asian Americans. For a set of comprehensive accounts of how Asian Americans have challenged definitions of identity and belonging through their participation in the U.S. judicial system, see Hyung-chan Kim's *A Legal History of Asian Americans, 1790–1990* (1994), Charles J. McClain's *In Search of Equality: The Chinese Struggle Against Discrimination in Nineteenth-Century America* (1994), and *Asian Americans and Congress: A Documentary History* (1996).

23. Although Yamaguchi's novel depicts a connection between the picture bride system and the smuggling of women into the U.S. for the purposes of prostitution, a significant number of women being smuggled into the country as prostitutes during the late-nineteenth and early twentieth centuries were Chinese, not Japanese, and "almost always imported as unfree labor, indentured, or enslaved; most were kidnapped, lured or purchased from poor parents by procurers in China" (Yung 27). See chapter 1—"Bound Feet: Chinese Women in the 19th Century"—of Judy Yung's *Unbound Feet: A Social History of Chinese Women in San Francisco* (1995), Lucie Cheng Hirata's "Free, Indentured, Enslaved: Chinese Prostitutes in Nineteenth-Century America" (1979), Sucheng Chan's "The Exclusion of Chinese Women, 1870–1943" (1991), and Huping Ling's *Surviving on the Gold Mountain: A History of Chinese American Women and Their Lives* (1998) for additional information on the practice of Chinese prostitution and the experiences of Chinese immigrant women.

24. Muñoz develops his conceptualization of disidentification, a concept that

attempts to move beyond binaries toward a theory of "identification that is both mediated and immediate, a disidentification that enables politics" (10), from the work of French linguist Michel Pecheux. Muñoz's work, which focuses on the ways in which queers of color identify with queerness despite the complications of the identity category, elaborates upon Pecheux's articulation of the three modes by which a subject is, in Althusserian terms, "interpellated." According to Muñoz, Pecheux offers, in addition to the "good" and "bad" subjects constructed via ideological practice in an Althusserian economy, a model of disidentification by which both assimilation and the "controlled symmetry of 'counterdetermination'" are resisted and negotiated (11). This mobilization of a third paradigm of response that is neither acquiescent to dominant ideology nor formed as "pure" resistance echoes Lisa Lowe's reading of Gramsci's theory of hegemony, counter-hegemony, and the space of the subaltern in "Heterogeneity, Hybridity, and Multiplicity."

25. Kandice Chuh provides a provocative and powerful articulation of the need for a deconstructive account of "Asian American" in her recently published *Imagine Otherwise: On Asian Americanist Critique* (2003). According to Chuh, we need to think about the ways in which "Asian American" signals "a momentary configuration of meaning that is impermanent and overdetermined" (28). To that end, Chuh emphasizes the field as a set of "collaborative antagonisms" rather than unified or representative of any kind of "concrete knowability" (28, 26).

Chapter 2: Dissecting the "Devil Doctor"

1. Comments by Chan et al. concerning the depiction of Fu Manchu as a homosexual menace are based upon the filmic representations of the Doctor, which must be differentiated from his textual representations in Rohmer's series. Frank Chin has elaborated upon the menace Fu Manchu poses: "Unlike the white stereotype of the evil black stud, Indian rapist, Mexican macho, the evil of the evil Dr. Fu Manchu was not sexual but homosexual" (66). Chin goes on to describe the reasons for such an assertion as ones based on a generic scene from the many film representations of Fu Manchu: "Dr. Fu, a man wearing a long dress, batting his eyelashes, surrounded by muscular black servants in loin cloths, and with his bad habit of caressingly touching white men on the leg, wrist, and face with his long fingernails is not so much a threat as he is a frivolous offense to white manhood" (66). The MGM movie *The Mask of Fu Manchu* (1932), starring Boris Karloff, stages Fu Manchu in all of the ways Chin asserts. For a discussion of the ways in which Chin mobilizes Fu Manchu as a trope for homosexuality, see Daniel Kim's "The Strange Love of Frank Chin" in *Q&A: Queer in Asian America* (1998).

2. Fu Manchu has become such a deeply embedded part of the Euro-Ameri-

can cultural unconscious that he has attained a quasi-mythical, quasi-historical status. His status as a literary creation has proliferated beyond the boundaries of the
stories in which he first made his appearance. Cay van Ash writes that "[t]he name
of Fu Manchu had [by 1932] become a household word, to the extent that many
people had a tentative belief in his physical existence" (215). Arguably, the most famous literary creation to ever step off the page and enter into the realm of belief
was Arthur Conan Doyle's fictional detective Sherlock Holmes, who is still the re-
cipient of letters addressed to "221 Baker Street." Although no one ever wrote to
Fu Manchu, a letter sent to the American State Department signed "President of
the Si-Fan" warranted the attention of the F.B.I., who wrote Rohmer for information about the organization.

3.   In fact, *President Fu Manchu* (1936) was conceived and written specifically
for Rohmer's American audience; Rohmer intended "to reward his American sup-
porters by transferring the activities of Fu Manchu to the United States" (van Ash
297). In addition, as William Wu has pointed out, the eventual pairing of Smith
with American protagonists denoted financial and commercial considerations.
With the size of the potential American reading market in mind, it made sense to
give the American stake in the adventures a more visible presence in the novels.

4.   From the beginning, the Fu Manchu books were published simultaneously
in London and New York.

5.   As Robert Lee asserts in *Orientals* (1999), the Anglo-Saxon alliance of the Fu
Manchu novels is paralleled by the "consolidat[ion of] the Oriental" such that na-
tional histories are "collapse[d] into an ahistorical cultural category of Oriental
Otherness" (115).

6.   Actually, since Rohmer did not initially conceive of the Fu Manchu stories
as a series of books, the distinction made between the first three novels and the
rest of the series stemmed from the distinct chronological gap between *The Hand
of Fu Manchu* (1917) and *Daughter of Fu Manchu* (1931) as well as changing publishing concerns. Pre-war trends in magazine fiction that demanded episodic,
"complete in one issue" serials evolved into opportunities for serializing book-
length novels conceived in a more coherent manner. As such, aside from the thirteen years which separate the first three books from the rest of the series, one of
the major differences between the early and later Fu Manchu novels rests in the
fact that while the post-1931 novels are written as novels, with the suspense of each
story being developed throughout the entire book, the structure of the first three
novels is clearly episodic, reflecting their status as compilations of short stories
published in book form. See Rachel Lee for a discussion of how to read Rohmer's
racial representations as a response to the journalistic milieu provided by maga-
zines like *Collier's*.

7. Fu Manchu began his movie career in the 1920s, a career which later expanded to include television, radio, and comic strips. While the Doctor made weekly appearances in newspaper cartoons during the 1930s, he also emerged as a character in Marvel comic books in 1973–74 as the "Master of Kung-fu" (Glaessner 13). In addition to the increased public exposure he acquired through movies and comic strips, Fu Manchu gained a couple of children along the way: Marvel produced a series of comic books featuring Shang-chi, the Eurasian son of Fu-Manchu. In *Daughter of the Dragon*, the female lead, obviously intended to be the same character as Fah Lo Suee, is instead called Princess Ling Moy. And in *Castle of Fu Manchu*, a Fu Manchu movie which, unlike the earlier films, is not based, however loosely, on an original Rohmer book, the Doctor apparently has a daughter named Lin Tang (there is no mention of Fah Lo Suee). For a sampling of original Fu Manchu newspaper comics of the 1920s and 1930s, see the reissued Malibu graphics compilation *Sax Rohmer: Two Complete Fu Manchu Adventures* (1989); for a discussion of Fu Manchu's influence on creating the pulp fiction characters of Dr. Wu-Fang and Dr. Yen Sin, see Don Hutchinson's *It's Raining Corpses in Chinatown* (1991).

8. Smith's colonial appointment to Burma is significant. As Maung Htin Aung writes in his study of Anglo-Burmese relations, "[t]he period 1890 to 1920 could be termed the Golden Period of British rule [in Burma]" (95). After four years of fighting, which the British government euphemistically referred to as the "Pacification of Burma," Burmese nationalism became dormant for about thirty years. During that time, Anglo-Burmese relations were represented as a model of imperial rule, where "the British officials did not air a sense of superiority, [and] the Burmese, in turn, did not come to acquire an inferiority complex against the new rulers" (96).

9. Fu Manchu's name was hyphenated in the first three novels of the series but the hyphen was eventually dropped from his name in the later books.

10. While Rohmer has not garnered much critical success in academic circles, his novels did enjoy a measure of praise in popular critical reviews of his books. *The Bookman* review of *The Insidious Dr. Fu-Manchu* sums up the novel as "a very creditable specimen of its kind, . . . [which] fulfills all the requirements the most exacting reader of that type of fiction could demand" (Phillips 306). A later review in *The New York Times Book Review* of *Tales of Secret Egypt* concludes that "If you like to dream over the fascinating Orient, with its hashish and perfumes, its veiled ladies and eunuchs, its harems and lattices, its bazaars and mosques, its tombs and its mummies, you will revel in these Eastern tales of Sax Rohmer's" (van Ash 358).

11. Christopher Frayling has distilled the plot elements of the first three Fu

Manchu novels into the following list:

> an initial show of force by the Burmese dacoits in a London setting;
> the attempted murder of a prominent Orientalist or Government scientist;
> a scene in Shen Ya's or John Ki's Limehouse opium den;
> the capture (and complicated escape) of Smith and Petrie;
> evidence of Smith's knowledge of the East, Fu's refined sense of honour and
>   expertise in "certain . . . obscure sciences which no university of today can
>   teach," and Petrie's medical skills (misjudged by Fu to be those of a near-
>   genius);
> a contrast between Smith's and Fu's codes of civilization;
> an elaborate machine of torture, described in meticulous detail, but seldom
>   fully used;
> a not-so-subtle hint of Karamaneh's divided loyalties and finally
> a chase, followed by Fu Manchu's "death." (70)

Robert Briney has identified each of the twenty-nine episodes contained in the first three novels as adventures where Nayland Smith and Dr. Petrie are either "a) menaced by one of Fu-Manchu's exotic death-traps, b) captured by his agents, or c) engaged in trying to foil a murderous attempt on the life of someone who Knows Too Much" (47–8).

12.   Elizabeth Sax Rohmer revealed that Rohmer "could not sit through the film versions of his work" and according to Frayling, "the Karloff adaptation (*The Mask of Fu Manchu*, MGM 1932) is more blatantly racist than anything Rohmer ever wrote ('Kill all the white men and take their women!')" (74).

13.   It is ironic to note that the "reincarnations" of Fu Manchu in Rohmer's later texts and mass culture tended in different directions. Rohmer's continual development of the Doctor resulted in further complicating the character of Fu Manchu while the many incarnations of the Doctor in popular culture were undeniably reductivist in their depictions of him.

14.   The popularity of sketches of Chinese resulted in record-breaking runs for several productions mounted on the music hall stage. Ernest Short in *Fifty Years of Vaudeville* (1946) reports that "[a]mong vaudeville shows, only *Chu-Chin-Chow* and *The Maid of the Mountains* have excelled the 1,075 performances of *A Chinese Honeymoon*" (88). John MacKenzie notes that many of the escapist musicals set in the Orient had "strikingly long runs, among the longest of the period[:] *The Geisha* (1896) ran for 760 performances, *San Toy* (1899) for 768, *Chinese Honeymoon* (1901) for 1,075 . . . *The Cingalee* (1904), a naval comedy called *The Flag Lieutenant* for 381, *Mr. Wu*, an Anglo-Chinese play for 403" (53).

15.   As James S. Moy writes in *Marginal Sights* (1993), "Well before Asians be-

gan to appear in America, the framework that would provide for their representation had been established. The Chinese, and Asians in general, first appear as representational issues during the nineteenth century, their constructed images emerging amidst a rapidly expanding world of visual texts" (4).

16. In an interview with *The New Yorker*, Rohmer candidly discusses the use of ethnic minorities in his fiction: "Sir Newman . . . bought a serial I had knocking about in the trunk, called 'The Sins of Severac Bablon,' for a new periodical, *Cassell's Magazine*. It was a kind of Robin Hood tale, with a rich Jew doing a poor Jew in the eye until the tables were neatly turned. From the Jews, I went on to the Chinese and Dr. Fu Manchu, but between times I wrote a hell of a lot of comic songs for George Robey, the comedian [known for his vaudevillian sketches of Chinamen]" ("Doctor's Blade" 37).

17. While Rohmer claimed ignorance of the Chinese, he was quite astute in evaluating the social and political contexts that rendered his Asian malefactor so popular to the public: "Conditions for launching a Chinese villain on the market were ideal. I wondered why it had never before occurred to me. The Boxer Rebellion had started off rumors of a Yellow Peril which had not yet died down. Recent events in Limehouse had again drawn public attention eastwards" (van Ash 75). In his clearly self-reflexive accounting of Fu Manchu's genesis, Rohmer also represented his creation of Fu Manchu as one augmented by "divine" or "supernatural" sanction of the project. According to Rohmer, he once asked a ouija board "How can I best make a living?" only to have the pointer repeatedly spell out the word C-H-I-N-A-M-A-N (van Ash 63).

18. Elaine Kim articulates this dynamic as the basic structure of the Fu Manchu-Nayland Smith relationship: "Fu Manchu is the diametrical opposite of the white hero: he is, in Rohmer's words, 'not a normal man. He is superman. Satan materialized and equipped with knowledge which few had ever achieved.' Ultimately, nothing can defeat the wholesome, warmly human British protagonists of the Fu Manchu novels—not superior intelligence, not ingenious weapons, not overwhelming numbers, not magic, because the battle is between good and primordial, Satanic, Chinese evil" (8).

19. The connection made between religion and violence in the Fu Manchu books prefigures contemporary ideas of the Middle East as a hotbed of religious terrorism. *The Mask of Fu Manchu* (1932) deals with this issue explicitly in the fundamentalist uprising that occurs when Lionel Barton destroys the tomb of El Mokanna. Richard Rubenstein distinguishes terrorism as a crime separate from warfare: "Descriptively, 'terrorism' suggests violent actions by individuals or small groups. Judgmentally, it implies illegitimacy. These meanings are closely related, since there are very few situations in which assassinations, bombings, kidnappings,

or bank robberies seem justified. By contrast, wars and revolutions are frequently considered not only justifiable, but holy. . . . According to this understanding, mass violence may sometimes be justified, individual violence virtually never" (10–18). Fu Manchu laments at various points in the novels that because of his position as an unrecognized minority in relation to the British and American governments, he is considered a criminal rather than a diplomat working on behalf of an internationally recognized organization. At times, the books do expose the hypocrisy of maintaining such distinctions between Fu Manchu's projects and the political activity of national governments represented by Smith. For representative examples of such narratives, see *The Drums of Fu Manchu* (1939) and *The Island of Fu Manchu* (1940).

20. Most of these examples are taken from *The Return of Dr. Fu Manchu* (1929), though such identificatory moments between Fu Manchu and Smith are interspersed throughout the series.

21. According to Orson S. Fowler, one of the most prominent phrenologists in the United States, "[white] men of ordinary talent possess a respectable endowment of these organs [frontal, coronal parts of the head]. The Hindoos [sic], Chinese, American Indians, and the African race, still less, but much more than the lower order of animals" (qtd. in Horseman 144).

22. Colonialism and imperialism are obviously related concepts, each denoting specific historical phases of the particular relations of domination active between European powers and other countries. Although the distinctions between the two are not always clearly demarcated, Shohat and Stam define the difference between the two modes of governmentality as such: "colonialism is the process by which the European powers reached positions of economic, military, political and cultural hegemony in much of Asia, Africa and the Americas. Colonialism took the form both of distant control of European settlement (French Indochina, the Belgian Congo, the Philippines), and of direct European settlement (Algeria, South Africa, Australia, the Americas). . . . [I]mperialism . . . refer[s] to a specific phase or form of colonialism, running roughly from 1870 to 1914, when conquest of territory gave way to a systematic search for markets and an expansionist exporting of capital" (15).

23. Miscegenation is not displaced in the texts; rather, it is confronted directly, although subsumed as part of an Orientalizing project. The penchant Oriental women have for forming sudden and mysterious attachments to Western men reinforces the feminization of the Orient as well as bolsters the image of Western masculinity.

24. Smith's response to characters like James Richter in *President Fu Manchu* (1936) and Kegan Van Roon in *The Return of Dr. Fu Manchu* (1929) are good examples of this practice.

25. This sympathetic rendering of part-Chinese characters might have much to do with the fact that *Emperor Fu Manchu* takes place in China. In the face of "Chinese-Chinese," McKay and Cameron-Gordon, both extensively influenced by American culture, are repositioned within the oppositional economy of the books. Also, the representation of the Chinese shifted according to changing political climates. See "The Political Appeal of Dr. Fu Manchu" by Peter Christensen for an account of how the Fu Manchu novels depicted the Devil Doctor differently during the World War II years and afterward.

26. According to Tsai Chin in her autobiography, the endings were not the only thing repeated in the Fu Manchu movies: "Apart from the name changes, the plots were all identical: perhaps that explains why I did not bother to read the script when I came to do the fifth film. Fu wants to conquer the world, forcing a Western scientist to assist him. The white and noble scientist always refuses to cooperate until Fu abducts his beautiful daughter. Then the scientist pretends to relent before destroying his evil opponent. End of picture—though as the credits roll, the menacing voice of Fu Manchu is heard warning his Western cinema audience that worse is yet to come" (144).

Chapter 3: De/Posing Stereotype on the Asian American Stage

1. See Sander Gilman's *Difference and Pathology* (1985) for a discussion of stereotype's oppositional nature.

2. As Lisa Lowe points out in *Immigrant Acts* (1996), "[t]o the extent that Asian American discourse articulates an identity in reaction to the dominant culture's stereotype, even if to refute it, the discourse may remain bound to and overly determined by the logic of the dominant culture" (71).

3. According to Shimakawa, examples of plays that address stereotype in this way include works like Wakako Yamauchi's *12–1–A* (1993), Elizabeth Wong's *Letters to a Student Revolutionary* (1989) and Frank Chin's *Chickencoop Chinaman* (1981) and *The Year of the Dragon* (1981). Shimakawa usefully points out the ways in which each of these texts focuses on the racialized formation of U.S. Americanness and dramatizes the exclusionary processes to which Asian Americans are subject in an effort to direct attention to the experiences of "real" Asian Americans. For more details, see chapter 3, " 'We'come a Chinatowng, Folks!' Resisting Abjection," in *National Abjection*.

4. Jon Erickson suggests that ownership depends upon an act of transgression, the deliberate trespassing of what demarcates "what is yours" from "what is theirs" (226). This process both increases and decreases the value assigned to any given act or object. Thus, the kinds of appropriation made possible are themselves "double" in nature.

5. There is a fascination with the "living dead" in the Fu Manchu novels, a fascination that manifests itself in the liberal use of the secret, catalepsy-inducing drug that engenders Barton's "death" at the beginning of *The Daughter of Fu Manchu*. Significantly, this interest is developed in much more detail in *The Drums of Fu Manchu* (1939), where the adventure involves uncovering voodoo rituals and Fah Lo Suee herself is rendered a zombie by her father.

6. As I have discussed in chapter 2, Rohmer effects a process of "discoloration" against both Fu Manchu and his daughter by emphasizing their association with darker peoples. This practice is visually manifested in filmic representations of Fu Manchu as well—see the MGM production of *The Mask of Fu Manchu* (1932) for an example of how African Americans are used to frame perceptions of "the Devil Doctor."

7. In *Performing Women* (1993), Gay Gibson Cima argues persuasively for the rejection of virtuosity in feminist performance, suggesting that "as initiators of novel and unpracticed performance styles (styles that necessarily carry with them vestiges of the old), the majority of female actors discussed herein reject virtuosity" (7). Similarly, Joseph Roach has demonstrated that virtuosity should actually be read as subjection given the ways in which it requires mastery of a particular repertoire to be deeply inscribed upon the body. These critical conceptions of the dangers of virtuosity have exciting implications for the performance of racial stereotypes as well, bolstering my theorization of impersonation as a performance that successfully exposes the limitations of seeing stereotype as a kind of racial imposture.

8. Dorinne Kondo argues that while "self-Orientalizing" (10) is a poignant problem experienced by subaltern peoples, such acts are particularly important to investigate in any consideration of the pleasures produced by performance.

9. In her vignette "Anna May Speaks (From the Grave)," Lisa See imagines an interior monologue in which the actress understands her relation to stereotype as one produced, in part, by the movie industry's practice of yellowface performance: "I got so weary of it all—of the scenarists' conception of the Chinese character. You remember Fu Manchu? *Daughter of the Dragon?* So wicked! I'm telling you this because I *knew* I was creating bad stereotypes. That's why I wanted the part of O'Lan so badly. *The Good Earth* showed Chinese people in a good light, but Thalberg wanted *white* actors for the leading roles. Today, when they say *I* perpetrated those stereotypes, I wonder" (226).

10. Hwang claims in his "Afterword" that although he was intrigued by "a two-paragraph story in *The New York Times*" (94) about the ill-fated affair between French diplomat Bernard Boursicot and Chinese opera singer Shi Pei-pu, he "purposely refrained from further research" into the story because "frankly, I didn't want the 'truth' to interfere with my own speculations" (95).

11. For a more detailed discussion of Hwang's use of Brechtian theatrical practice, see my "Betrayed into Motion: The Seduction of Narrative Desire in *M. Butterfly*" (1994).

12. The "openness" of the gender drag performed by Song has been noted by critics both as problematic and provocative for the ways in which it foregrounds Gallimard's own investment in continuing to deny, despite evidence to the contrary, Song as being anything other than his fantasy of the Perfect Woman. In a specific example of such complicated recognition, Gabrielle Cody asserts that actor "[B. D.] Wong deliberately plays Butterfly as a man-playing-at-being-a-woman, self-consciously endowing her with Gallimard's fantasy of how an Oriental woman should behave—the equivalent in the West of third rate transvestitism" (26).

13. The most openly disjunctive performance in the entire play can be ascribed to the actor playing Comrade Chin who then undertakes the role of Suzuki, Butterfly's "faithful servant" in the ironic re-telling of Puccini's operatic tale. Her spectacularly disjunctive performance is marked by completely unbelievable dialogue—she tells Butterfly, "Girl, he's a loser. What'd he ever give you? Nineteen cents and those ugly Day-Glo stockings?" (12)—and deliberately underplayed action.

14. I locate the play's potential to disrupt stereotype and effect a political critique in Hwang's use of theatrical strategies that destabilize both the framing of narrative and the merging of character and identity. In adapting *M. Butterfly* for David Cronenberg's 1993 film, Hwang wrote out all such strategies and the end result is a "straight" love story about "two people composing the opera of their lives." Hwang's interview with Dorrine Kondo reveals that although he attempted to find "filmic equivalents" to the "theatrical devices and metaphors" of the play, director David Cronenberg preferred to make a much more naturalistic picture about "the delusion of romantic love" (Kondo 216, 217).

15. Williamson Chang traces his "painful experience" watching the play to Song's inability to evolve from cipher to character as easily as he effected his gender transformation: "I could not identify with Song, he was not 'male' in my sense of the word—as someone whose character I would aspire to or identify with . . . For an Asian male sitting throughout the evening, it was the lack of psychological involvement that was noticeable. As has become the standard framework for dramas about East meets West, Asian males are again simply not there, they are *invisible*" (181–82; emphasis original).

16. Shimakawa draws on a number of theorists—among them, Homi Bhabha, Elizabeth Grosz, Judith Butler, and, most prominently, Luce Irigaray—in framing the concept of critical mimesis. See in particular chapter 4 of *National Abjection*.

Chapter 4: Bodily Negotiations

1. Much of the best discussion of how to "read" the body is being done by dance theorists. As a representative sampling, see Susan Leigh Foster's introduction to *Choreographing History* (1995) and Sondra Horton Fraleigh's *Dance and the Lived Body* (1987).

2. According to Martha J. Cutter, in Chinese American literature, "translation" is "an impossible necessity" whose relevance moves beyond the actual act of linguistic translation to become "a symbolic trope" that "evokes the concept of a crossing of borders, a permeation of barriers erected between what seem to be separate and disjunctive cultural and linguistic entities" (581).

3. For a discussion of Brecht's key concepts, see Reinhold Grimm's "Alienation in Context: On the Theory and Practice of Brechtian Theater" (1997); Peter Brookner's "Key Words in Brecht's Theory and Practice of Theatre" (1994); and Elin Diamond's "Brechtian Theory/Feminist Theory: Toward a Gestic Feminist Criticism" (1988).

4. Kirk Denton raises the question of reading and interpretation in his review of *Mulberry and Peach*: "For those of us who study modern Chinese literature, the question begs: is Nieh Hualing a Chinese writer, a Taiwanese writer, or an overseas Chinese writer? Drawing from such diverse literary traditions as she does, based on which tradition are we to view her novel? . . . But perhaps we should see her novel in a larger context [of the literature of exile] . . ." (qtd. in Wong, "Stakes" 133).

5. Written while Nieh worked as a consultant for the Iowa Writers' Workshop, *Mulberry and Peach* was banned in China, partially serialized in Taiwan, and published in its entirety in Hong Kong. Refer to Sau-ling C. Wong's "The Stakes of Textual Border-Crossing: Sinocentric, Asian American, and Feminist Critical Practices on Hualing Nieh's *Mulberry and Peach*" (2001) for a fuller discussion of the novel's publication history.

6. For examples of such criticism, see Pai Hsien-yung's "The Wandering Chinese: The Theme of Exile in Taiwan Fiction" (1976) and Shiao-ling Yu's "The Themes of Exile and Identity Crisis in Nie Hualing's Fiction" (1993).

7. The blurring boundaries between Asian and Asian American literature are further documented by Sau-ling C. Wong in her provocative article "Denationalization Reconsidered: Asian American Cultural Criticism at a Theoretical Crossroads" (1995). While Wong welcomes the process of denationalization, she argues that uncritical participation in such a practice can lead to a number of risky consequences: "unwitting subsumption into master narratives (despite a mandate to subvert master narratives built into the ethnic studies approach), and depoliticization occluded by theoretical self-critique" (12).

8. Another way to approach *Mulberry and Peach* as an Asian American text

would be to consider ways in which Asian American literature and Chinese literature both constitute, albeit very differently, a type of "minority discourse" (which
Abdul R. JanMohamed and David Lloyd identify as "the product of damage, of
damage more or less systematically inflicted on cultures produced as minorities by
the dominant culture" [7]). Rey Chow, in "Against the Lures of Diaspora: Minority Discourse, Chinese Women, and Intellectual Hegemony," argues that "the notion of modern Chinese literature . . . depends, implicitly, on the notion of a minority discourse in the postcolonial era. . . . Modern Chinese literature['s . . .]
problems are symptomatic of the histories of non-Western cultures' struggles for
cultural as well as national autonomy in the aftermath of Western imperialism.
Because postcolonial literatures are linked to the hegemonic discourse of the West
as such, they are, in spite of the typical nativist argument for their continuity with
the indigenous traditions, always effectively viewed as a kind of minority discourse
whose existence has been victimized and whose articulation has been suppressed"
(25).

9. The original English language translation of *Mulberry and Peach* utilizes
British spelling, a practice maintained in the Beacon Press edition of the novel.

10. Although the existence of multiple personalities in a single body is almost
always seen as a sign of psychological illness, Allucquere Rosanne Stone highlights
the degrees in consciousness that may characterize those who have a "multiple personality disorder." Some, like Mulberry, undergo blackouts and suffer from memory gaps when the other personality takes over. Others, such as Peach, "do not suffer blackouts and . . . claim to retain awareness of what the alter personalities are
doing when they are out" (37). While those who are conscious of what their alter
personalities are doing still fear being subject to the same kind of pathologization
imposed on those who cannot remember what happens during their memory gaps,
Stone argues that "[t]heir accustomed mode of existence, sharing a single body
with several quasi-independent personalities, is emblematic of a fair percentage of
everyday life at the close of the mechanical age" (37).

11. Sau-ling C. Wong identifies mobility as a significant concern in Asian
American literature. Despite the traditional yoking of mobility with ideas of freedom in the American cultural imagination, Asian American writers evince a "keen
collective awareness of immobility as a historical given rather than a private frustration . . . [and their] preoccupation with mobility often takes the form of images
of *im*mobility" (*Reading Asian American Literature* 123). According to Wong,
"[p]erhaps the only generalization we can safely make about directionality is that,
when an Asian American mobility narrative consciously alludes to Westward
movement as a possible structuring principle, the effect is typically ironic as in
Nieh's *Mulberry and Peach* and Mukherjee's *Jasmine*" (127).

12. The issues concerning Mulberry/Peach's invisibility and the ways in which

the INS agent considers Peach's identity false are accentuated by reading the two women as lesbian partners. While Mulberry's early relationship with her lesbian friend Lao-shih disappears from the picture as Mulberry travels, and both Mulberry and Peach continue to participate in various heterosexual relationships with men, their relationship with one another raises the issue of female homoeroticism. According to renee hoogland: "Only by being relegated to, in Butler's words, a 'domain of unthinkability and unnameability' can the lesbian be culturally present: as an 'abiding falsehood,' as a 'copy, imitation, a derivative example, a shadow of the real" (161).

Chapter 5: Shamanism and the Subject(s) of History

1. All of these imagined scenarios are based on the testimony of comfort women, which have been collected in a number of different sources. See George Hicks's *The Comfort Women: Japan's Brutal Regime of Enforced Prostitution in the Second World War* (1994), Dai-Sil Kim Gibson's "They Are Our Grandmas" (1997), Sangmie Choi Schellstede's *Comfort Women Speak: Testimony by Sex Slaves of the Japanese Military* (2000), Keith Howard's *True Stories of the Korean Comfort Women* (1996), and Rosa Marie Henson's *Comfort Woman: A Filipina's Story of Prostitution and Slavery Under the Japanese Military* (1999).

2. Keller suggests she had both reactions herself when engaging in this exercise while writing *Comfort Woman:* she wrestled with both an instinctive "first response" which is "How should I know?" even as she found herself identifying with these women to such an extent the experience became "scary" and something she tried to resist "by postponing writing certain sections for weeks" ("Reader's Guide" 5).

3. In *A Gift of the Emperor,* the narrator Soon-ah wakes in a panic because she believes the ghost of her friend Kyung Hwa has returned from the dead to take her with her to the grave (79–80). In *A Gesture Life*—Lee's novel about the life of Franklin Hata, whose placid existence in the idyllic and affluent town of Bedley Run masks a past wherein Hata's previous relationship with a Korean comfort woman while he worked as a medical officer in the Japanese army surfaces in disturbing ways—the wronged K. also returns to visit Hata: "Last night she lightly pattered up and down the hallway in her bare feet, pausing outside my bedroom door. I knew it was she. I sat up and told her to come in and she stepped to the foot of my lone twin bed. Though she sat down I couldn't feel any press of her weight, and once again, for a moment, I was almost sure she was a spectral body or a ghost. But I am not a magical man, and never have been. I am unversed in the metaphysical, have long become estranged from it, and if this can be so, I be-

lieve the metaphysical is as much unversed in me. We have a historical pact. And as deeply as I wished she were some wondrous, ethereal presence, that I was being duly haunted, I knew that she was absolute, unquestionably real, a once-person-hood come wholly into being" (286). Ghosts emerge as a trope in Korean American comfort woman literature, although their use, function, and elaboration vary from text to text. Park's evocation of Kyung Hwa's ghost represents Soon-ah's guilt for not demonstrating the courage of her friend and surviving what seems an unsurvivable ordeal. In *A Gesture Life,* Lee's deployment of K.'s ghostly presence is more integral than Park's to the structure and meaning of the novel. By materializing K only at the end but revealing the ways in which she has always been the structuring presence of Franklin's life after the war, Lee articulates the materiality of ghostliness as a trope through which to understand the impact of the comfort woman's experience. As I will demonstrate in this chapter, Keller's novel represents the most ambitious articulation of ghosts as an emerging trope for writing and reading the culturally and ethnically specific traumas experienced by Korean comfort women.

4. The kind of acknowledgment Gordon suggests we pursue here is structurally analogous to Foucault's notion of "subjugated knowledges," information systems "that have been disqualified as inadequate to their task or insufficiently elaborated: naïve knowledges, located low down on the hierarchy, beneath the required level of cognition or scientificity" (82).

5. In addition to the oral histories and memories noted in my first footnote, a number of scholarly studies in English have also appeared: see George Hicks's *The Comfort Women: Japan's Brutal Regime of Enforced Prostitution in the Second World War* (1994), Yuki Tanaka's *Hidden Horrors: Japanese War Crimes in World War II* (1998), Yoshimi Yoshiaki's *Comfort Women: Sexual Slavery in the Japanese Military During World War II* (2000), and the special issue of *positions: east asia cultures critique* edited by Chungmoo Choi entitled *the comfort women: colonialism, war, and sex* (1997).

6. Although Korean women comprised approximately 80% of the comfort women population during the war, data reveals that a wide variety of women—including Japanese, Taiwanese, Chinese, Indonesian, Dutch, Burmese, Malay, White Russian, Filipina, Vietnamese, and Burmese—were used by the Japanese military. George Hicks estimates that if we assume a ratio of comfort women to soldiers as 1 : 50, then there were about 139,000 comfort women in service during the war. Yoshimi Yoshiaki acknowledges that we have no documents from which to derive accurate numbers; however, the range of numbers would be between 50,000 and 200,000 (93–94).

7. For nuanced articles on the Japanese response to comfort women's demands

for apology and reparations, see Norma Field's "War and Apology: Japan, Asia, the Fiftieth, and After" (1997) and Won Soon Park's "Japanese Reparations Policies and the 'Comfort Women' Question" (1997). For an argument about how U.S. hegemony is complicit in the sexual enslavement of Asian women, see Lynn Thiesmeyer's "U.S. Comfort Women and the Silence of the American Other" (1996). Thiesmeyer argues that U.S. discourses blame the sexual slavery/exploitation of Asian women "on a single agent, Asia itself: they exploit women there 'because' they are Asian" (58). Such a response displaces U.S. American responsibility and complicity in perpetuating the sexual oppression of Asian women, a phenomena that continues to this day in the sex industries of Thailand and Vietnam that cater to predominantly Western men; the rape of thousands of women by American servicemen, and even the establishment of U.S. Government Jurisdiction offices on Okinawa set up to inspect the health of prostitutes seen as "belonging" to U.S. military bases. According to Thiesmeyer, "In point of fact, in the international community it is quite possible, even encouraged, to discuss Asian male victimization of women. Yet our feeding-frenzy on both sides of the Pacific about the comfort women is, as the surviving comfort women point out, fifty years too late, calling into question whether next it will be fifty years too late for our present sex slaves. It is precisely this partial disclosure that reveals the gap in our own discourse: we do not allow such descriptions of western males into our public speech" (49). As Thiesmeyer's argument makes explicit, U.S. discourses on comfort women tend to overlook the complicity of the U.S. in the sexual slavery of Asian women, both then and now. While this complicity does not absolve Asian nations from their own responsibility in perpetuating or overlooking the sexual oppression of Asian women, it does suggest that the "comfort zones" created by such discourses warrant more critical investigation.

8.   The issue of reparations involves a number of factors in addition to financial restitution and apology—see Won Soon Park's "Japanese Reparations Policies and the 'Comfort Women' Question" (1997).

9.   In other words, we must learn to be sensitive to the ways in which Keller attunes herself to the "nameless masses" of women killed by "abnormal causes" in order to "translate them into a political rhetoric" that doesn't then turn around and re-silence them in the name of expedience.

10.   The issue of economic independence emerges as a critical motivating factor for almost all of the shamans studied by Young-sook Kim Harvey in *Six Korean Women: The Socialization of Shamans* (1979). For a discussion of the performative dimensions of gender and spirituality in shamanism, see "The Sham in Shaman" in Laurence Senelick's *The Changing Room: Sex, Drag, and Theatre* (2000).

11.   As Mohanty charges, "assumptions of privilege and ethnocentric universal-

ity on the one hand, and inadequate self-consciousness about the effect of western scholarship on the 'third world' in the context of a world system dominated by the west on the other, characterize a sizable extent of western feminist work on women in the third world. . . . It is in this process of discursive homogenization and systematization of the oppression of women in the third world that power is exercised in much of recent western feminist writing, and this power needs to be defined and named" (197–98).

12.   Deborah Gewertz and Frederick Errington call this process "occidentalizing the world" and suggest that studying "the primitive" in order to analyze ourselves very often results in the uncomfortable dictum of "We Think, Therefore They Are."

13.   Keller contributes to the formation of a transnational feminism, which Pamela Thoma defines as "those various forms of feminist practices and alliances that oppose particular and global versions of economic and cultural hegemony and seek social change for women in different locations" (29).

14.   One of the hegemonies resisted, ironically enough, might be an Asian American studies history that, according to David K. Yoo, has neglected or in large part overlooked the significance of religion in the construction of Asian Americanness. See "Introduction" to *New Spiritual Homes: Religion and Asian Americans* (1999). In diasporic Hmong communities, shamanism is considered a critical site for maintaining ethnic identity and resisting assimilation, even as it is particularly vulnerable to the encroachments of western discourses of health and logic: "People have been trying to make us lose our shaman beliefs for a long time. Before the Vietnam War, there were some French missionaries that came across to our people and converted some to Catholicism. Some shamans even became priests and then forced other Hmong people to convert. . . . I think for those who are living in the U.S. now, in ten years they won't be practicing the shaman religion anymore. That is very bad because that is a part of our tradition that is being destroyed. Not only that, it is the *main* core of our culture. What do we have in our culture if we don't have shamanism? It is our tradition, our religion, our medicine—and maybe it will soon be gone" (Faderman and Xiong 116). In Korea, shamanism in particular has a long history of resisting colonial and neo-colonial efforts to stamp it out or co-opt it as part of a larger, national project of establishing the ideologies by which a modern Korea might be governed. See "Rituals of Resistance: The Manipulation of Shamanism in Contemporary Korea" (1994) by Kwang-Ok Kim and "The Cultural Politics of 'Superstition' in the Korean Shaman World: Modernity Constructs Its Other" (2001) by Laurel Kendall.

15.   According to Laurel Kendall in *Shamans, Housewives, and Other Restless Spirits* (1985), *mudang* is a commonly used Korean term for both shamans and

hereditary priests. However, due to the fact that, as a term, *mudang* is both imprecise and derogatory, Kendall (along with Harvey) chooses to use the "more polite and localized title *mansin*" (xi), a choice that I am also making in this chapter.

16. "Sympathetic magic" is a term I have borrowed from Michael Taussig's *Mimesis and Alterity: A Particular History of the Senses* (1993). Impersonation is a kind of performance that enacts sympathetic magic, which Taussig defines as "this notion of the copy, in magical practice, affecting the original to such a degree that the representation shares in or acquires the properties of the represented" (47–48).

17. By positioning the reader as a mediator of Beccah's and Akiko's stories, Keller's novel, in a way, asks the reader to occupy the structural location of the shaman who mediates between the spirit world and the world of the living.

18. Induk belongs in a sorority with characters like Mari in Hisaye Yamamoto's "The Legend of Miss Sasagawara" (1988), Rosa in Cynthia Ozick's *The Shawl* (1990), and Sethe in Toni Morrison's *Beloved* (1987), all of whom perform acts deemed "mad" by society but whose actions actually call into question the "madness" of the situations—Japanese internment, the Holocaust, and slavery—in which they find themselves.

19. Beccah's feelings of shame, catalyzed by both what her classmates articulate and what she is unable to say in response, result from Akiko's out-of-place shamanic activity at the school. That Beccah's shame results partially from her own silence resonates with the complex negotiation of shame and silence comfort women have had to navigate in order to pursue reparations: "former comfort women have been shamed and pressured not to talk about their histories. . . . The injunction of silence operates through the imposition of shame in which the rape is seen as an intensely private matter" (J. Kim 73).

20. This suggestion about the violence of the word is perhaps depicted most (in)famously in Maxine Hong Kingston's *The Woman Warrior* (1975), when the heroine has words cut into her back. The comfort women's situation demonstrates that the names by which the women are "hailed" as sexual slaves lead directly to the physical assault of rape.

21. Keller offers here an extreme example of what Tzvetan Todorov differentiates as "private" and "public" discourse: "the two discourses, which are characterized by a call for totality similar to that by the two languages of a bilingual, differ in vocabulary, partially in syntax, but especially in the way they are used. Private discourse is governed by the requirement that may be called the truth of correspondence: statements must describe the world or designate the position of the speaking subject in the most precise manner possible. Public discourse, by contrast, is governed by the quest for the truth of conformity: in order to be assessed, an utterance is not compared with an empirical experience but with other dis-

courses, given in advance and known to all, with an opinion that is right about everything" ("Dialogism and Schizophrenia" 205).

22. According to Hahm Pyong-choon, "[s]hamanistic parents keep their child in constant bodily contact. . . . The dialectic between [the child] as subject and others as object is not emphasized, and is not considered essential for the sound personality development of the child" (66).

23. As King-Kok Cheung has argued in *Articulate Silences* (1993), Asian American women writers have, as part of their efforts to "question the authority of language (especially language that passes for history) and speak to the resources as well as the hazards of silence," emphasized the ways in which "silences—textual ellipses, nonverbal gestures, authorial hesitations (as against moral, historical, religious, or political authority)—can also be articulate" (3, 4).

24. This strategy of impersonation is reminiscent of what Darlene Clark Hine has termed a "culture of dissemblance" cultivated by Black women in response to a history of institutionalized rape under slavery. According to Hine, a culture of dissemblance entails "the appearance of openness and disclosure but actually shield[s] the truth of . . . inner lives and selves" (292). This might be applied to Akiko throughout her multiple transformations but perhaps most effectively to her performances as shaman, whereby she appears to act out (uncontrollable-ness being a substitute for openness) her inner demons but nonetheless acknowledges within herself a series of inner selves that are hidden from view, either by the spectacular nature of the impersonation or the inability of others to read the cultural contexts of her performances.

25. Kathleen Brogan in *Cultural Haunting* (1998) asserts that in *Comfort Woman,* bad forms of possession "all require the relinquishing of language or voice" (155) while good forms of possession involve reconnecting with the ancestral-spiritual.

26. This is supported by a number of other researchers including Claude Lévi-Strauss, G. Devereaux, Bou-Yong Rhi, Larry Peters, and Douglas Price. For a concise summary of these findings, see Merete Jakobsen, *Shamanism: Traditional and Contemporary Approaches to the Mastery of Spirits and Healing* (1999) and Kim Kwang-il's "*Kut* and the Treatment of Mental Disorders" (1988).

27. Several different types of shamans exist in Korea. According to Kim Tae-gon, these can be divided into four categories: A. *Mudang,* B. *Tan'gol,* C. *Simbang,* and D. *Myongdu.* Aside from categorizing the shamans of Korea into four discrete types, one of the major distinctions between them derives from whether or not they are *kangsin* (charismatic) shamans who enter their office after being possessed by spirits or hereditary shamans whose priestly functions are handed down from generation to generation. In *Comfort Woman,* Keller is clearly depicting Akiko as a

mudang, although she also bears characteristics of being a *myongdu* shaman whose precondition involves being possessed by the spirit of a dead person and who then shares the same name as that of the spirit possessing her. For more on the distinctions between these various types of Korean shamans, see "Regional Characteristics of Korean Shamanism" in *Shamanism: The Spirit World of Korea* (1988).

28. The power of the shaman stems, in part, from her marginalized position. Thus, the re-integration of shamans in Korean society is partial, recognized but not always respected. Akiko's decision not to take back her name reflects her awareness of how, as shaman, she can never return to the identity she claimed before and must occupy a position that at once reveals her connection to community while acknowledging her peripheral positionality in relation to it. To think of herself as Akiko is to remember and perform her own continued decentering of self— a characteristic crucial to her success as a shamanic impersonator.

29. The ways in which (potential) shamans can be driven crazy not by the spirits that haunt them but by the people they live with who may not understand the nature of their affliction is conveyed in the following verbal exchange between filmmaker and shaman in the documentary *An Initiation Kut for a Korean Shaman:*

> SHAMAN. Her [the initiate Chini's] maternal aunt was a destined shaman. High spirits had descended to make a shaman but it was left half done because her sisters all thought she was crazy. They had her put away. She used to go down under a highway overpass, set down a bowl of water, and pray. She was behaving just like someone on the verge of becoming a shaman. But Chini's mother thought she was crazy and they slapped her into a mental hospital, a place for crazy people. She ranted and raved, so she was beaten and had drugs forced down her throat. Now she's a dimwit.
>
> FILMMAKER. If they had kept Chini in a place like that, wouldn't she have gone crazy too?
>
> SHAMAN. You bet, she would have lost her wits.

30. Mansin Ahjuma's character is obviously informed by Keller's research on shamanism. Her ambivalent position as a former shaman who struggles to denounce her previous calling in light of her conversion is patterned on the life and experiences of Deaconess Chang, one of the six shamans in Harvey's study. Although Deaconess Chang has renounced her former identity as a shaman in favor of being a born-again Christian, she characterizes herself as a site wherein a continued contest between God and the Devil takes place: "I'm being used by both Satan and God . . . . My poor body and soul are the arena of their power contest. In their battle to possess me, neither God nor Satan has any pity for me. I just

can't take it sometimes" (Harvey 210). This sentiment is lifted almost verbatim by Keller in her depiction of Mansin Ahjuma's explanation of her own sometimes-tortured condition as a former shaman who has been saved from "starvation and damnation" by Christian missionaries: "Damn jealous, those men. The Satan General and the Jesus God fight over me, she said, thrusting her chest forward. I am the arena of their power contest. And in their battle to possess me, neither has any pity for me. I just can't take it sometimes" (59). What we know from Harvey's study is that while Deaconess Chang belongs to a vibrant prayer group and is used to having her testimony of conversion utilized by her church family as part of their proselytizing endeavors, there are significant moments of tension and strain that undergird the relationship and cause us to question the "salvation" that Christian belief offers the former shaman. As her own admission acknowledges, Deaconess Chang's status as a "saved" woman is constantly in question and part of a process that requires continual vigilance and effort. Harvey notes in her study that during her sessions with Deaconess Chang, a member of the prayer group was always present and such surveillance resulted in feelings of constraint on the part of both researcher and Deaconess Chang. Clearly, by relying so heavily on this particular former shaman's experience in delineating the character of Mansin Ahjuma, Keller suggests that relinquishing one's status as a shaman in favor of a Christian identity results in a conflicted state wherein some of the symptoms of *sinbyong*, albeit not recognized as such, reoccur. Some fundamental aspect of Korean identity is thus denied and can only be maintained by the vigilant surveillance of the Christian faith community.

31. Keller's use of a doubled discourse to narrate cultural differences through generational distinction, particularly her emphasis on the unreliable perspective of Beccah, is an example of the "double-telling" that King-Kok Cheung has argued is characteristic of Hisaye Yamamoto's stories.

32. This counters one trend in the race to pursue reparations for comfort women, where women are defined by their comfort women experience in such a way as to focus almost exclusively on their period of captivity.

33. Buddhism was introduced to Korea in 372 A.D. through Koguryo, one of the three early kingdoms. Confucianism, which was influential in "molding the Korean ethos of the Yi dynasty," was introduced in Korea during the second century B.C. when Emperor Wu of China established colonies in the Korean peninsula (Kang 7–8). Invading Japanese soldiers brought Christianity to Korea in 1592 although Korean visitors to Peking who converted to Roman Catholicism and returned to Korea to baptize others laid a more substantive foundation for the religion in the eighteenth century. Dr. Horace N. Allen, a Presbyterian medical missionary, established the first Protestant church missions in Korea in 1884. For a

summary of when and how these three religions were imported to Korea, see the first chapter of Wi Jo Kang's *Religion and Politics in Korea Under the Japanese Rule* (1987).

34. In contemporary Korea, shamanistic folk rituals have been revived under the aegis of the Popular Culture Movement *(Minjung Munhwa Undong)* in order to foster a nationalistic spirit that departs from the government's notion of what constitutes modern Korean identity.

35. According to Kwang-Ok Kim, the appeal of Christianity as a religion of dissent in contemporary Korea has lost ground to indigenous popular religion, in large part because the Christian community has constructed a self-contradictory image: Christian churches have achieved expansion as a result of their cooperation with authoritarian regimes, and their emphasis on "nationalism" is seen as a tool of the dictatorial government. In Korean American diasporic communities, though, the role of Christian churches occupies a significantly different space and performs different roles: as sites of Korean cultural reinforcement, they are partially responsible for maintaining a strong level of ethnic affiliation amongst Korean Americans and fostering resistance to assimilation. According to Pyong Gap Min, Korean Americans maintain a higher level of ethnic attachment than any other Asian ethnic group, in part because most of them are affiliated with Korean ethnic churches. Min notes that a significant number of Korean immigrants who are affiliated with Korean immigrant churches were not Christians in Korea. Min deduces that the reasons for their membership are "practical" in nature: Korean immigrant churches "help maintain social interaction" (214) by serving as meeting places and helping to maintain Korean cultural traditions through language and other programs.

36. While postmodernity's disruption of binary logic and rejection of totalizing meta-narratives have produced some liberating strategies for the formation of counter-hegemonic discourse, its accompanying collapse of distinctions has also proven problematic for minority subjects and critics who seek to maintain the validity of the self as it operates in real-world contexts. As David Palumbo-Liu notes in *Asian/American* (1999), "[t]he positively inflected notion of equality under postmodern hybridity is complemented in its negative formation by a paranoid and indeed schizophrenic sense that what was formerly Other is now the Same . . . everything and everybody is mixed, pastiched, multiple" (322). Clearly, this "equality" of condition can be spun two ways: as a way of challenging the reification of Western theory and practice or as a way of denying the cultural, social, and political differences driving counter-hegemonic practices.

37. As Marita Sturken in *Tangled Memories* (1997) tells us, "we need to ask not whether a memory is true but rather what its telling reveals about how the past affects the present" (2).

38. *Chongshindae* is a term used in South Korea to refer to military comfort women. Hyunah Yang specifies that the *chongshindae* "actually consisted of two groups, one used as laborers and the other to accommodate the sexual needs of Japanese soldiers" (68). The Japanese used the official terms *jugan ianfu* ("military comfort women") and *deshintai* ("volunteer corps"). Other colloquial terms referring to comfort women include: *nigyu-ichi* (which means "29:1," specifying the ideal comfort woman to soldier ratio), *chosen poji* ("Korean pussy"), and *p'i* (a vulgar Chinese term for "vagina").

Chapter 6: Impersonation and Other Disappearing Acts

1. For discussions of the various formulas associated with spy and detective fiction, see John Cawelti and Bruce Rosenberg's *The Spy Story* (1987), John Cawelti's *Adventure, Mystery, and Romance* (1975), and Julian Symons's *Mortal Consequences* (1973). Although many critics insist on reading spy fiction as a subcategory of detective fiction, Martin Green categorizes "espionage and private eye fiction, insofar as they send their protagonists traveling," as "adventure tales" (157–58).

2. In *The Technology of Espionage* (1978), Lauran Paine traces the ways in which technology has changed the nature of espionage, especially after WWII. Such a change transforms not only the practice of espionage but also the practitioner: "The individual spy has not been as indispensable a part of the espionage operation over the succeeding generation as he was previously, although he has remained important. What he has inevitably become is a vastly more skilled technician" (12).

3. According to some critics (and fans), the danger of not meeting reader expectations by subverting the conventions of the formula story can result in some devastating outcomes. Tzvetan Todorov suggests with regard to detective fiction that it "has its norms; to 'develop' them is also to disappoint them: to 'improve' upon detective fiction is to write 'literature,' not detective fiction. The whodunit par excellence is not the one which transgresses the rules of the genre, but the one which conforms to them" (*The Fantastic* 43). Similarly, another critic offers the following advice to writers who might be tempted to write "literature" instead of a spy story: "Mistakes to avoid—making the hero an anti-hero, killing off your hero, letting the hero figure out which door hides the tiger too early in the tale, letting the bad guys win. Now you can do any one or all of these things, but if you do you no longer have a spy thriller: you have written a serious novel that can be sold only to intellectuals, a small, miserable, nitpicking, poverty-stricken audience that you will starve to death trying to please" (Coonts; qtd. in Smith 655 and White).

4. According to Palmer, "It is because the hero is an 'outsider' that he is usually given a dubious status: a lawyer like Perry Mason, who has to skate on very thin

ice; a PI, who can never be quite sure what his relationship to the police is; a spy, who will always be disowned by the employers when it comes to the crunch, in order to avoid an international scandal" (25).

5.   In his essay "Living On: Border Lines" (1991), Jacques Derrida also gestures to the paradoxical function of the self-reflexivity necessary to the process Tani describes and *Native Speaker* enacts: "What are we doing when, to practice a 'genre,' we quote a genre, represent it, stage it, expose its *generic law,* analyze it practically? Are we still practicing the genre? Does the 'work' still belong to the genre it recites? But inversely, how could we make a genre work without referring to it [quasi]quotationally, indicating at some point, 'See, this is a work of such-and-such a genre'? Such an indication does not belong to the genre and makes the statement of belonging an ironical exercise. It interrupts the very belonging of which it is a necessary condition" (259).

6.   Phelan maintains that the ideology of the visible is based on several presumptions: "1) Identities are visibly marked so the resemblance between the African-American on the television and the African-American on the street helps the observer see they are members of the same community; 2) The relationship between representation and identity is linear and smoothly mimetic. What one sees is who one is; 3) If one's mimetic likeness is not represented, one is not addressed; 4) Increased visibility equals increased power" (7).

7.   Sau-ling Cynthia Wong identifies this feeling of doubleness as one that is quite common in Asian American literature. See her chapter "Encounters with the Racial Shadow" in *Reading Asian American Literature: From Necessity to Extravagance* (1993).

8.   For a discussion of Lelia as a "speculum of whiteness, a figure who helps [Henry] focus the white lens through which he views various apparently 'Korean' aspects of his background," see Tim Engles's " 'Visions of Me in the Whitest Raw Light': Assimilation and Doxic Whiteness in Chang-rae Lee's *Native Speaker*" (1997).

9.   The ways in which *Native Speaker* is not like a spy story go beyond its language. David Stafford's *The Silent Game* (1991) argues that spy novels are "novels of crisis" which symbolize "national vulnerabilities and fears" by depicting agents in "extraordinary moments of great national or international destiny: saving the country from invasion, protecting the vital plans of top-secret weapons, destroying the enemy's imminent conspiracies" (3).

10.   This surety on Lelia's part is ironized by the difficulty that linguists of recent years have had with the very concept of a native speaker. See Paikeday, *The Native Speaker Is Dead!* (1985), and Coulmas, *A Festschrift for Native Speaker* (1981).

11.   This inscrutability is clearly racially marked and noted in Lelia's later in-

ability to "read" Ahjuma: "She doesn't seem like she's anything. I keep looking for something, but even when she's with your father there's nothing in her face" (62).

12. John C. Hawley asserts that the "struggle for masculine self-definition" (185) in the works of Gus Lee, Li-young Lee, and Chang-rae Lee manifests itself most visibly in the vexed relationships between sons and fathers.

13. Another reason for Henry's attraction to Lelia is her lack of performative ability: "When she play-acts, horses around, she is silly and awkward, completely unconvincing. She must be the worst actor on earth. And perhaps most I loved this about her, her helpless way, love it still, how she can't hide a single thing, that she looks hurt when she is hurt, seems happy when happy. That I know at every moment the precise place where she stands. What else can move a man like me, who would find nothing as siren or comforting?" (147).

14. This unwilling/unwitting transformation remarks upon one of the key lessons of *Invisible Man* (1952). The narrator's discovery and subsequent imperson-ation of the character Rinehart prefigure Henry's metamorphosis as Luzan's pa-tient. As Anne Anlin Cheng has argued so convincingly, "Rinehart as an event of visual performance demonstrates first that the act of identification is dependent on representation, and thus draws our attention to the power dynamics of viewer and spectatorship; second, that the act of representation involves simultaneously, on a deeper level, an act of disidentification. To impersonate Rinehart is to *become* Rinehart" (57).

15. As Jill Dolan asserts in her study of spectatorship, "Historically, in North American culture, this spectator has been assumed to be white, middle-class, het-erosexual, and male. That theatre creates an ideal spectator carved in the likeness of the dominant culture whose ideology he represents is the motivating assump-tion behind the discourse of feminist performance criticism" (1). Following Dolan's study, Josephine Lee theorizes the implications of an Asian American spectator in *Performing Asian America* (1997).

16. Rebecca Schneider suggests that constructed categories still have "operative reality effects" and such effects reflect "[t]he degree to which the 'real' is a ruse of performance" (156).

17. See Margaret Eddershaw's "Actors on Brecht" (1994) for a discussion of the implications of Brechtian theory and practice for the performer.

18. In his article, Cawelti lists a number of writers who have created protago-nists who reflect the concerns of a variety of minority groups. See *Multicultural Detective Fiction: Murder from the "Other" Side* (1999) edited by Adrienne Johnson Gosselin and *Diversity and Detective Fiction* (1999) edited by Kathleen Gregory Klein for two excellent collections on the work of specific minority and women writers who are re-working the conventions of the detective story. See Stephen

Soitos's *The Blues Detective* (1996) for a study of the ways in which African Americans have utilized "African American detective tropes on both classical and hard-boiled detective conventions to create a new type of detective fiction" (3).

19. The familiarity of form produces unstable results, as Patricia Linton brings to our attention in her article about Linda Hogan's "resistant" text *Mean Spirit* (1991): "By appropriating well-established genres, writers . . . make their narratives sites of cultural negotiation, in which both writer and reader have much at stake. The ethnic writer risks assimilation by willful or complacent readers, while the Eurocentric reader risks both the destabilization of a coherent worldview and the morally ambiguous status of the cultural interloper" (22).

20. For a discussion of the fears of and accusations against the Japanese that led to internment, see Ronald Takaki's *Strangers from a Different Shore* (1989), pp. 379–405. Ironically, Japanese Americans who worked in Intelligence were operating on behalf of the U.S. government and according to historian Roger Daniels, "the feats of the Japanese American intelligence specialists [have] received almost no public notice" (247). Members of the JACL "function[ed] as counterespionage" by agreeing to report "[a]ny act or word prejudicial to the United States committed by any Japanese" (209) to the FBI, Naval Intelligence, Sheriff's Office, and local police. Also, JAs were recruited to work at the Military Intelligence Service (MIS) language school "translat[ing] captured documents, monitor[ing] radio traffic, [and] interrogat[ing] prisoners" (247).

21. For more on the Yellow Peril phenomenon, see William Wu's *The Yellow Peril: Chinese Americans in American Fiction* (1982).

22. Both Cawelti and Roth trace the lineage of the spy story to Rohmer's Dr. Fu Manchu.

23. In addition to Lee, Hwang, and Chang, R. A. Shiomi in *Yellow Fever* (1984) writes a parodic and humorous revision of the conventional hard-boiled detective story and Wayne Wang's *Chan Is Missing* (1982) depicts a highly ironic sleuthing expedition that turns up no solutions. See also Jessica Hagedorn's preface to the collection *Charlie Chan Is Dead* (1993).

24. Stefano Tani argues that "every innovation in the detective story genre has occurred in reaction to the current that had long been the dominant one and that later seemed closed to variation" (36). Drawing on the observations of Russian formalist critic Jurij Tynjanov, who identifies the series of stages whereby any literary practice undergoes "automatization" and revision, Tani posits that the "anti-detective novel and its frustrating nonsolution (or parodic solution)" will eventually "be exhausted [and] ready to be replaced by some opposite constructive principle" (37).

25. Psychoanalyst Charles Rycroft argues that "[i]n the ideal detective story

the detective or hero would discover that he himself is the criminal for whom he has been seeking" (115). See Roth's chapter on "Crime, Criminal, Community" in *Foul and Fair Play* (1995) for an extended exploration of the similarities and differences between the hero and criminal.

26. Min Song's review in *Amerasia Journal* criticizes the novel for a "singular unwillingness to grant depth" to its female characters.

Coda

1. For more on the Asian American movement and the development and evolution of panethnic coalitions, see William Wei, *The Asian American Movement* (1993); David Yamane, *Student Movements for Multiculturalism: Challenging the Curricular Color Line in Higher Education* (2001); Karen Umemoto, " 'On Strike!': San Francisco State College Strike 1968–69: The Role of Asian American Students" (1989); Glenn Omatsu, " 'The Four Prisons' and the Movements of Liberation: Asian American Activism from the 1960s to 1990s" (1994); *Legacy to Liberation: Politics and Culture of Revolutionary Asian Pacific America* (2000, eds. Fred Ho et al.), and Pei-te Lien, *The Making of Asian America Through Political Participation* (2001).

Works Cited

Accardo, Annalucia and Alessandro Portelli. "A Spy in the Enemy's Country: Domestic Slaves as Internal Foes." *The Black Columbiad: Defining Moments in African American Literature and Culture.* Eds. Werner Sollors and Maria Diedrich. Cambridge, MA: Harvard UP, 1994. 77–87.

Altick, Richard D. *The Shows of London.* Cambridge, MA: Belknap P of Harvard UP, 1978.

Anderson, Benedict. *Imagined Communities.* 1983. Rev. ed. London: Verso, 1991.

Apter, Emily. "Acting Out Orientalism: Sapphic Theatricality in Turn-of-the-Century Paris." *Performance and Cultural Politics.* Ed. Elin Diamond. London: Routledge, 1996. 15–34.

Aung, Maung Htin. *The Stricken Peacock: Anglo-Burmese Relations 1752–1948.* The Hague, Neth.: Martinus Nijhoff, 1965.

Barrault, Jean-Louis. *Reflections on the Theatre.* Trans. Barbara Wall. London: Rockliff, 1951.

Bennett, Juda. *The Passing Figure: Racial Confusion in Modern American Literature.* New York: Peter Lang, 1998.

Berger, Harry, Jr. "Bodies and Texts." *Representations* 17 (1987): 144–66.

Bhabha, Homi K. "Of Mimicry and Man: The Ambivalence of Colonial discourse." *The Location of Culture.* London: Routledge, 1994. 85–92.

———. "The Other Question: Stereotype, Discrimination and the Discourse of Colonialism." *The Location of Culture.* London: Routledge, 1994. 66–84.

Blair, Rhonda. " 'Not . . . but' / 'Not-Not-Me': Musings on Cross-Gender Performance." *Upstaging Big Daddy: Directing Theater as if Gender and Race Matter.*

Eds. Ellen Donkin and Susan Clement. Ann Arbor: U of Michigan P, 1993. 291–309.

Bordo, Susan. "The Body and the Reproduction of Femininity: A Feminist Appropriation of Foucault." *Gender/Body/Knowledge: Feminist Reconstructions of Being and Knowing.* Eds. Alison M. Jaggar and Susan R. Bordo. New Brunswick, NJ: Rutgers UP, 1989. 13–33.

————. "Reading the Slender Body." *Body/Politics: Women and the Discourses of Science.* Eds. Mary Jacobus, Evelyn Fox Keller, and Sally Shuttleworth. New York: Routledge, 1990. 83–112.

Bow, Leslie. *Betrayal and Other Acts of Subversion: Feminism, Sexual Politics, Asian American Women's Literature.* Princeton, NJ: Princeton UP, 2001.

Brecht, Bertolt. *Brecht on Theatre: The Development of an Aesthetic.* Ed. and trans. John Willett. New York: Hill and Wang, 1964.

Brien, Alan. "My Enemy's Enemies." *New Statesman* 24 May 1985: 32.

Briney, Robert. "Sax Rohmer: An Informal Survey." *The Mystery Writer's Art.* Ed. Francis M. Nevins Jr. Bowling Green, OH: Bowling Green U Popular P, 1970.

Brogan, Kathleen. *Cultural Haunting: Ghosts and Ethnicity in Recent American Literature.* Charlottesville: U of Virginia P, 1998.

Brookner, Peter. "Key Words in Brecht's Theory and Practice of Theatre." *The Cambridge Companion to Brecht.* Eds. Peter Thompson and Glendyr Sacks. Cambridge: Cambridge UP, 1994. 185–200.

Browder, Laura. *Slippery Characters: Ethnic Impersonators and American Identities.* Chapel Hill: U of North Carolina P, 2000.

Bulosan, Carlos. *America Is in the Heart.* 1946. Seattle: U of Washington P, 1973.

Butler, Judith. *Bodies That Matter: On the Discursive Limits of "Sex."* New York: Routledge, 1993.

————. *Gender Trouble: Feminism and the Subversion of Identity.* New York: Routledge, 1990.

————. "Performative Acts and Gender Constitution: An Essay in Phenomenology and Feminist Theory." *Performing Feminisms: Feminist Critical Theory and Theatre.* Ed. Sue-Ellen Case. Baltimore, MD: Johns Hopkins UP, 1990. 270–82.

————. "Variations on Sex and Gender: Beauvoir, Wittig and Foucault." *Feminism as Critique: On the Politics of Gender.* Eds. Seyla Benhabib and Drucilla Cornell. Minneapolis: U of Minnesota P, 1987.

Carlson, Marvin. *Performance: A Critical Introduction.* New York: Routledge, 1996.

Castle of Fu Manchu. Dir. Jesse Franco. Perf. Christopher Lee, Tsai Chin, and Richard Greene. 1972. DVD. Blue Underground, 2003.

Caughie, Pamela L. *Passing and Pedagogy: The Dynamics of Responsibility.* Urbana: U of Illinois P, 1999.

Cawelti, John G. *Adventure, Mystery, and Romance: Formula Stories as Art and Popular Culture.* Chicago: U of Chicago P, 1975.

———. "Canonization, Modern Literature, and the Detective Story." *Theory and Practice of Classic Detective Fiction.* Eds. Jerome H. Delamater and Ruth Prigozy. Westport, CT: Greenwood, 1997. 5–20.

———. "The Concept of Formula in the Study of Popular Literature." *Popular Fiction: An Anthology.* Ed. Gary Hoppenstand. New York: Longman, 1998. 730–36.

Cawelti, John G. and Bruce A. Rosenberg. *The Spy Story.* Chicago: U of Chicago P, 1987.

Cha, Theresa Hak-Kyung. *Dictee.* New York: Tanem, 1982.

Chambers, Iain. *Border Dialogues: Journeys in Postmodernity.* London: Routledge, 1990.

Chan Is Missing. Dir. Wayne Wang. Perf. Marc Hayashi and Wood Moy. New Yorker, 1982.

Chan, Jeffery Paul, et al. "Introduction." *The Big Aiiieeeee!: An Anthology of Chinese American and Japanese American Literature.* New York: Penguin, 1991.

Chan, Sucheng. "The Exclusion of Chinese Women, 1870–1943." *Entry Denied: Exclusion and the Chinese Community in America, 1882–1943.* Ed. Sucheng Chan. Philadelphia, PA: Temple UP, 1991. 94–146.

———, ed. *Entry Denied: Exclusion and the Chinese Community in America, 1882–1943.* Philadelphia, PA: Temple UP, 1991.

Chang, Leonard. *Over the Shoulder: A Novel of Intrigue.* New York: Ecco, 2001.

Chang, Williamson B. C. "*M. Butterfly:* Passivity, Deviousness, and the Invisibility of the Asian American Male." *Bearing Dreams, Shaping Visions: Asian Pacific American Perspectives.* Eds. Linda A. Revilla, Gail M. Nomura, Shawn Wong, and Shirley Hune. Pullman: Washington State UP, 1993. 181–84.

Chen, Tina. "Betrayed into Motion: The Seduction of Narrative Desire in *M. Butterfly.*" *Critical Mass: A Journal of Asian American Cultural Criticism* 1.2 (1994): 129–54.

———. "Dissecting the Devil Doctor: Stereotype and Sensationalism in Sax Rohmer's Fu Manchu." *Re/collecting Early Asian America.* Eds. Josephine Lee, Imogene Lim, and Yuko Matsukawa. Philadelphia, PA: Temple UP, 2002. 218–37.

Cheng, Anne Anlin. "The Melancholy of Race." *The Kenyon Review* 19.1 (Winter 1997): 49–70.

Chesler, Phyllis. *Women and Madness.* New York: Avon, 1973.

Cheung, King-Kok. *Articulate Silences: Hisaye Yamamoto, Maxine Hong Kingston, Joy Kogawa.* Reading Women Writing Series. Ithaca, NY: Cornell UP, 1993.

Chin, Frank. *Bulletproof Buddhists and Other Essays.* Honolulu: U of Hawai'i P in association with UCLA Asian American Studies Center, 1998.

———. *"The Chickencoop Chinaman" and "The Year of the Dragon": Two Plays.* Seattle: U of Washington P, 1981.

———. "Come All Ye Asian American Writers of the Real and the Fake." *The Big Aiiieeeee!: An Anthology of Chinese American and Japanese American Literature.* Eds. Jeffery Paul Chan, Frank Chin, Lawson Fusao Inada, and Shawn Wong. New York: Penguin, 1991. 1–92.

———. "Confessions of a Chinatown Cowboy." *Bulletin of Concerned Asian Scholars* 4.3 (1972): 58–70.

Chin, Tsai. *Daughter of Shanghai.* New York: St. Martin's, 1988.

Chin, Tung-Pok with Winifred C. Chin. *Paper Son: One Man's Story.* Philadelphia, PA: Temple UP, 2000.

Choi, Chungmoo. "Guest Editor's Introduction." *positions: east asia cultures critique* 5.1 (Spring 1997): v–xiv.

Chow, Rey. "Against the Lures of Diaspora: Minority Discourse, Chinese Women, and Intellectual Hegemony." *Gender and Sexuality in Twentieth-Century Chinese Literature and Society.* Ed. Tonglin Lu. N.p.: SUNY P, n.d. 21–45.

Choy, Philip P., Lorraine Dong, and Marlon K. Hom, eds. *The Coming Man: Nineteenth-Century American Perceptions of the Chinese.* Seattle: U of Washington P, 1995.

Christensen, Peter. "The Political Appeal of Dr. Fu Manchu." *The Devil Himself: Villainy in Detective Fiction and Film.* Eds. Stacy Gillis and Philippa Gates. Westport, CT: Greenwood P, 2002. 81–90.

Chu, Patricia P. *Assimilating Asians: Gendered Strategies of Authorship in Asian America.* Durham, NC: Duke UP, 2000.

Chuh, Kandice. "Discomforting Knowledge, or Korean 'Comfort Women' and Asian Americanist Critical Practice." *Journal of Asian American Studies (JAAS)* 6.1 (2003): 5–23.

———. "Guest Editor's Introduction: On Korean 'Comfort Women'." *Journal of Asian American Studies (JAAS)* 6.1 (2003): 1–4.

———. *Imagine Otherwise: On Asian Americanist Critique.* Durham, NC: Duke UP, 2003.

Cima, Gay Gibson. *Performing Women: Female Characters, Male Playwrights, and the Modern Stage.* Ithaca, NY: Cornell UP, 1993.

Clegg, Jenny. *Fu Manchu and the "Yellow Peril": The Making of a Racist Myth.* Stoke-on-Trent: Tratham Books, 1994.

Cody, Gabrielle. "David Henry Hwang's *M. Butterfly:* Perpetuating the Misogynist Myth." *Theatre* 20 (1989): 24–27.

Cohen, Ed. "Posing the Question: Wilde, Wit, and the Ways of Man." *Performance and Cultural Politics.* Ed. Elin Diamond. New York: Routledge, 1996. 35–47.

Conquergood, Dwight. "Performance Theory, Hmong Shamans, and Cultural Politics." *Critical Theory and Performance.* Eds. Janelle G. Reinelt and Joseph R. Roach. Ann Arbor: U of Michigan P, 1992. 41–64.

Coulmas, Florian. "Introduction: The Concept of Native Speaker." *A Festschrift for Native Speaker.* Ed. Florian Coulmas. The Hague, Neth: Mouton, 1981. 1–28.

———. "Spies and Native Speakers." *A Festschrift for Native Speaker.* Ed. Florian Coulmas. The Hague, Neth: Mouton, 1981. 355–68.

Covell, Alan Carter. *Ecstasy: Shamanism in Korea.* Elizabeth, NJ: Hollym International Corp., 1983.

Craig, Patricia and Mary Cadogan. *The Lady Investigates: Women Detectives and Spies in Fiction.* London: Victor Gollancz, 1981.

Crane, David. "A Personal Postscript, an Impostured Preface." *Pedagogy: The Question of Impersonation.* Ed. Jane Gallop. Theories of Contemporary Culture. Bloomington: Indiana UP, 1995. ix–xiv.

Cutter, Martha J. "An Impossible Necessity: Translation and the Recreation of Linguistic and Cultural Identities in Contemporary Chinese American Literature." *Criticism* 34 (1997): 581–612.

Dallery, Arleen B. "The Politics of Writing (the) Body: *Écriture Féminine.*" *Gender/Body/Knowledge: Feminist Reconstructions of Being and Knowing.* Eds. Alison M. Jaggar and Susan R. Bordo. New Brunswick, NJ: Rutgers UP, 1989. 52–67.

Daniels, Roger. *Asian America: Chinese and Japanese in the United States Since 1850.* Seattle: U of Washington P, 1988.

Daughter of the Dragon. Dir. Lloyd Corrigan. Perf. Anna May Wong, Warner Oland, Sessue Hayakawa. Paramount, 1931.

de Man, Paul. *Allegories of Reading: Figural Language in Rousseau, Nietzche, Rilke, and Proust.* New Haven, CT: Yale UP, 1979.

Dempster, Elizabeth. "Women Writing the Body: Let's Watch a Little How She Dances." *Grafts: Feminist Cultural Criticism.* Ed. Susan Sheridan. London: Verso, 1988. 35–54.

Derrida, Jacques. "Living On: Border Lines." *A Derrida Reader: Between the Blinds.* Ed. Peggy Kamuf. New York: Columbia UP, 1991. 254–68.

Diamond, Elin. "Brechtian Theory/Feminist Theory: Toward a Gestic Feminist Criticism." *TDR* 8.1 (1988): 82–94.

———. "Refusing the Romanticism of Identity: Narrative Interventions in Churchill, Benmussa, Duras." *Performing Feminisms: Feminist Critical Theory and Theatre*. Ed. Sue-Ellen Case. Baltimore, MD: Johns Hopkins UP, 1990. 92–108.

Dolan, Jill. *The Feminist Spectator as Critic*. Ann Arbor: U of Michigan Research P, 1988.

Eddershaw, Margaret. "Actors on Brecht." *The Cambridge Companion to Brecht*. Eds. Peter Thomson and Glendyr Sacks. Cambridge: Cambridge UP, 1994. 254–72.

Eliade, Mircea. *Shamanism: Archaic Techniques of Ecstasy*. Trans. Willard R. Trask. New York: Bollingen/Pantheon, 1964.

Ellison, Ralph. *Invisible Man*. 1952. Rpt. New York: Vintage, 1990.

———. *Shadow and Act*. New York: Random House, 1964.

Engles, Tim. " 'Visions of Me in the Whitest Raw Light': Assimilation and Doxic Whiteness in Chang-rae Lee's *Native Speaker*." *Hitting Critical Mass: A Journal of Asian American Cultural Studies* 4.2 (1997): 27–48.

Erickson, Jon. "Appropriation and Transgression in Contemporary American Performance: The Wooster Group, Holly Hughes, and Karen Finley." *Theatre Journal* 42.2 (1990): 225–37.

Espiritu, Yen Le. *Asian American Panethnicity: Bridging Institutions and Identities*. Philadelphia, PA: Temple UP, 1992.

———. *Asian American Women and Men: Labor, Laws, and Love*. Thousand Oaks, CA: Sage Publications, 1997.

Fabi, M. Giulia. *Passing and the Rise of the African American Novel*. Urbana: U of Illinois P, 2001.

Faderman, Lillian with Ghia Xiong. *I Begin My Life All Over: The Hmong and the American Immigrant Experience*. Boston: Beacon, 1998.

Fanon, Frantz. *The Wretched of the Earth*. 1957. Trans. Constance Farrington. New York: Grove Weidenfeld, 1963.

Fenkl, Heinz Insu. "Reflections on Shamanism." *New Spiritual Homes: Religion and Asian Americans*. Ed. David K. Yoo. Honolulu: U of Hawai'i P, 1999. 188–201.

Field, Norma. "War and Apology: JapaN, Asia, the Fiftieth, and After." *positions: east asia cultures critique* 5.1 (Spring 1997): 1–50.

Foster, Susan Leigh. Ed. *Choreographing History*. Bloomington: Indiana UP, 1995.

Foucault, Michel. *Discipline and Punish*. New York: Vintage, 1979.

————. *Power/Knowledge*. Ed. Colin Gordon. Trans. Colin Gordon, Leo Marshall, John Mepham, and Kate Soper. New York: Pantheon, 1980.

Fraleigh, Sondra Horton. *Dance and the Lived Body: A Descriptive Aesthetics*. Pittsburgh, PA: U of Pittsburgh P, 1987.

Frayling, Christopher. "Criminal Tendencies—II: Sax Rohmer and the Devil Doctor." *London Magazine* 13.2 (1973): 65–80.

Fusco, Coco. *the bodies that were not ours and other writings*. London and NY: Routledge and inIVA, 2001.

————. *English Is Broken Here: Notes on Cultural Fusion in the Americas*. New York: The New P, 1995.

Gallop, Jane. "Im-Personation: A Reading in the Guise of an Introduction." *Pedagogy: The Question of Impersonation*. Ed. Jane Gallop. Theories of Contemporary Culture. Bloomington: Indiana UP, 1995. 1–18.

Gewertz, Deborah and Frederick Errington. "We Think, Therefore They Are? On Occidentalizing the World" in *Cultures of United States Imperialism*. Eds. Amy Kaplan and Donald E. Pease. Durham, NC: Duke UP, 1993. 635–55.

Gibson, Dai-Sil Kim. "They Are Our Grandmas." *positions: east asia cultures critique* 5.1 (1997): 255–74.

Gilman, Sander L. *Difference and Pathology: Stereotypes of Sexuality, Race, and Madness*. Ithaca, NY: Cornell UP, 1985.

————. *Disease and Representation: Images of Illness from Madness to AIDS*. Ithaca, NY: Cornell UP, 1988.

Glaessner, Verina. *Kung Fu*. New York: Bounty, 1974.

Gordon, Avery F. *Ghostly Matters: Haunting and the Sociological Imagination*. Minneapolis: U of Minnesota P, 1997.

Gosselin, Adrienne Johnson, ed. *Multicultural Detective Fiction: Murder from the "Other" Side*. New York: Garland, 1999.

Gotanda, Philip Kan. *Yankee Dawg You Die*. New York: Dramatists Play Service, Inc., 1991.

Green, Martin. *Seven Types of Adventure Tale: An Etiology of a Major Genre*. University Park: Pennsylvania State UP, 1991.

Grimm, Reinhold. "Alienation in Context: On the Theory and Practice of Brechtian Theater." *A Bertolt Brecht Reference Companion*. Ed. Siegfried Mews. Westport, CT: Greenwood, 1997.

Grosz, Elizabeth. *Volatile Bodies: Toward a Corporeal Feminism*. Bloomington: Indiana UP, 1994.

Guillermo, Emil. "America Was in the Heart, but the FBI Was in His Life." *SFGate.com* 8 Oct. 2002. 15 Nov. 2002 <http:/www.sfgate.com/cgi-bin/article?=/gate/archive/2002/10/08/eguillermo.DTL>.

Hagedorn, Jessica. "Preface." *Charlie Chan Is Dead: An Anthology of Contemporary Asian American Literature.* New York: Penguin, 1993. vii–xiv.

Hahm, Pyong-choon. "Shamanism and the Korean World-View, Family Life-cycle, Society and Social Life." *Shamanism: The Spirit World of Korea.* Eds. Richard W. I. Guisso and Chai-shin Yu. Berkeley, CA: Asian Humanities P, 1988. 60–97.

Hamamoto, Darrell Y. *Monitored Peril: Asian Americans and the Politics of TV Representation.* Minneapolis: U of Minnesota P, 1994.

Hara, Marie. "Honeymoon Hotel, 1895." *Bananaheart and Other Stories.* Honolulu, HI: Bamboo Ridge, 1994. 7–18.

Harvey, Young-sook Kim. *Six Korean Women: The Socialization of Shamans.* St. Paul, MN: West Publishing Company, 1979.

Hawley, John C. "The Search for the Father in Asian American Literature." *Ideas of Home: Literature of Asian Migration.* Ed. Geoffrey Kain. East Lansing: Michigan State UP, 1997. 183–96.

Heilbrun, Carolyn. "Keynote Address: Gender and Detective Fiction." *The Sleuth and the Scholar: Origins, Evolution, and Current Trends in Detective Fiction.* Eds. Barbara A. Rader and Howard G. Zettler. New York: Greenwood, 1988. 1–10.

Henson, Rosa Marie. *Comfort Woman: A Filipina's Story of Prostitution and Slavery Under the Japanese Military.* Lanham, MD: Rowman & Littlefield, 1999.

Hicks, George. *The Comfort Women: Japan's Brutal Regime of Enforced Prostitution in the Second World War.* New York: Norton, 1994.

Hine, Darlene Clark, ed. *Black Women's History: Theory and Practice.* Brooklyn, NY: Carlson, 1990.

Hirata, Lucie Cheng. "Free, Indentured, Enslaved: Chinese Prostitutes in Nineteenth-Century America." *Signs: Journal of Women in Culture and Society* 5.1 (1979): 3–29.

Ho, Fred, Carolyn Antonio, Diane Fujino, and Steve Yip, eds. *Legacy to Liberation: Politics and Culture of Revolutionary Asian Pacific America.* San Francisco, CA: Big Red Media and AK P, 2000.

Hong, Catherine. "In Brief—*Native Speaker* by Chang-rae Lee." *Vogue* 185.4 (1995): 236.

Hongo, Garrett. "Introduction." *Under Western Eyes: Personal Essays from Asian America.* New York: Anchor/Doubleday, 1995. 1–33.

hoogland, renée c. "The Gaze of Inversion: The Lesbian as Visionary." *Vision in Context: Historical and Contemporary Perspectives on Sight.* Eds. Teresa Brennan and Martin Jay. New York: Routledge, 1996. 155–68.

Horseman, Reginald. *Race and Manifest Destiny: The Origins of American Racial Anglo-Saxonism.* Cambridge, MA: Harvard UP, 1981.

"How to Tell Japs from the Chinese." *Life* 14 December 1941: 14.

Howard, Keith. *True Stories of the Korean Comfort Women.* New York: Cassell Academic, 1996.

Hutcheon, Linda. *Irony's Edge: The Theory and Politics of Irony.* London: Routledge, 1994.

———. *A Poetics of Postmodernism: History, Theory, Fiction.* New York: Routledge, 1988.

Hutchinson, Don. *It's Raining Corpses in Chinatown.* Mercer Island, WA: Starmont, 1991.

Hwang, David Henry. *M. Butterfly.* New York: Plume, 1989.

An Initiation Kut for a Korean Shaman. Dir. Laurel Kendall and Diana S. Lee. U of Hawai'i P, 1991.

Jakobsen, Merete Demant. *Shamanism: Traditional and Contemporary Approaches to the Mastery of Spirits and Healing.* New York: Berghahn, 1999.

JanMohamed, Abdul R. *Manichean Aesthetics: The Politics of Literature in Colonial Africa.* Amherst: U of Massachusetts P, 1983.

———and David Lloyd. "Introduction: Minority Discourse—What Is to Be Done?" *Cultural Critique* 7 (1987): 7–21.

Johnson, Barbara. "Writing." *Critical Terms for Literary Study.* Eds. Frank Lentricchia and Thomas McLaughlin. Chicago: Chicago UP, 1990. 39–49.

Kang, Wi Jo. *Religion and Politics in Korea Under the Japanese Rule.* Lewiston, NY: Edwin Mellen, 1987.

Karamcheti, Indira. "Caliban in the Classroom." *Pedagogy: The Question of Impersonation.* Ed. Jane Gallop. Theories of Contemporary Culture. Bloomington: Indiana UP, 1995. 138–46.

Keller, Nora Okja. *Comfort Woman.* New York: Viking, 1997.

Kendall, Laurel. "The Cultural Politics of 'Superstition' in the Korean Shaman World: Modernity Constructs Its Other." *Healing Powers and Modernity: Traditional Medicine, Shamanism, and Science in Asian Societies.* Eds. Linda H. Connor and Geoffrey Samuel. Westport, CT: Bergin and Garvey, 2001. 25–41.

———. *The Life and Hard Times of a Korean Shaman: Of Tales and the Telling of Tales.* Honolulu: U of Hawai'i P, 1988.

———. *Shamans, Housewives, and Other Restless Spirits: Women in Korean Ritual Life.* Honolulu: U of Hawai'i P, 1985.

Kim, Daniel Y. "The Strange Love of Frank Chin." *Q & A: Queer in Asian America.* Eds. David L. Eng and Alice Y. Hom. Philadelphia, PA: Temple UP, 1998. 279–303.

Kim, Elaine. *Asian American Literature: An Introduction to the Writings and Their Social Context.* Philadelphia, PA: Temple UP, 1982.

Kim, Hyun Sook. "History and Memory: The 'Comfort Women' Controversy." *positions: east asia cultures critique* 5.1 (1997): 73–106.

Kim, Hyung-chan. *A Legal History of Asian Amerians, 1790–1990*. Westport, CT: Greenwood, 1994.

———, ed. *Asian Americans and Congress: A Documentary History.* Westport, CT: Greenwood, 1996.

Kim, Jodi. "Haunting History: Violence, Trauma, and the Politics of Memory in Nora Okja Keller's *Comfort Woman." Hitting Critical Mass: A Journal of Asian American Cultural Criticism* 6.1 (1999): 61–78.

Kim, Kwang-il. "*Kut* and the Treatment of Mental Disorders." Trans. Suh Kik-on and Im Hye-young. *Shamanism: the Spirit World of Korea.* Eds. Richard W. I. Guisso and Chai-shin Yu. Berkeley, CA: Asian Humanities P, 1988. 131–61.

Kim, Kwang-Ok. "Rituals of Resistance: The Manipulation of Shamanism in Contemporary Korea." *Asian Visions of Authority: Religion and the Modern States of East and Southeast Asia.* Eds. Charles F. Keyes, Laurel Kendall, Helen Hardacre. Honolulu: U of Hawai'i P, 1994. 195–220.

Kim, T'ae-gon. "Regional Characteristics of Korean Shamanism." Trans. Yi Yu-jin. *Shamanism: The Spirit World of Korea.* Eds. Richard W. I. Guisso and Chai-shin Yu. Berkeley, CA: Asian Humanities P, 1988. 119–30.

Kingston, Maxine Hong. *The Woman Warrior: Memoir of a Girlhood Among Ghosts.* New York: Viking, 1975.

Klein, Kathleen Gregory, ed. *Diversity and Detective Fiction.* Bowling Green, OH: Bowling Green State U Popular P, 1999.

Klinkenborg, Verlyn. Rev. of *Native Speaker. New Yorker* 10 July 1995: 76–77.

Kondo, Dorinne. *About Face: Performing Race in Fashion and Theater.* New York: Routledge, 1997.

Koshy, Susan. "The Fiction of Asian American Literature." 1996. Rpt. *Asian American Studies: A Reader.* Eds. Jean Yu-Wen Shen Wu and Min Song. New Brunswick, NJ: Rutgers UP, 2000. 467–96.

Kott, Jan. *The Memory of the Body.* Evanston: Illinois UP, 1992.

Kramsch, Claire. "The Privilege of the Nonnative Speaker." *PMLA* 112 (1997): 359–69.

Kummer, Werner. "Malinche, Patron Saint of Informants?" *A Festschrift for Native Speaker.* Ed. Florian Coulmas. The Hague, Neth: Mouton, 1981. 175–94.

Lacan, Jacques. *Four Fundamental Concepts of Psycho-Analysis.* Ed. Jacques-Alain Miller. Tr. Alan Sheridan. New York: Norton, 1978.

Lagden, Sir Godfrey. *The Native Races of the Empire.* London: W. Collins, 1924.

Lee, Chang-rae. *A Gesture Life.* New York: Riverhead, 1999.

———. *Native Speaker.* New York: Riverhead, 1995.

Lee, Josephine. *Performing Asian America: Race and Ethnicity on the Contemporary Stage.* Philadelphia, PA: Temple UP, 1997.

Lee, Rachel. "Journalistic Representations of Asian Americans and Literary Responses, 1910–1920." *An Interethnic Companion to Asian American Literature.* Ed. King-Kok Cheung. Cambridge: Cambridge UP, 1997. 249–73.

Lee, Robert G. *Orientals: Asian Americans in Popular Culture.* Philadelphia, PA: Temple UP, 1999.

Lewis, I. M. *Religion in Context: Cults and Charisma.* Cambridge: Cambridge UP, 1986.

Lévi-Strauss, Claude. *Structural Anthropology.* New York: Basic, 1963.

Lien, Pei-te. *The Making of Asian America Through Political Participation.* Philadelphia, PA: Temple UP, 2001.

Ling, Huping. *Surviving on the Gold Mountain: A History of Chinese American Women and Their Lives.* Albany: State U of New York P, 1998.

Linton, Patricia. "The Detective Novel as a Resistant Text: Alter-Ideology in Linda Hogan's *Mean Spirit.*" *Multicultural Detective Fiction: Murder from the "Other" Side.* Ed. Adrienne Johnson Gosselin. New York: Garland, 1999.

Liu, Eric. *The Accidental Asian: Notes of a Native Speaker.* New York: Random House, 1998.

Loewen, James W. *The Mississippi Chinese: Between Black and White.* Cambridge, MA: Harvard UP, 1971.

Lowe, Lisa. *Immigrant Acts: On Asian American Cultural Politics.* Durham, NC: Duke UP, 1996.

Lye, Colleen. "*M. Butterfly* and the Rhetoric of Antiessentialism: Minority Discourse in an International Frame." *The Ethnic Canon: Histories, Institutions, and Interventions.* Ed. David Palumbo-Liu. Minneapolis: U of Minnesota P, 1995. 260–89.

M. Butterfly. Dir. David Cronenberg. Perf. Jeremy Irons and John Lone. Warner Bros. 1993.

Ma, Sheng-mei. *The Deathly Embrace: Orientalism and Asian American Identity.* Minneapolis: U of Minnesota P, 2000.

MacDonald, Janice. "Parody and Detective Fiction." *Theory and Practice of Classic Detective Fiction.* Eds. Jerome H. Delamater and Ruth Prigozy. Westport, CT: Greenwood P, 1997. 61–72.

MacKenzie, John M. *Propaganda and Empire: The Manipulation of British Public Opinion 1880–1960.* Studies in Imperialism. Manchester: Manchester UP, 1984.

Manalansan, Martin F. "*Biyuti* in Everyday Life: Performance, Citizenship, and Survival Among Filipinos in the United States." *Orientations: Mapping Studies in the Asian Diaspora.* Eds. Kandice Chuh and Karen Shimakawa. Durham, NC: Duke UP, 2001. 153–71.

————, ed. *Cultural Compass: Ethnographic Explorations of Asian America.* Philadelphia, PA: Temple UP, 2000.

Marchetti, Gina. *Romance and the "Yellow Peril": Race, Sex, and Discursive Strategies in Hollywood Fiction.* Berkeley: U of California P, 1993.

The Mask of Fu Manchu. Dir. Charles Brabin. Perf. Boris Karloff, Myrna Loy, and Lewis Stone. MGM, 1932.

Mason, Tom, ed. *Sax Rohmer: Two Complete Fu Manchu Adventures.* Newbury Park, CA: Malibu Graphics, 1989.

McClain, Charles J. *In Search of Equality: The Chinese Struggle Against Discrimination in Nineteenth-Century America.* Berkeley: U of California P, 1994.

Merry, Bruce. *Anatomy of the Spy Thriller.* Montreal, Can: McGill-Queen's UP, 1977.

Mey, Jacob. " 'Right or Wrong, my Native Speaker.' Estant les Régestes du Noble Souverain de l'Empirie Linguistic avec un Renvoi au mesme Roy." *A Festschrift for Native Speaker.* Ed. Florian Coulmas. The Hague, Neth: Mouton, 1981. 69–84.

Miller, Stuart C. *The Unwelcome Immigrant: The American Image of the Chinese, 1785–1882.* Berkeley: U of California P, 1969.

Min, Eun Kyung. "Reading the Figure of Dictation in Theresa Hak Kyung Cha's *Dictee.*" *Other Sisterhoods: Literary Theory and U.S. Women of Color.* Urbana: U of Illinois P, 1998. 309–24.

Min, Pyong Gap. "Korean Americans." *Asian Americans: Contemporary Trends and Issues.* Ed. Pyong Gap Min. Thousand Oaks, CA: SAGE Publications, 1995. 199–231.

Mirikitani, Janice. "American Geisha." *Shedding Silence.* Berkeley, CA: Celestial Arts, 1987. 21–24.

Mohanty, Chandra Talpade. "Under Western Eyes: Feminist Scholarship and Colonial Discourses." *Colonial Discourse and Post-colonial Theory.* Eds. Patrick Williams and Laura Chrisman. New York: Columbia UP, 1994. 196–220.

Morrison, Toni. *Beloved.* 1987. New York: Plume, 1998.

Moy, James S. *Marginal Sights: Staging the Chinese in America.* Studies in Theatre History and Culture. Iowa City: U of Iowa P, 1993.

Moya, Paula M. L. *Learning From Experience: Minority Identities, Multicultural Struggles.* Berkeley: U of California P, 2002.

Muñoz, José Esteban. *Disidentifications: Queers of Color and the Performance of PoLitics.* Minneapolis: U of Minnesota P, 1999.

Munson, C. B. "Japanese on the West Coast." *Asian American Studies: A Reader.* Eds. Jean Yu-Wen Shen Wu and Min Song. New Brunswick, NJ: Rutgers UP, 2000. 84–92.

Mura, David. *Where the Body Meets Memory: An Odyssey of Race, Sexuality and Identity.* New York: Anchor, 1996.

Murch, Alma Elizabeth. *The Development of the Detective Novel.* Westport, CT: Greenwood P, 1958.

Nicolson, Marjorie. "The Professor and the Detective." *The Art of the Mystery Story.* Ed. Howard Haycraft. New York: Carroll & Graf, 1974. 110–27.

Nieh, Hualing. *Mulberry and Peach.* Boston: Beacon, 1988.

Ng, Fae Myenne. *Bone.* New York: Hyperion, 1993.

Nguyen, Viet Thanh. *Race and Resistance: Literature and Politics in Asian America.* Oxford: Oxford UP, 2002.

Okihiro, Gary Y. *The Columbia Guide to Asian American History.* New York: Columbia UP, 2001.

———. *Common Ground: Reimagining American History.* Princeton, NJ: Princeton UP, 2001.

Omatsu, Glenn. " 'The Four Prisons' and the Movements of Liberation: Asian American Activism from the 1960s to 1990s." *The State of Asian America: Activism and Resistance in the 1990s.* Ed. Karin Aguilar San Juan. Boston: South End P, 1994. 19–69.

Otsuka, Julie. *When the Emperor Was Divine.* New York: Alfred A. Knopf, 2002.

Owen, Kathleen Belin. " 'The Game's Afoot': Predecessors and Pursuits of a Postmodern Detective Novel." *Theory and Practice of Classic Detective Fiction.* Eds. Jerome H. Delamater and Ruth Prigozy. Westport, CT: Greenwood P, 1997. 73–84.

Owens, Craig. "The Medusa Effect, or, The Specular Ruse." *Beyond Recognition: Representation, Power, and Culture.* Eds. Scott Bryson, et al. Berkeley: U of California P, 1992. 191–200.

———. "Posing." *Beyond Recognition: Representation, Power, and Culture.* Eds. Scott Bryson, et al. Berkeley: U of California P, 1992. 201–17.

Ozick, Cynthia. *The Shawl.* 1989. New York: Vintage, 1990.

Pai, Hsien-yung. "The Wandering Chinese: The Theme of Exile in Taiwan Fiction." *Iowa Review* 7.2–3 (1976): 205–12.

Paikeday, Thomas M. *The Native Speaker Is Dead!* Toronto: Paikeday Publishing, 1985.

Paine, Lauran. *The Technology of Espionage.* London: Robert Hale, 1978.

Palmer, Jerry. *Thrillers: Genesis and Structure of a Popular Genre.* London: Edward Arnold, 1978.

Palmer, Spencer J. *Korea and Christianity: The Problem of Identification with Tradition.* Seoul: Hollym Corp., 1967.

Palumbo-Liu, David. *Asian/American: Historical Crossings of a Racial Frontier.* Stanford, CA: Stanford UP, 1999.

———. "The Minority Self as Other: Problematics of Representation in Asian-American Literature." *Cultural Critique* 28 (1994): 75–102.

Park, Therese. *A Gift of the Emperor.* Duluth, MN: Spinsters Ink, 1997.

Park, Won Soon. "Japanese Reparations Policies and the 'Comfort Women' Question." *positions: east asia cultures critique* 5.1 (1997): 107–34.

Pavey, Ruth. Rev. of *Native Speaker. New Statesman & Society* 25 August 1995: 32.

Phelan, Peggy. "Thirteen Ways of Looking at *Choreographing Writing." Choreographing History.* Ed. Susan Leigh Foster. Bloomington: Indiana UP, 1995. 200–10.

———. *Unmarked: The Politics of Performance.* London: Routledge, 1993.

Phillips, Ralph Hobart. "Sax Rohmer's 'The Insidious Dr. Fu-Manchu'." *The Bookman* Nov. 1913: 305–6.

Picture Bride. Dir. Kayo Hatta. Miramax, 1995.

Porter, Dennis. *The Pursuit of Crime: Art and Ideology in Detective Fiction.* New Haven, CT: Yale UP, 1981.

Renan, Ernest. "What Is a Nation?" *Nation and Narration.* Ed. Homi K. Bhabha. London: Routledge, 1990. 8–22.

Rev. of *Tales of Secret Egypt. The New York Times Book Review* 6 July 1919: 358.

Roach, Joseph. *Cities of the Dead: Circum-Atlantic Performance.* New York: Columbia UP, 1996.

Robertson, Pamela. *Guilty Pleasures: Feminist Camp from Mae West to Madonna.* Durham, NC: Duke UP, 1996.

Rohmer, Sax. *The Daughter of Fu Manchu.* 1931. New York: Zebra Kensington, 1986.

———. "The Doctor's Blade." *The New Yorker.* 29 Nov 1947. 37.

———. *The Drums of Fu Manchu.* Garden City, NY: Crime Club-Doubleday, Doran & Company, 1939.

———. *Emperor Fu Manchu.* London: Herbert Jenkins, 1959.

———. *Fu Manchu's Bride.* Garden City, NY: Crime Club-Doubleday, Doran & Company, 1933.

———. *The Hand of Fu Manchu. The Book of Fu Manchu.* New York: McBride, 1929. 1–89.

———. *The Insidious Dr. Fu Manchu.* 1913. New York: Pyramid, 1970.

———. *The Island of Fu Manchu.* 1940. New York: Pyramid, 1971.

———. *The Mask of Fu Manchu.* 1932. New York: Pyramid, 1970.

———. *President Fu Manchu.* Garden City, NY: The Sun Dial P, 1936.

———. *The Return of Dr. Fu Manchu. The Book of Fu Manchu.* New York: McBride, 1929. 91–187.

———. *Shadow of Fu Manchu.* Garden City, NY: Doubleday & Co., 1948.

————. *The Trail of Fu Manchu.* 1934. New York: Pyramid, 1966.

Roth, Marty. *Foul and Fair Play: Reading Genre in Classic Detective Fiction.* Athens: U of Georgia P, 1995.

Rubenstein, Richard E. *Alchemists of Revolution: Terrorism in the Modern World.* New York: Basic, 1987.

Rycroft, Charles. "The Analysis of a Detective Story." *Imagination and Reality: Psychoanalytic Essays, 1951–1961.* London: Hogarth, 1968. 114–28.

Said, Edward W. *Orientalism.* New York: Vintage, 1979.

Saiki, Patsy Sumie. *Japanese Women in Hawai'i: The First 100 Years.* Honolulu, HI: Kisaku, 1985.

Sandemeyer, Elmer C. *The Anti-Chinese Movement in California.* 1939. Urbana: U of Illinois P, 1991.

Saxton, Alexander. *The Indispensable Enemy: Labor and the Anti-Chinese Movement in California.* Berkeley: U of California P, 1971.

Schellstede, Sangmie Choi. *Comfort Women Speak: Testimony by Sex Slaves of the Japanese Military.* New York: Holmes and Meier, 2000.

Schneider, Rebecca. "After Us the Savage Goddess." *Performance and Cultural Politics.* Ed. Elin Diamond. London: Routledge, 1996. 157–78.

Schwartz, Hillel. *The Culture of the Copy: Striking Likenesses, Unreasonable Facsimiles.* New York: Zone, 1996.

"Secret Egypt." *New York Times Book Review* 6 July 1919: 358.

See, Lisa. *On Gold Mountain.* New York: Vintage, 1995.

Senelick, Laurence. *The Changing Room: Sex, Drag, and Theatre.* London: Routledge, 2000.

Shimakawa, Karen. *National Abjection: The Asian American Body Onstage.* Durham, NC: Duke UP, 2002.

Shiomi, R. A. *Yellow Fever.* Toronto: Playwrights Canada, 1984.

Shohat, Ella and Robert Stam. *Unthinking Eurocentrism: Multiculturalism and the Media.* London: Routledge, 1994.

Short, Ernest Henry. *Fifty Years of Vaudeville.* London: Eyre & Spottiswoode,1946.

Silence Broken: Korean Comfort Women. Dir. and written by Dai-Sil Kim Gibson. PBS, 2000.

Silverman, Kaja. *The Threshold of the Visible World.* New York: Routledge, 1996.

Smith, Myron J. Jr. and Terry White. *Cloak and Dagger Fiction: An Annotated Guide to Spy Thrillers.* Third Edition. Bibliographies and Indexes in World Literature. Westport, CT: Greenwood, 1995.

Smith, Sidonie. *Subjectivity, Identity, and the Body: Women's Autobiographical Practices in the Twentieth Century.* Bloomington: Indiana UP, 1993.

Soitos, Stephen. *The Blues Detective: A Study of African American Detective Fiction.* Amherst: U of Massachusetts P, 1996.

Son, Diana. "R.A.W. ('Cause I'm a Woman)." *Contemporary Plays by Women of Color.* Eds. Kathy A. Perkins and Roberta Uno. New York: Routledge, 1996. 284–96.

Song, Min. Review of *Native Speaker. Amerasia Journal* 23.2 (1997): 185–88.

Spanos, William V. "The Detective and the Boundary: Some Notes on the Postmodern Literary Imagination." *Early Postmodernism: Foundational Essays.* Ed. Paul A. Bové. Durham, NC: Duke UP, 1995. 17–39.

Stafford, David. *The Silent Game.* Athens: U of Georgia P, 1991.

Stallybrass, Peter and Allon White. *The Politics and Poetics of Transgression.* Ithaca, NY: Cornell UP, 1986.

Stetz, Margaret D. and Bonnie B. C. Oh. "Introduction." *Legacies of the Comfort Women of World War II.* Armonk, NY: M. E. Sharpe, 2001. xi–xvi.

Stone, Allucquere Rosanne. "Identity in Oshkosh." *Posthuman Bodies.* Eds. Judith Halberstam and Ira Livingston. Bloomington: Indiana UP, 1995. 23–37.

Sturken, Marita. *Tangled Memories: The Vietnam War, the AIDS Epidemic, and the Politics of Remembering .* Berkeley: U of California P, 1997.

Symons, Julian. *Mortal Consequences.* New York: Viking, 1973.

Takaki, Ronald. *Strangers from a Different Shore: A History of Asian Americans.* New York: Penguin, 1989.

Tanaka, Yuki. *Hidden Horrors: Japanese War Crimes in World War II.* Boulder, CO: Westview, 1998.

Tani, Stefano. *The Doomed Detective: The Contribution of the Detective Novel to Postmodern American and Italian Fiction.* Carbondale: Southern Illinois UP, 1984.

Taussig, Michael. *Mimesis and Alterity: A Particular History of the Senses.* New York: Routledge, 1993.

Thiesmeyer, Lynn. "U.S. Comfort Women and the Silence of the American Other." *Hitting Critical Mass: A Journal of Asian American Cultural Criticism* 3.2 (1996): 47–67.

Thoma, Pamela. "Cultural Autobiography, Testimonial, and Asian American Transnational Feminist Coalition in the 'Comfort Women of World War II' Conference." *Frontiers: A Journal of Women's Studies* 21.1 and 2 (2000): 29–54.

Thompson, Jon. *Fiction, Crime and Empire: Clues to Modernity and Postmodernism.* Urbana: U of Illinois P, 1993.

Todorov, Tzvetan. "Dialogism and Schizophrenia" in *An Other Tongue.* Ed. Alfred Arteaga. Durham, NC: Duke UP, 1994. 203–14.

———. *The Fantastic: A Structural Approach to a Literary Genre.* Ithaca, NY: Cornell UP, 1975.

Torgovnick, Marianna. *Gone Primitive: Savage Intellects, Modern Lives.* Chicago: U of Chicago P, 1990.

Trinh, Minh-ha T. *Woman, Native, Other.* Bloomington: Indiana UP, 1989.

Tuan, Mia. *Forever Foreigners or Honorary Whites?: The Asian Ethnic Experience Today.* New Brunswick, NJ: Rutgers UP, 1998.

Umemoto, Karen. " 'On Strike!': San Francisco State College Strike 1968–69: The Role of Asian American Students." *Amerasia Journal* 15.1 (1989): 3–41.

van Ash, Cay and Elizabeth Sax Rohmer. *Master of Villainy: a Biography of Sax Rohmer.* Bowling Green, OH: Bowling Green U Popular P, 1972.

Wald, Gayle. *Crossing the Color Line: Racial Passing in Twentieth-Century U.S. Literature and Culture.* Durham, NC: Duke UP, 2000.

Wang, Ling-chi. "Re: 'Honorary White' references." Online posting. 21 Oct. 2002. AAAS Community. 21 Oct 2002. <AAASCommunity@yahoogroups.com>.

Watson, Colin. *Snobbery with Violence: English Crime Stories and Their Audience.* London: Eyre Metheun, 1979.

Weglyn, Michi. *Years of Infamy: The Untold Story of America's Concentration Camps.* 1976. Seattle: U of Washington P, 1996.

Wei, William. *The Asian American Movement.* Philadelphia, PA: Temple UP, 1993.

Wiegman, Robin. *American Anatomies: Theorizing Race and Gender.* Durham, NC: Duke UP, 1995.

Wilde, Oscar. 1895. *An Ideal Husband.* New York: Penguin, 1999.

Wong, Elizabeth. "China Doll." *Contemporary Plays by Women of Color.* Eds. Kathy A. Perkins and Roberta Uno. New York: Routledge, 1996. 310–16.

Wong, K. Scott, and Sucheng Chan, eds. *Claiming America: Constructing Chinese American Identities During the Exclusion Era.* Philadelphia, PA: Temple UP, 1998.

Wong, Sau-ling C. "Denationalization Reconsidered: Asian American Cultural Criticism at a Theoretical Crossroads." *Amerasia Journal* 21.1–2 (1995): 1–27.

———. *Reading Asian American Literature: From Necessity to Extravagance.* Princeton, NJ: Princeton UP, 1993.

———. "The Stakes of Textual Border-Crossing: Sinocentric, Asian American, and Feminist Critical Practices on Hualing Nieh's *Mulberry and Peach.*" *Orientations: Mapping Studies in the Asian Diaspora.* Eds. Kandice Chuh and Karen Shimakawa. Durham, NC: Duke UP, 2001. 130–52.

Wordsworth, William. *The Prelude: A Parallel Text.* Ed. J.C. Maxwell. London: Harmondsworth, 1971.

Wu, William F. *The Yellow Peril: Chinese Americans in American Fiction 1850–1940.* New York: Archon, 1982.

Yamada, Mitsuye. *Camp Notes and Other Writings.* New Brunswick, NJ: Rutgers UP, 1992.

Yamaguchi, Yoji. *Face of a Stranger.* New York: HarperCollins, 1995.

Yamamoto, Hisaye. *Seventeen Syllables and Other Stories.* New Brunswick, NJ: Rutgers UP, 1988.

Yamamoto, Traise. *Masking Selves, Making Subjects: Japanese American Women, Identity, and the Body.* Berkeley, CA: U of California P, 1999.

Yamane, David. *Student Movements for Multiculturalism: Challenging the Curricular Color Line in Higher Education.* Baltimore, MD: Johns Hopkins UP, 2001.

Yang, Hyunah. "Revisiting the Issue of Korean 'Military Comfort Women': The Question of Truth and Positionality." *positions: east asia cultures critique* 5.1 (1997): 51–72.

Yi, Du-hyun. "Role Playing Through Trance Possession in Korean Shamanism." *Shamanism: The Spirit World of Korea.* Eds. Richard W. I. Guisso and Chai-shin Yu. Berkeley. CA: Asian Humanities P, 1988. 162–80.

Yoo, David K. "Introduction: Reframing the U.S. Religious Landscape." *New Spiritual Homes: Religion and Asian Americans.* Ed. David K. Yoo. Honolulu: U of Hawai'i P, 1999. 1–18.

Yoon, Won Kil. *The Passage of a Picture Bride.* Riverside, CA: Loma Linda UP, 1989.

Yoshiaki, Yoshimi. *Comfort Women: Sexual Slavery in the Japanese Military During World War II.* Trans. Suzanne O'Brien. New York: Columbia UP, 2000.

Yu, Shiao-ling. "The Themes of Exile and Identity Crisis in Nie Hualing's Fiction." *Nativism Overseas: Contemporary Chinese Women Writers.* Ed. Hsin-sheng C. Kao. Albany: State U of New York P, 1993. 127–56.

Yung, Judy. *Unbound Feet: A Social History of Chinese Women in San Francisco.* Berkeley: U of California P, 1995.

Zaleski, Jeff. Review of *Over the Shoulder,* by Leonard Chang. *Publisher's Weekly* 18 December 2000: 57.

Index

In this index an "f" after a number indicates a separate reference on the next page, and an "ff" indicates separate references on the next two pages. A continuous discussion over two or more pages is indicated by a span of page numbers, e.g., "57–59." *Passim* is used for a cluster of references in close but not consecutive sequence.

ASIAN AMERICA

Before Internment: Essays in Pre-War Japanese American History

YUJI ICHIOKA, EDITED BY ARIF DIRLIK, EIICHIRO AZUMA, AND
GORDON CHANG, FORTHCOMING.

Sexual Naturalization: Asian Americans and Miscegenation

SUSAN KOSHY, FORTHCOMING.

*Better Americans in a Greater America: Japanese American Internment,
Redress, and Historical Memory*

ALICE YANG-MURRAY, FORTHCOMING.

Five Faces of Exile: The Nation and Filipino Intellectuals

AUGUSTO FAUNI ESPIRITU, 2005.

Dhan Gopal Mukerji, *Caste and Outcast*

EDITED AND PRESENTED BY GORDON H. CHANG, PURNIMA MANKEKAR,
AND AKHIL GUPTA, 2002.

*New Worlds, New Lives: Globalization and People of Japanese Descent in the
Americas and from Latin America in Japan*

EDITED BY LANE RYO HIRABAYASHI, AKEMI KIKUMURA-YANO, AND JAMES
A. HIRABAYASHI, 2002.

*Japanese Pride, American Prejudice: Modifying the Exclusion Clause of the
1924 Immigration Act*

IZUMI HIROBE, 2001.

Chinese San Francisco, 1850–1943: A Trans-Pacific Community

YONG CHEN, 2000.

Dreaming of Gold, Dreaming of Home: Transnationalism and Migration Between the United States and South China, 1882–1943

MADELINE Y. HSU, 2000.

Imagining the Nation: Asian American Literature and Cultural Consent

DAVID LEIWEI LI, 1998.

Morning Glory, Evening Shadow: Yamato Ichihashi and His Internment Writings, 1942–1945

EDITED, ANNOTATED, AND WITH A BIOGRAPHICAL ESSAY BY GORDON H. CHANG, 1997.

Mary Kimoto Tomita, *Dear Miye: Letters Home from Japan, 1939–1946*

EDITED, WITH AN INTRODUCTION AND NOTES, BY ROBERT G. LEE, 1995.

Beyond the Killing Fields: Voices of Nine Cambodian Survivors in America

USHA WELARATNA, 1993.

Making and Remaking Asian America

BILL ONG HING, 1993.

Righting a Wrong: Japanese Americans and the Passage of the Civil Liberties Act of 1988

LESLIE T. HATAMIYA, 1993.